Monument sacred to the memory of more than 400 members of the *Arbeiders Jeugd Centrale* (Young Workers Center), who died during the war 1940–1945.

De Paasheuvel, Vierhouten.

Dedicated to all victims of genocide.

Thou shalt love thy neighbour even as thyself.
Leviticus 19 (Tyndale)

Thou shalt not follow a multitude to do evil.
Exodus 23 (Tyndale)

When you see a man being dragged to be killed, go to his rescue and save those being hurried away to their death.
Proverbs 24:11 (New English Bible)

HIDDEN LETTERS

May 1940 German victory parade through Amsterdam, showing the tower of Westerkerk church.

HIDDEN LETTERS

Annotated by Deborah Slier and Ian Shine
Letters translated by Marion van Binsbergen-Pritchard

Star Bright Books
New York

Published in the United States of America by Star Bright Books, Inc., New York.
The name Star Bright Books and the Star Bright Books logo are registered
trademarks of Star Bright Books, Inc. Please visit www.starbrightbooks.com.

ISBN-13: 978-1-887734-88-2

Meticulously and painstakingly printed in India by Thomson Press (I) Ltd. to whom we offer many thanks. 9 8 7 6 5 4 3 2 1

Designed by Choi and Shine Design Studio

Coedited by Jenefer Coates and Alice van Keulen-Woudstra

Library of Congress Cataloging-in-Publication Data

Slier, Philip, 1923-1943
    Hidden letters / annotated by Deborah Slier; Ian Shine; translated by Marion Pritchard;
        p. cm.
    Includes index.
    ISBN-13: 978-1-887734-88-2
    ISBN-10: 1-887734-88-0
    1. Slier, Philip, 1923-1943--Correspondence. 2. Molengoot Labor Camp. 3. World War,
    1939-1945--Personal narratives, Dutch. 4. World War, 1939-1945--Jews--Netherlands. 5.
    Netherlands--History--German occupation, 1940-1945. 6. Holocaust, Jewish (1939-1945)--
    Netherlands. 7. Jews--Netherlands--Correspondence. I. Shine Deborah Slier, II Shine, Ian III. Title.

D805.5.M63S54 2006
    940.53'09492—dc22

                                                        2005056290

CONTENTS

MAP OF THE NETHERLANDS IN 1942 SHOWING CITIES AND CAMPS

Scale: The Afsluitdijk (Barrier Dyke) is 30 kilometers (19 miles) long.

This dyke was built in 1932. It separated the North Sea from the Zuiderzee, converting it into Lake IJsselmeer.

■ Cities or villages

● Camps

PREFACE

Hidden Letters is a profoundly compassionate report on the tragedy that befell a young Dutch Jew and his extended family during the Holocaust. It is also a thoroughly documented scientific analysis of how and why young Philip Slier and so many other innocents were destroyed by the German Nazis and their local helpers. We bear witness to the process of destruction as slow and methodical, starting with the exclusion of Jews in German-occupied Netherlands from work and school (which made them eligible for a work camp) all the way to their concentration in Westerbork, the dreaded Dutch transit camp. From there, the road led directly to Auschwitz or to one of the death camps. Philip Slier, an attractive and intelligent young man, tried to escape his fate but had no luck. He left behind an extraordinary legacy, however, in the letters that he wrote to his parents almost daily from the work camp which were found accidentally more than fifty years later during the demolition of an old tenement building in Amsterdam. This collection, carefully studied by Deborah Slier (a close relative of Philip Slier) and her husband, constitutes one of most valuable contemporary sources on Jewish life, and on Dutch life in general, during the war. It shows, as similarly honest documents show everywhere, that the behavior of the non-Jewish Europeans toward the victims of the Holocaust ranged all the way from the abominable to the self-sacrificing and the heroic. The death or survival of the majority of Jews was, however, not a decision of the denunciators or of those who hid Jews, but that of the German Nazis and the local authorities. It was also the consequence of the fortunes of war. In this respect, the Dutch Jews were not among the luckier ones.

The two authors completed precise research on life in occupied Netherlands, on the Holocaust, the revolt in Sobibor, and the history of the Slier family. The translations are excellent as are the many photographs and maps. In brief, like the *Diary of Anne Frank*, this is a masterpiece.

István Deák
Seth Low Professor Emeritus of History
Columbia University
New York

ACKNOWLEDGMENTS

While working on this book, I received friendly assistance of a kind that I have never encountered before. Almost without exception everyone that I approached for help gave me more than I asked, so that I came away dazed and enormously grateful. If the level of frank, friendly comments that I have received from the people listed below, mostly Dutch, is representative of that country as a whole, then the Netherlands is surely a beacon to the world. In particular, this book owes more to Elma Verhey than to anyone else. She gave me unstinting help, advice and friendship. Elma put me in touch with Tootje Loonstijn Renger, Karel van der Schaaf, Günter Brandorff, Roel Gritter and Dick Slier; she found the Hardenberg police file on Philip Bromet and much more. Elma was the stimulus to the publication of these letters in Dutch in 1999 and to this book in English. In addition, her article in *Vrij Nederland* spurred investigation and discussion about the work camps and concentration camps in the Netherlands.

I have been stunned by the effort so many people extended to help this book and I am deeply grateful to everyone whom I have listed below. Guido Abuys, the archivist at Westerbork provided valuable information, advice, documents and a photo at short notice. Aleksandr kindly provided an instant translation of the Black Book. Michlean Amir and Vincent Slatt, of the United States Holocaust Memorial Museum tried hard to find Zygielbojm's WJC telegram of December 2, 1942. Drs.* David Barnouw of NIOD made corrections to the manuscript. Richard Blake translated several documents. Hennie Wesseling-Bolk helped unravel the Salomonson genealogy. Günter Brandorff provided the history and photos of the de Bruins, as well as family histories and local information about Hardenberg. He made me aware of the letter from Lion Salomonson and gave me a photograph of him as well as the letter from Jules Scharis (a fellow prisoner in camp Molengoot) to the Veurink family, who still live in the same house in Heemseveen. Hans A. Heese Cartoef, a newly found cousin, supplied family information, documents, and photos. Professor Dr. Johannes Houwink ten Cate spent a long time discussing the Jewish Council and suggested useful sources to pursue. Barbara H. Cole made many corrections and offered helpful suggestions. Jan Fikken supplied information about the work camps. Jen Foray served as a valued consultant. Jane Fresco told me about the Gallery, about her brother Bernard Cohen, and gave me permission to include his photo. Drs. Harco Gijsbers at NIOD was exceedingly helpful. He read the manuscript, gave information, suggested corrections, and located photographs and documents. Miriam Gloger of the New York Public Library found sources, photos and translator Aleksandr. Roel Gritter supplied maps, information, advice, photographs, his booklet, permission to use his material, and in conversation added much useful detail. Manus de Groot found the letters and appreciated their significance and preserved them. Andre Idzinga at Oude Vriezenveen Museum Archives provided information and photographs. Professor Karin Hofmeester guided me to inaccessible photos of the Roodveldts. Noa Kats at Yad Vashem supplied photographs. Kees Koetsier and Richard Oerle of Nauta Dulith generously provided helpful guidance. Jelka Kröger from the Jewish Historical Museum in Amsterdam gave time and supplied photographs and documents. Dr. Laurel G. Leff generously gave advice and allowed me to quote from her material. The daughters of Philip Mechanicus kindly allowed me to quote from their father's book, *In Depot*, and supplied his photo. Ross Mellows provided photographs and information about 1940-era Primus stoves. Hans Moonen provided scans of all the propaganda pamphlets shown, and shared his vast knowledge of them at a time when he was very harassed, and moreover obtained scans of the German propaganda leaflet that came from the Stapersma Netherlands Collection. Joost de Moor, Secretary of the AJC Research Foundation has given valued help with this book, correcting errors and omissions and supplying a copy of Piet Tigger's book of AJC songs and provided the moving AJC memorial photograph. He also put me in touch with Flip's first girl-friend Truus Tokkie-Sant who kindly supplied some fine photos and many memories. Brother Bryan Paquette, OCD of the Institute of Carmelite Studies was generous with his time and graciously gave permission to reproduce Edith Stein's letter and supplied information about her. Ellen Pasman of Pasman, Veldheer and Bos spent a great deal of time giving good advice. Kathy Paton removed many errors with sensitivity and went to great trouble to correct the final manuscript. Eddie and Jules Philips, whose father Arthur, was both Flip's and my first cousin, gave permission to use family photographs. Jules and Joke Philips filled gaps in family histories, gave family photos and provided a guided tour of Westerbork. Maren Read of the United States Holocaust Memorial Museum showed amazing patience with my many requests. She suggested and supplied many photographs. Martin Redi at the United Nations Photo Archives supplied a photograph of Raphael Lemkin when I had all but given up. Tootje Loonstijn-Renger and Gerrit Renger could not have been more supportive or more generous with their time and photographs and material. Elisabeth Renger kindly allowed me to reproduce her ration card. Dick Slier supplied advice, photos and the history of the

---

*Drs. is the title for the first university degree which is the Dutch equivalent of a Masters degree. The second university degree is a Ph.D., which in Dutch is abbreviated Dr.

Molengoot monument. The South African Sliers have given strong support and provided photos which they had guarded carefully for over 80 years. Yvonne was the chief guardian, and Lionel supplied recollections and astute comments. They gave me the Red Cross reports on Flip and his parents and a handwritten family tree that Nol Slier had given to them when he visited shortly before he died. Tina Trent took on more than her share of extra work while I pursued sources for this book. Marcel van Dam gave photographs of coins. Alice van Keulen-Woudstra gave friendship and eagle-eyed critical comments, unending information and suggestions, and discovered the source of the *Unknown Soldier* poem. She identified Henk Schenk, deciphered Flip's jokes and meanings after reading the large and small print on every letter and every document and checked and rechecked facts. She is amazing. Drs. Carry van Lakerveld explained what happened once the transports left Westerbork. The van der Schaafs (Karel van der Schaaf and Sippy Boersma) provided their company, their car, their time, and their photos whether in their own collection, or on loan to the Friesland Resistance Museum in Leeuwarden or to others. During the war, Karel offered everyone a helping hand and he and Sippy still do. J. van der Sleen generously supplied photographs and information about Nieuwlande. Clementine van Stiphout of the Amsterdam Municipal Archives was very supportive and went out of her way to assist me in locating a photo of Louis Slier. Eduard Victor generously supplied copies of documents. Hans van der Werff put me in touch with Jozef Vomberg, an erstwhile S-prisoner [S for *Straf*, punishment] in Westerbork (he was arrested in 1944). Joe now seems like an old friend. He has given hours of unending advice, suggestions and corrections. He generously allowed me to make use of his translation of Flip's letters and he has translated many other documents including Professor Cohen's memoir which provides a sobering glimpse of the callousness of the Dutch and Allied governments. Joe has devoted much energy over many years to ensure that the wartime record is accurate. Henrika Veurink-Jolversma and Hermina Broekroelofs-Vrijlink provided photos, memories, and kindness.

I have tried to identify and thank everyone who helped Flip and who helped me in compiling this book. I apologize if I have missed anyone. I would be happy to hear from anyone who has information about Flip, his family, his friends, or fellow prisoners. I would be grateful to have errors or omissions corrected. I would be grateful for Joop van Amstel and Nico Groen's real names and for confirmation that Uncle Max was indeed Uncle Joseph. I would like to learn more about the Peekel and Bleekveld families of Vrolik Street, about Mr. Biederman of *Algemeen Handelsblad,* De Brave, Brilleman, Charlie Bird, Jules Scharis and the eight runaway boys from Sellingen. Should there be a second edition, I would be pleased to include new information, photos and documents. If the melancholy list of friends and family who did not come back contains errors, it would be good to learn that someone lost has been found. The Dutch often use the term "did not come back" because it was very difficult to know whether someone had been killed or had emigrated or was in some Soviet gulag. Even today people are still looking for family members who disappeared. I met with six death camp survivors hoping to get information about Flip; I am most grateful to Thomas Toivi Blatt, Selma Wijnberg-Engel, Samuel Lerer, Esther Terner-Raab, Jules Schelvis, and Kurt Thomas who shared their memories, photos and documents.

Jenny Coates made a huge contribution, corrected scores of errors and mistakes, suggested many changes in layout, style, presentation of ideas and organization of all the material so that the book is now quite transformed and very greatly improved. The advice was brilliant and invaluable and was followed almost invariably.

And finally a warm thank-you to Marion Pritchard for translating Flip's letters. As she was Flip's coeval, and lived and worked in Amsterdam, and as she is fluent in English, Dutch, and Yiddish, she was perfectly qualified to catch his meaning, his sarcasm, and his compassion. I am very grateful for her many kindnesses and patience when answering endless questions about the Netherlands during the German occupation. Marion has helped many people. She rescued children in the Netherlands during the war, she comforted refugees in UNRRA camps after the war, and she later worked with Jewish refugees in Boston. She taught at Clark University and has been a psychoanalyst practicing in Vermont. Whenever she has encountered injustice, she has fought it and offered a helping hand to the victim. She received a Yad Vashem medal in 1981 for rescuing, hiding, and looking after 150 children and families and she has received shoals of honors and awards. The *U.S. News* & *World Report* selected her as one of world's 50 heroes of the past 50 years. I feel privileged that she calls me a friend.

Deborah Slier
New York, 2007

Flip (Philip) Slier in August 1942

FLIP'S CLOSEST RELATIVES AND FRIENDS

Official name	Relationship	Known as
Andries Slier	Father's brother married to Aunt Anna van Es	Uncle Andries
Alfred Sallie Salomonson	Mother's brother married to Aunt Jenny (Jeanie Muriel) Gestetner	Uncle Alfred
Betje Benjamins-Slier	Grandmother	Grandma
Debora Slier	Father's sister, unmarried	Aunt Bora
Dick van der Schaaf	Friend	Dick
Duifje Slier	Father's sister, unmarried	Aunt Duifje
Elisabeth de Vries	Girlfriend	Bep
Gerard Elzas	Friend	Harry
Grietje Slier-Philips	Father's sister married to Uncle Eduard Philips	Aunt Grietje
Heintje de Lange	Friend	Henny
Johanna Sophie Salomonson-Samas	Mother's sister married to Uncle Bram (Abraham) Samas	Aunt Jo
Jonas Slier	Father's brother married to Aunt Anna Plas	Uncle Jonas
Joseph Slier	Father's brother married to Aunt Cato (Catherina) Vleeschhouwer	Uncle Max
Nico Groen	Friend	Nico
Juliette Anna Salomonson Schaap	Mother's sister married to Uncle Karel (Koopman) Schaap	Aunt Juul
Karel van der Schaaf	Friend	Karel
Rosalie Johanna Salomonson	Mother's oldest sister	Aunt Rosalie
Rudolf de Bruin	Mother's cousin	Ru
Seline & Leendert (Eliazar) Slier	Flip's parents	Pa & Ma
Simon Loonstijn	Friend	Siem
Truus Sant	Girlfriend	Truus
Veurink family	Friendly farm family	
Vrijlink family	Friendly farm family	Vr.

Throughout this book the order of names are: nickname, first name (in brackets), maiden name and then the last name. Thus Aunt Jo is given as Jo (Johanna) Salomonson-Samas, whereas in the Netherlands she would be called Johanna Samas-Salomonson. The only exception is Alice van Keulen-Woudstra, whose singular contribution requires it thus.

INTRODUCTION

In 1997, Mr. Manus de Groot, foreman of Deegen & Son Demolition Company, was pulling down a house at 128 Vrolik Street[A]* in Amsterdam. He found two bundles of letters hidden in the ceiling of the bathroom on the third floor. He supposed they were important because there were so many of them—86 letters and postcards and one telegram. They had been written in 1942 by Flip (Philip) Slier from a forced labor camp to his parents, when he was 18½ years old. Mr. de Groot took the letters home and as he read through them he could feel the boy's increasing fear and was deeply moved. Having earlier worked on a job at NIOD (the Dutch National Institute of War Documentation), Mr. de Groot decided to hand the letters to them, on condition that he be told what had happened to the boy and his family and whether there were any survivors. This book is his answer.

The significance of the letters was immediately apparent to Drs. David Barnouw, NIOD's expert on Anne Frank, and he in turn alerted Elma Verhey, expert, journalist and author of *Om het Joodse Kind* (About the Jewish Children) and *Kind van de Rekening* (The Accounting). Elma researched the letters' background, transcribed them, and wrote about them in the Dutch weekly magazine, *Vrij Nederland*.

The letters first came into my possession in 1999. At that time, most of Flip's allusions and references were lost on me, but it was the desire to understand and know more that led me to eventually produce this book. I have tried to discover the people and recreate the circumstances of one boy's life during the German occupation of the Netherlands more than 60 years ago. As my explorations widened and deepened, Flip's world gradually came into focus. Once I had photographs, documents, and local knowledge, it became easier to understand the conditions under which Flip was living in camp, to understand his fears, and above all, to appreciate his spirit, courage, optimism, and generosity. The lovable and admirable person that emerged was to become my close companion for the next seven years.

I have not edited the letters. Flip's originality in spelling and grammar, his errors, crossing-outs, and emphases have been retained to preserve the letters' original content, character and layout. The parts of his letters that were most unusual or distinctive—all his signatures and "daaaags!!" [good byes] that provide a barometer of his changing moods—have been scanned, copied and pasted so that they appear as they do in each original letter. In addition there are scanned copies of parts of 15 letters from Flip and his family and friends.

Where a correction was needed, it has been added within square brackets and explanations are given in annotations or in the source notes.

My father and Flip's father were brothers; both were born in Amsterdam. In 1922 my father emigrated from the Netherlands to South Africa, from where he must have kept up a lively correspondence with his family because I knew the names and faces of many Dutch relatives whose photos filled his green album. I remember the day in 1940 when I came home from school to find my mother in tears because the Netherlands had been invaded. And I remember a postcard that arrived about two years later from an uncle, saying that he was in a camp, he was well, but please send food. After the war, a letter arrived from the Red Cross announcing that all my father's brothers and sisters had died in concentration camps and my grandmother had died in Westerbork camp in the Netherlands. It was the only time I ever saw my father weep.

For one year after the German invasion on May 10, 1940, life on Vrolik Street had gone on much as usual. The Germans tightened their noose so slowly and so cleverly that the president of the Jewish Council, Abraham Asscher, later stated that when the Jewish Council was established in February 1941, the German "attitude to the Jews was by no means clearly hostile." A.J. Herzberg stated that the head of Westerbork camp, First Lieutenant Gemmeker, generally treated the Jews courteously, ". . . occasionally giving the impression that he no more hated Jews than a butcher hates cows."[B]

The German policy towards the Netherlands was to fortify the coast against any Allied invasion, integrate the country into the Greater Reich, steal food, money and goods, put the Dutch to work as slave labor, and purge the entire country of Jews. By 1942, Jews were prohibited from almost all types of work. Once they were unemployed, they were sent to one of about 50 work camps set up throughout the Netherlands, which were, in reality, holding pens. In the spring of 1942, at the age of 18, Flip was one of 7,000 Jews sent to a Dutch work camp. From there he wrote to friends and family almost daily, and his letters now provide a unique eyewitness account of life in camp Molengoot.

In October 1942, the camps were emptied. The inmates were sent to Westerbork transit camp and from there they

---

*An alphabetical superscript indicates that the source is given in the notes beginning on page 166.

were deported to Poland. Between 1941 and 1944 about 104,000 Jews were deported, while 24,000 went into hiding or, as the Dutch say, became *onderduikers* (literally under-divers). Beginning in 1943, the Germans summoned 800,000 Dutch non-Jews to work as slave labor in Germany, and many volunteered to fight in the German army (page 44), but a great many declined the invitation and they too became *onderduikers* whose names were posted by the police as wanted (page 71). The *onderduikers* were sustained by hundreds of thousands of their fellow countrymen who willingly opened their doors, their pockets, and their pantries to strangers, thereby reducing their own living space, privacy, and food. In addition, for hiding *onderduikers*, they risked barbaric German punishment, which was concentration camp or death. Unfortunately there were many who did not follow the biblical command to "save those being hurried away to their death," and many *onderduikers* were betrayed. In the autumn of 1944, in retaliation for a countrywide rail strike, the Germans imposed a food and fuel embargo that caused the death of 22,000 from starvation.[4] Having an extra mouth to feed was a heavy burden.

When I first went to the Netherlands in 1953, I stayed with my cousin, Arthur Philips, and his wife Willy (Wilhelmina Magdalena). We got on well and Willy and I spent most days together. We talked and talked, but the war—which had ended only a few years before—was never a topic of conversation. Willy did not tell me that she and Arthur had been hidden during the war, or that her three sisters and a brother had been killed. In fact she never even mentioned that she had had any sisters, although she did tell me of the time the police came to arrest her mother for deportation. Willy had begged them to take her as well, but they refused as she was not on their list. It was only when talking to Jules Philips (Willy and Arthur's son) half a century later, in 2005, that I learned that Arthur had been in the Dutch army when Germany invaded the Netherlands in 1940, that a bullet had broken his shoulder, which had put him in a rehabilitation hospital for a year. One of the nurses there, Johanna Vink suggested that Minke Honij would hide him, which she did throughout the war. Willy herself was hidden by Johanna's parents, but like many people in hiding, Willy moved countless times. Among the people who hid her was a young woman named Betje Bosboom. Betje was reported to the Germans and summarily shot. After the war Johanna married Willy's brother who was hidden in a chicken coop.

Flip's letters make light of his hardships. They tell how his good friends Karel and Dick van der Schaaf helped to make life easier. As go-betweens, they carried food, clothing, money, messages, and goodwill to Flip and to scores of friends in the work camps. Eventually they themselves were ordered to work in Germany, but instead they became *onderduikers* in Friesland. I could not have imagined how much pleasure would spring from meeting Karel and his wife Sippy. They radiated such goodwill when I met them in 2004 that I felt immediate love for them and it was easy to understand what the van der Schaafs had meant to Flip. We have since spent many happy days, indeed many weeks, together talking about Flip and their common friends in East Amsterdam. Karel produced dozens of photos, and he, Sippy and I spent hours identifying people and comparing his photos with those in my father's album.

Flip often wrote about his two closest friends in camp, Nico Groen, who probably did not survive (Truus Sant heard that he had been arrested in the Hague), and Simon Loonstijn, who sent a postcard on January 30, 1944, from Monowitz (a sub-camp of Auschwitz) to friends in The Hague (p. 155). I have had the good fortune to enjoy the friendship of Simon's sister, Tootje Loonstijn, and her husband, Gerrit Renger. They have been lovely and made available all their photos and Simon's letters, and they taught me much about life under German occupation. It was from them that I heard of Professor R. P. Cleveringa, and about the two school teachers in Amsterdam, Mrs. M. L. Hoefsmit and Mrs. C. W. Ouweleen, who hid 12 children and who, late one night, received a knock at the door from a neighbor who complained, "Your *onderduikers* are making so much noise that my *onderduikers* can't get to sleep."

Flip, Simon and others received generous help from local farmers, especially the Vrijlink family and the Veurink family whose farm was only 200 yards from the camp. In 1942 Gees Vrijlink wrote to the Loonstijns, ". . . we absolutely cannot stand by and see someone else go hungry." Flip wrote, "Pa and Ma, you cannot imagine what nice people the Vrijlinks are . . . They are really lovely to us . . . like a mother to us." On October 27, 2005, I met the Vrijlink family and was able to thank them for what they had done. I also had the pleasure of toasting Hermina Vrijlink on her seventy-seventh birthday and enjoying the company of her brother Seine who has hardly changed since the day the photo of him and Flip was taken 63 years ago (page 113). It is easy to understand how Flip appreciated the sweetness that he and all the Vrijlinks radiate.

Flip returned to Amsterdam in 1942 to be with his family and friends even though he could have accepted the Vrijlinks' offer of a hiding place. He could possibly have hidden in Nieuwlande, a small community about 15 miles north of his camp where the Vrijlinks' friend, the Reverend Frits Slomp[4] together with Councillor Johannes Post and his brother Marinus encouraged people to open their doors to *onderduikers*. Almost every household in Nieuwlande responded and hid one or more Jews, taking in 300 in all. It is not known how many other Slomps, Posts, Van der Schaafs, Veurinks and Vrijlinks did the same all over the Netherlands, for such people tend to hide their light under a bushel. Many stories will never be told, many heroic acts will go unsung, and many kindnesses unthanked. Indeed, had Flip's letters not been found, this one particular story would have remained hidden as well. But thanks to Manus de Groot, the courage of a few people will be long remembered alongside the more public thunderclaps of protest from Cleveringa, a professor; van Hasselt, a student; Visser, a judge; de Jong, an archbishop; and the dock-workers of Amsterdam.

I started this book because I felt the need to uncover Flip's world and understand all his references and allusions. But I did not anticipate that it would be satisfying to do so, to peel off the layers to reveal the details, even the painful details. It was satisfying to discover his finger print (page 125) and his joke on the barrack window (page 71) or the probable reason why he did not sign three letters (page 118). For a reason that I do not understand, there is a sort of satisfaction in seeing the very haystack in which he hid (page 154), or seeing his arrest card at Vught. I expected that his fate and the fate of his friends and family would be terrible, and haunting; and it was. I could not avoid thinking that had my father not had the good fortune to be unemployed in 1922, it would be my eyes and my brother's, mother's, father's and sisters' eyes that would be gazing out of this book alongside Flip's. It was very gratifying to discover how likeable Flip was and how likeable his friends were, and are. I came to know him and appreciate his optimism, his compassion, his humor, his lack of hatred, his affection for family and friends, whether Jews or Christians, and his pleasure at standing close to a good-looking farmer's daughter to whom he expressed, as to all the Vrijlinks, whole-hearted thanks: "We can never be grateful enough to Gees."

Deborah Slier
New York, 2007

TIME LINE FROM FLIP'S BIRTH TO HIS ARRIVAL IN CAMP

1. Book burning was staged in Munich (*above*) and several German cities. In Berlin, the book burning university students were told:

"The future German man will not just be a man of books, but a man of character. It is to this end that we want to educate you . . . to overcome the fear of death, and to regain respect for death."

Joseph Goebbels, May 10 1933

In 1933, Joseph Roth pointed to Prussian control of Germany and Hitler's adoption of the Prussian project "to burn the books, to murder the Jews and to revise Christianity."*A*

Joseph Roth, Sept/Nov 1933

"Where they burn books, they will, in the end, burn human beings too."

Heinrich Heine, 1821

1923 Flip (Philip) Slier is born in Amsterdam.
Adolf Hitler states his philosophy in *Mein Kampf* (My Struggle), that he begins in 1923 in prison while serving a sentence for treason.
In Germany it sells 8,000,000 copies and makes Hitler a millionaire.

1932 The Nazi party is democratically elected, winning 37 percent of the votes.

1933 Hitler is appointed Chancellor by President Hindenburg, who openly admitted that he had never read a book in his life. The Nazis set fire to the Reichstag,*B* blame van der Lubbe, a Dutch communist, declare a state of emergency, and arrest all communist deputies. In a snap election, Hitler wins 44 percent of the votes. He bans all political parties, trade unions, judges, and newspapers who oppose him, boycotts Jewish shops and begins to exclude Jews from the civil service. Students burn books by Brecht, Einstein, Freud, London, Mann, Marx, Remarque and Wells.[1]

1934 Germany signs a non-aggression treaty with Poland.

1935 Germany occupies Saarland, conscripts 500,000 into army.*C*
Nuremberg laws deprive Jews of German citizenship.
"Germany will not annex or achieve union with Austria and will respect the demilitarization of the Rhineland."—Adolf Hitler

1936 Germany occupies the Rhineland.
The Gestapo*D* is placed above the law. Jehovah's Witnesses are arrested.

Cartoon by David Low, London *Evening Standard*, July 8, 1936

STEPPING STONES TO GLORY

1937   "The German Government has further given the assurance to the Netherlands that it is prepared to recognize and guarantee the inviolability and neutrality of these territories."—Adolf Hitler

Every local authority in Germany compiles a list of children of African descent. 385 are identified and all are sterilized.
German doctors begin killing mentally and physically disabled people under the 1933 euthanasia law.
Systematic takeover of Jewish property begins.

1938   Mar: Germany occupies Austria, with the connivance of Seyss-Inquart.

Apr: The German occupying government holds a plebiscite which retroactively approves the annexation of Austria.

30 Sept: Munich Agreement: Britain, France, and Italy agree to let Germany annex 11,000 square miles of German-speaking Czechoslovakia (Sudetenland); in return Czechoslovakia is guaranteed that there will be no unprovoked aggression from Germany.

Oct: Jewish children are expelled from German schools.
Driver's licenses of all Jews in Germany are confiscated.

9–10 Nov: *Kristallnacht* . Throughout Germany gangs are encouraged to attack Jews and their property. 7,000 businesses are destroyed, Jewish libraries are burned in public, 100 synagogues are set ablaze, 91 Jews are killed and 26,000 are sent to concentration camps.

1939   30 Jan: "If the international Jewish financiers in and outside Europe should succeed in plunging the nations once more into a world war, then the result will not be the Bolshevizing of the earth, and thus the victory of Jewry, but the annihilation of the Jewish race in Europe!"—Adolf Hitler

Mar: Germany invades Czechoslovakia in violation of the Munich agreement.

Aug: Hitler again guarantees the neutrality of the Netherlands.

20 Aug: Hitler and Stalin sign a mutual non-aggression pact that grants the USSR eastern Poland, Finland, the Baltic states and Bessarabia.

1 Sept: 1,800,000 German troops invade Poland.
"All representatives of the Polish intelligentsia are to be exterminated."
—Adolf Hitler

3 Sept: World War II begins as Great Britain, the Commonwealth, and France, declare war on Germany.

5 Sept: The Netherlands and the United States proclaim neutrality.

17 Sept: USSR invades eastern Poland.

27 Sept: Poland surrenders.

GERMAN EXPANSION 1934-1938

Saarland

1934

1935

1936

1938

1939

In February 1938, Hitler had Artur Seyss-Inquart (*above left*) made interior minister of Austria. He was a pro-Nazi Austrian lawyer, a diligent Catholic, and a WW I veteran who committed high treason, handing his country over to Hitler who then appointed him governor of Austria. In 1939, Hitler appointed him deputy governor of Poland and a minister without portfolio in the German government. In 1940, Hitler appointed him Reich Commissioner of the Netherlands. In 1945, in his last will, Hitler appointed him Foreign Minister of Germany. He was hanged by the International Military Court in Nuremberg on October 16, 1946.

Hanns Rauter (*above right*) was an Austrian Nazi, an SS general, the head of the SS and the police in the Netherlands. He took orders from his personal friend Heinrich Himmler in Berlin, who was the head of all the SS, the Gestapo and the concentration camps. Officially Rauter reported to Seyss-Inquart but both of them were competing for control of the elimination of the Jews from the Netherlands. After the war Rauter was tried in The Hague by a Dutch court and executed on March 25, 1949.

A stamp alluding to Seyss-Inquart's name. The Dutch for 6¼ is "*zes en een kwart*" which sounds close to Seyss-Inquart. And the quarter suggests a fraction of unbalance to mock his limp. Perforated sheets of these stamps were dropped by the British Royal Air Force (RAF) between February 8 and August 20, 1941.

1940   Jan: By January 1, 1940, 61,000 prominent Poles (leaders, professors, teachers, bankers, etc.) have been killed by the Germans.[A]

Mar: Soviets kill 17,000 Polish officers in the Katyn Forest. Large numbers of Poles were continually killed by the Soviets and the Germans.

Apr: Germany invades Denmark and Norway.

10 May: Without provocation or warning,[B] Germany invades the Netherlands, Belgium, and Luxemburg, countries that posed no political, territorial, or economic threat and whose borders she had pledged to respect.

14 May: During surrender negotiations, Rotterdam is bombed indiscriminately; 800 civilians are killed and 78,000 are made homeless. Germany invades France.

15 May: The Netherlands surrenders.

On Friday, May 10, 1940, the *Algemeen Handelsblad* announced that the Netherlands and Germany were at war. Flip and his father worked as typesetters at this newspaper. The Dutch Queen and the royal family as well as members of her government escaped to England.

1940 26 May: German troops overrun northern France. Many British, French and
Polish troops are trapped. By June 4, 338,226 British, French, and Polish
troops are rescued from Dunkirk, 25 miles north of Calais.

29 May: Hitler appoints Artur Seyss-Inquart head of the German authority in
the Netherlands.

22 June: France surrenders.

Most of following events take place in the Netherlands:

1 July: The first anti-Jewish decree: Jews are banned from Air Raid Service.

Aug: No Jews may be hired or promoted in the civil service.

Sept: Germans define a Dutch Jew as anyone with one Jewish grandparent,
whereas in Germany two Jewish grandparents are required.
Jews are banned from street markets in Amsterdam.

Oct: Civil servants must declare which of their grandparents were Aryan.
Six Protestant churches protest against the Aryan declaration.
IDs are issued to everyone over age 15.
Jewish businesses must register with German authorities.

Nov: Jewish civil servants, teachers, and university professors are dismissed.
Frans van Hasselt at Delft and R. P. Cleveringa in Leiden speak out
against German dismissals of Jewish faculty.
Students at Delft and Leiden strike. The Germans close both
universities and arrest Frans van Hasselt and R. P. Cleveringa.

1941 Jan: Jews are banned from all cinemas.
Jews are required to register with the German authority.
Everyone with Jewish parents or grandparents is required to register.

Feb: Archbishop de Yong enjoins Catholics not to join the Dutch National
Socialist Parties.
Seyss-Inquart orders the enclosing of the Jewish area of Amsterdam.
Germans encourage Dutch Nazis to provoke fights in Rotterdam, The
Hague, and Amsterdam.
The Germans demand the formation of a Jewish Council.
First raid is made against Jews; 425 are arrested including Flip's cousin,
Philip Samas.
General strike in Amsterdam is led by the Union of Dock Workers in
protest against the arrest of Jews.
Doctors must declare if they are Jewish.

Mar: Jewish businesses must have a German administrator.
Jews are prohibited from donating blood.
Office for Jewish "Emigration" is opened. In practice the office serves
to collect the names and addresses of Jews.

The first major arrest of Dutch Jews was in retaliation for the death of a Dutch Nazi. The Germans randomly arrested 425 Jewish men between the ages of 16 and 40. The men were beaten and 390 were sent to Buchenwald; from there, 389 were sent to Mauthausen and killed. One man, Max Nebig, survived at Buchenwald because he was protected.[A]

"Wednesday, February 25, 1941. The notorious Green Police closed off Apollo Lane in Amsterdam, dragged a number of Jews living on this avenue out of their dwellings and carried them off to an unknown destination. Unsuspecting pedestrians who wanted to enter Apollo Lane were met with a roaring: *'Bist du Jude?'* (Are you a Jew?). Those who answered in the affirmative were referred to the police van. It was appalling."[B] Resistance newspaper, *Het Parool.*

1. In June 1940, the Germans set up a Pigeon Brigade that counted 32,709 pigeons in Amsterdam and put them under surveillance. In addition to forbidding them to fly, they demanded that any that were caught be turned in to the mayor's office.[A]

Perforated sheets of these stickers were dropped on the Netherlands on the night of March 25, 1941. They were intended as morale boosters for the Dutch.

1941

Apr: Jews are prohibited from entering hotels, restaurants, theaters, parks, and public meeting halls.
"Jews Forbidden" and "Jews Not Wanted" signs begin to appear.
The Jewish Weekly, a new Jewish newspaper with a German-appointed editor appears; all other Jewish papers are banned.
Jews are required to hand in their radios.

May: Jews are banned from the stock exchange.
Jewish doctors, dentists, attorneys, and pharmacists may not treat or work for gentiles.
Certain streets in Amsterdam are designated "Jewish streets."
Jewish farms must be registered and sold.
Jews are banned from swimming pools, public parks, and racetracks.

June: Jews may not own pigeons. The Germans forbid all pigeons to fly.[1]
Jews must surrender their bank accounts to the Lippmann, Rosenthal bank which had been Jewish owned until the Germans took over but they did not Aryanize the name in the hope of misleading people.
Jews are barred from using public transport.

11 June: Second major raid is made against Jews: 277 Jewish men are arrested and sent to Mauthausen camp. Among them are young trainees from the Jewish agricultural training farm, Werkdorp Wieringermeer. The trainees addresses had been requested from the Jewish council by Klaus Barbie.

22 June: Germany invades Russia.

July: All emigration is forbidden.

Aug: All assets, bank accounts, insurance policies, jewelry, and property owned by Jews must be registered.

Sept: Jewish children may only attend separate Jewish schools.
"Jews Forbidden" signs appear in libraries, reading rooms, concert halls, zoos, theaters, public markets, parks, cafes, cabarets, and museums.

Oct: Jewish Council starts card index of all Jews.
Jews are banned from all bridge, dance, and tennis clubs.

Nov: Germans cancel work permits of most Jews, making them unemployed.
The Jewish Weekly announces that unemployed Jewish men will be sent to labor camps.
Non-Dutch Jews must register for "voluntary" emigration to Poland.
Jews may not change addresses or travel without permission.
Jewish street markets are established in Amsterdam.

7 Dec: Japanese attack Pearl Harbor.

11 Dec: Germany and Italy declare war on the United States.

1942 Jan: At the Wannsee Conference, Adolf Eichmann, Reinhard Heydrich, and 14 German officials lay out their plans to exterminate Europe's 11 million Jews. One of the attendees, Karl Eberhard Schöngarth, later became head of the SD[4] in the Netherlands.
Jews are not permitted to drive cars.
Jewish identity card must be stamped "j."
Call-up of unemployed Jews begins; they are sent to labor camps.
Evacuation of Jews from the provinces to Amsterdam begins.
Non-Dutch Jews are sent to Westerbork camp.

Mar: First of four decrees confiscating Jewish property is issued.
Jews are forbidden to remove or dispose of household articles.
Marriages between Jews and non-Jews are banned.

19 Apr: Protests against German anti-Jewish policies are read out in Catholic and Protestant churches.

25 Apr: Flip is sent to Molengoot work camp near Hardenberg in the northeast of the Netherlands.

1945 5 May: Germany surrenders unconditionally to the Netherlands.

8 May: Germany surrenders unconditionally to the Allies.

2 Sept: Japan surrenders unconditionally to the Allies. End of World War II.

Men dragging cut stone at Mauthausen, where the life expectancy of a prisoner was four months.

Legend over Molengoot camp entrance:
Government Work Camp
MOLENGOOT

Statue "De Dokwerker" by Mari Andriessen, on Jonas Daniel Meijerplein in Amsterdam, commemorating the 1941 dock workers' strike.

VOICES OF PROTEST

The Amsterdam dock workers' strike of February 1941 and the rail workers' strike that started September 17, 1944, were the only general strikes against the Germans to occur in any occupied country throughout World War II. There were also a great many individual protests throughout the Netherlands, including those by church, university, government, and student leaders.

Utrecht's **Archbishop Monsignor Dr. Johannes de Jong** (1885-1955), along with many other Dutch church officials, publicly warned against the dangers of Nazi ideology and repeatedly criticized Nazi decrees from the pulpit. On July 11, 1942, ten Christian churches sent a telegram to the Germans, expressing a "sense of outrage against the deportation of Jews . . . which went against the deepest moral feelings of the Dutch people and counter to the divine commandments of justice and charity." They added an additional plea for converts. De Jong instigated a pastoral letter to be read from every Catholic pulpit, which forbade Catholics from joining any Nazi organization, unless they explicitly denied Nazi ideology, "under pain of being refused the sacraments." It was the church's threat to read the letter out in every church that particularly enraged the Germans. This spirit of resistance was also expressed by Carmelite schools that refused to expel Jewish pupils as the Germans demanded. The Germans took their revenge on the Catholics in particular because they considered Archbishop de Jong to be the least compliant. They arrested many Jewish converts to Catholicism. Archbishop de Jong twice pleaded with Seyss-Inquart to spare them, but they were sent to Westerbork where one of them, Edith Stein, a Carmelite nun from Echt, refused an offer of rescue, saying she wanted to share the lot of her brothers and sisters.

On November 26, 1940, **Professor Mr. Rudolph P. Cleveringa***, the Dean of the Law Faculty at Leiden University, gave a speech in the great auditorium protesting the German's dismissal of a Jewish colleague, Professor Meijers: "This Dutchman, this noble and true son of our people, this man, this father to his students, this scholar, whom foreign usurpers have suspended from his duties . . . I told you that I would not speak of my feelings: I will keep my word even though they threaten to burst like boiling lava through all the cracks which I feel at moments could open under the pressure in my head and heart. In keeping with the traditions of the Netherlands, the written constitution declares that every Dutchman is eligible for appointment to every office and to every dignity and every function, and places him, independent of his religion, in the enjoyment of the same civic and civil rights. According to Article 43 of the Rules of Land Warfare, the occupying force is obliged to honor the laws of the country *sauf empêchement absolu* (without any impediment whatsoever). We cannot but conclude that absolutely no reason exists for the occupying forces not to leave Meijers where he was. This implies that ejecting him from his position in the manner of which I have informed you and similar measures affecting others (among them, the first who comes to mind being our friend and colleague David) can only be felt by us as injustice." A student began to sing the national anthem, and the entire audience joined in. The students went on strike. The Germans closed the university and imprisoned Cleveringa in Scheveningen prison and Vught concentration camp, and Meijers in Theresienstadt. When the university reopened after the war, both Cleveringa and Meijers returned. In 1946, University Rector Cleveringa presented Winston Churchill with an honorary Ph.D.

Mr. Lodewijk Ernst Visser was born in Amersfoort in 1871. He was appointed president of the Dutch Supreme Court on January 3, 1939. On May 10, 1940, Visser denounced the Germans from the bench for their "treacherous attacks" and "murder." He maintained that Jews were no different from non-Jews and legally could not be differentiated from any other Dutch citizens, and that it was contrary to the Dutch Constitution as well as a violation of international law to do so. He was dismissed on November 23, 1940. In December 1940, Visser became chairman of the Jewish Coordinating Committee, which advised Dutch Jews to deal with the Dutch authorities rather than with the Germans. He refused to accept an ID stamped with a "j." His son, Ernst Lodewijk, also refused. Visser opposed cooperation with the Germans and recommended defiance, not compliance. He said that the attitude of the Jewish Council to oblige the occupier and meekly obey his orders was craven. He denounced the opening of separate Jewish schools. He tried to plead directly with General Hanns Rauter, head of the SS, on behalf of the hostages who were taken to Mauthausen, and he protested in every way that he could. Visser also wrote articles for the resistance newspaper *Het Parool*. Although he had not been an observant Jew, he began walking on the Sabbath in Sabbath clothes, carrying a prayer book. Visser died of a heart attack on February 17, 1942, three days after receiving a letter from the Jewish Council threatening him with deportation if his protests continued. His 41-year-old son was killed in Mauthausen on September 2, 1942, for refusing to wear a yellow star.

J. B. F. (Frans) van Hasselt was born February 26, 1913. He was president of the student association at Delft University where, following the German dismissal of Jewish faculty, he delivered an inspiring roar of protest, ending with, "Blessed are they that suffer persecution for righteousness' sake: for theirs is the kingdom of heaven." All the students went on strike. Van Hasselt was arrested, sent to Scheveningen and died in Buchenwald on September 10, 1941.

*Mr. is the Dutch abbreviation for Master of Law.

THE JEWISH COUNCIL

In February 1941, the Germans encouraged local Nazis to attack Jews in The Hague, Rotterdam, and Amsterdam. The Jews defended themselves well and in Amsterdam one storm trooper died from his wounds. The Germans arrested Ernst Cahn and Alfred Kohn, two owners of the Koco Ice Cream Parlor from which Jewish activists launched their response. On March 3, 1941, Cahn was executed by a firing squad commanded by Klaus Barbie. Thinking it unfair for both sides to be armed, the Germans demanded that the Jews form a Council to disarm and control their people and to enforce German orders. Abraham Asscher, the director of a large diamond company, and David Cohen (*opposite, below*), professor of Ancient History at the University of Amsterdam, were joint chairmen. Cohen had been the head of the committee to help refugees fleeing the Nazis, and following *Kristallnacht,* he helped organize the transport of 10,000 children (the *Kindertransport*) from Germany, Austria, and Czechoslovakia to England, with a stopover in Holland. The project was initiated by a Dutch gentile, Mrs. Gertrude Wijsmuller.

Asscher and Cohen asked prominent Jews from professional and religious organizations to serve on the board, and most accepted. The Council was supposed to represent Jewish interests and be a buffer between the Germans and the Jews, as Jews were prohibited from contacting the German authorities directly.

From the beginning, the German authorities demanded that the Council ensure compliance with all the regulations that were published in a weekly newspaper, *Het Joodsche Weekblad (The Jewish Weekly)*, whose editor, Jacques de Leon, was appointed by the Germans. This was the only Jewish newspaper allowed. The paper dealt exclusively with Jewish affairs and did so in an authoritarian way; the text was prescribed and censured. The Council was required to compile a registry of the names and addresses of all Jews, and ensure that the exact number of people that the Germans stipulated reported for work or for "transportation to Germany." The Germans left it up to the Council to decide how to ensure compliance. When Asscher and Cohen complained that a target number was too difficult to achieve, the Germans reminded them of Mauthausen. The Council tried to soften the effects of the decrees where it could. It employed about 8,000 people who were given exemptions from deportation until further notice. It suggested exemption categories and loopholes; it also facilitated the delivery of mail and supplied food and clothing to the needy.

The Council had a central office in Amsterdam, and several regional offices that were closed in 1942 when all Jews were forced to move to Amsterdam. The Amsterdam branch of the Jewish Council urged people to obey their call-up summonses. It stated that "the most severe punishment will occur" if they did not show up. However, the regional branch in Enschede urged people to disobey the call-up summonses and go into hiding. Due to the support of a local Protestant minister, Leendert Overduin, 38 percent of the Jews of Enschede survived the war, which was roughly double the national average. The leaders of the Jewish Council in Enschede were Sig Menco, Gerard Sanders, and Isedoor van Dam (*below*). When the Germans ordered the Warsaw Jewish Council to supply 6,000 Jews a day for deportation in July 1942, Adam Czerniaków, the head of the Council, committed suicide. When the Germans ordered Elias Barzilai, the Grand Rabbi of Athens, to submit a list of all Jews, he destroyed the lists and advised the community to flee or go into hiding. And Archbishop Damaskinos of Athens ordered his priests to assist the Jews.

After the war, the German Chief-of-Police of Amsterdam, Willy Lages, was questioned by Jacob Presser, author of *Ashes in the Wind: The Destruction of Dutch Jewry:*

> "How was the Jewish Council used?"
> "In every possible way."
> "Did you find them easy to work with?"
> "Very easy indeed."

In 1946 Asscher and Cohen were arrested and charged with collaborating with the enemy, but the proceedings were dropped and there was no trial. In 1947 a Jewish court of honor (*Ereraad*), was created to try Asscher and Cohen for collaborating with the enemy and assisting in the identification, isolation, and deportation of the Jews from Holland. The court found them guilty, concluding that their conduct was blameworthy on four counts and severely blameworthy on the fifth. They were banned from holding any office in any Jewish organization, whether paid or unpaid, for the rest of their lives.

Two post-war experts, L. de Jong and Jacob Presser, criticized the Jewish Council for taking care of its own and assisting the rich at the expense of the poor. Jane Fresco, Bernard Cohen's (page 27), sister says that most people called the *Joodse Raad* (Jewish Council), *Joods Veraad* (Jewish treason). However, the Netherland's expert on the Jewish Council, Professor Houwink ten Cate, was of the opinion that the Council did what it could under difficult circumstances.[A]

Isedoor van Dam

New Edition: Volume 1 No 1 - 11 April 1941 (14 Nisan 5701)

The Jewish Weekly

PUBLISHED BY THE JEWISH COUNCIL OF AMSTERDAM

Under the directorship of A. Asscher and Prof. Dr. D. Cohen

Introduction

With permission from the German authorities and edited by the Jewish Council, *The Jewish Weekly* will appear from today onwards under the responsibility of the undersigned.

In addition to news items and pieces of information, this paper will contain articles that will bring discussions of the Jewish religion, Jewish science, and Jewish culture to its readers. In this way and through this paper, the editors, to whom we have already granted permission to operate under our direction, hope to have found a way to inform readers about everything considered important for them to know at this time.

With this newspaper, we hope to provide the Dutch Jews with leadership and information—leadership that will strive to look after their interests, where and whenever possible, and information that will make it easier for them to receive official and other news from a reliable source. Through this, rumors will lose their force and eventually be laid to rest, something which is necessary for our daily work.

In order to achieve this peace of mind, we call on everyone. We are now experiencing a difficult time together. We can bear it if we draw strength from Judaism, which it amply provides, and if we remain calm, thus allowing ourselves to do our duty to ourselves, our family, and our neighborhood. May this newspaper help us with this.

A. ASSCHER
Prof. Dr. D. COHEN

OFFICIAL

Composition of the Jewish Council for Amsterdam

The Reich's Commissioner's Special Representative for Amsterdam has established a Jewish Council for Amsterdam, whose chairmen are A. Asscher and Prof. Dr. D. Cohen. The Council is also led by the following: J. Arons, N. de Beneditty, A. van den Bergh, Alb. B. Gomperts, I. de Haan, A. de Hoop, Mr. M. L. Kan, Mr. I. Kisch, A. Krouwer, Mr. S. J. van Lier, A. J. Mendes da Costa, Prof. Dr. J. L. Palache, Mr. Dr. M. L. Prins, Chief Rabbi L. H. Sarlouis, Dr. D. M. Sluys, A. Soep Bzn., I. S. Voet,° and Dr. L. H. J. Vos.

°I. S. Voet resigned one week later.

Portion of the front page of the first edition of *Het Joodsche Weekblad* (The Jewish Weekly), published April 11, 1941.

Senior Officials of the Jewish Council:
Sitting from left to right: Abraham Asscher; David Cohen (co-presidents of the Council); name?; name?; A. van Dam (head of buildings); Rabbi Philip Frank; Dr. D. M. Sluys; S. J. van Lier; A. B. Gomperts; A. J. Mendes da Costa. *Standing left to right*: Meijer de Vries (secretary general); Dr. A. van der Laan; J. Brandon; name?; name?; A. Soep; name?; Prof. Dr. J. Brahn (representative of German Jews); A. Krouwer (chief accountant); name?; Prof. J. I. Palache.

MAUTHAUSEN

Mauthausen concentration camp was located in hilly country on the north bank of the Danube, 861 feet above sea level, near Linz, Austria. The camp, with 49 sub-camps, was centered in a picturesque wooded area close to a stone quarry. Mauthausen hung like a specter over Dutch Jews. In 1941, death notices began to be received in the Netherlands, making explicit the fate of those men arrested in the February raid. In June 1941, Klaus Barbie[A] politely asked David Cohen for the addresses of 200 students from the agricultural training school at Wieringermeer, so that he could notify them that they could return to the school. Cohen naively handed over the addresses. The students were arrested and sent to Mauthausen, where they were all killed.

Although Mauthausen was equipped with a small gas chamber that at times was used for prisoners no longer able to work, most were given a slower and more painful death. The camp policy of *"Vernichtung durch Arbeit"* (extermination by work) was Heinrich Himmler's invention. Prisoners were given little food and forced to work with the most primitive tools or with their bare hands.

Prisoners were tortured and punished for breaking the rules or purely for sport. In 1944, 47 Allied underground agents were caught when they parachuted into the Netherlands and were sent to Mauthausen: ". . . the prisoners arrived in September 1944 and were led barefoot to the quarry . . . At the bottom of the very uneven steps, stones were loaded on the backs of these poor men and they had to carry them to the top. The first journey was made with stones weighing about 60 pounds and accompanied by blows. On the second journey the stones were still heavier, and whenever the poor wretches sank under their burden, they were kicked and hit with a bludgeon or shot . . . In the evening 21 bodies were strewn along the road. The other 26 were shot the following morning."[B]

According to Christian Bernadac, a French resistance fighter who was imprisoned at Mauthausen, "suicides by jumping off the cliff were very frequent." In one single day, 55 Jews leaped off the cliff of the quarry, one after the other. At the Nuremberg International Military Tribunal, SS Alois Höllriegl testified that "From the guard watchtower I saw two SS who were striking the prisoners, and was able to note that they wanted to force them to leap off the cliff, or else they pushed them."[C]

It was at Mauthausen that the practice of freezing prisoners to death was invented. Commandant Karl Chmielewski of Gusen I, a subcamp four miles away, who savoured this method of execution, once gave his son a birthday gift of 50 Jews for target practice. In January 1943, he was posted as the commandant of Vught concentration camp in the Netherlands when it was opened as a punishment camp for Dutch Jews.

Of the one million members of the SS (Hitler's elite paramilitary corps), more than 19,000 served at Mauthausen, a posting that appealed to those who preferred their opponents to be starved, unarmed prisoners, rather than angry Russians at the front who followed the Geneva Conventions about as carefully as the Germans themselves. Between 1939 and 1945, approximately 250,000 prisoners were killed at Mauthausen.[D] The names and dates of birth and death of all 1,629 victims who were Dutch citizens is given in *Mauthausen: a Memorial Book,* by Henny E. Dominicus and Alice B. van Keulen-Woudstra. It includes biographies and photographs of all who could be found. The 1,629 comprise

338 from the Amsterdam raid on February 22-23, 1941
227 from the Amsterdam raid on June 11, 1941
103 from the raid in and around Enschede on September 14, 1941
60 from a raid in Gelderland on October 8-9, 1941
39 Dutch of the 47 agents captured in September 1944[E]
11 from *Aktion Kugel* (Action Bullet), March 1944-February 1945

851 other Dutch citizens, including people sent to Mauthausen for various reasons, and prisoners who survived the death marches from Auschwitz and other camps. It was in this camp that 21-year-old Philip Samas (Flip's cousin) died on October 3, 1941. His 25-year-old brother, Salomo Samas, died in Graeditz, Germany, on February 29, 1944. Both names are engraved on the Dutch monument in Mauthausen. When the Americans liberated the camp on May 5, 1945, they found approximately 78,754 men, of whom 13,701 were Jews, and 2,252 women, of whom 611 were Jews.

Stairway of death, Mauthausen quarry

FLIP (PHILIP) SLIER

Flip (Philip) Slier was born on December 4, 1923, on the top floor of 128 Vrolik Street in Amsterdam. When the Germans invaded, he was a 17-year-old apprentice typesetter for the *Algemeen Handelsblad*, a daily newspaper where his father also worked. He was 5 feet 7¾ inches tall, weighed 156 pounds, had black hair and gray eyes. He was a good-natured, gregarious young man who was described by his friend Karel van der Schaaf as *brutaal*—that is, audacious. He played the flute and the mandolin, liked singing, and had a good sense of humor. Truus Sant, his first girl friend said: "Flip was crazy about me, and Harry Elzas was jealous and his parents gave us a lot of trouble because I wasn't Jewish. I played the drum while he played the flute in the AJC band." Flip was an avid photographer. Many of the photos of family and friends in this book were taken by him. The AJC (*Arbeiders Jeugd Centrale:* Worker's Youth Center) was a Dutch socialist organization with a section for 12 to 16-year-olds called Red Falcons, and the Red Guards for those over 16. They held weekly political meetings, they did not drink or smoke; they were interested in art, literature, music, and outdoor activities; and on the weekends, they went hiking and camping and took holidays in the countryside. In 2007, Truus reminisced over lunch in the Amsterdam woods: "One day I was walking alone in the

Flip Slier about 1940

park when I met an AJC boy, Chris Brand, who walked along with me. Flip's father passed by and reported to Flip that I was out with another boy, and that was the end of Flip and me. I still saw Flip after that, but we were no longer together. Flip wrote a poem to me." She then recited it.[1]

On Thursday April 23, 1942, Flip received a letter like the one below from the Jewish Council ordering him to take a train on Saturday, April 25, to Hardenberg. (80 miles east of Amsterdam), and from there he walked the two miles to the camp.

Left to right: Flip, Truus; ? name; Harry Elzas

```
JOODSCHE RAAD VOOR AMSTERDAM
------------------------------        Amsterdam, 8 Januari 1942.

Nieuwe Keizersgracht 58
Tel: 55003, 55136, 54970.

Afd. III  A.Z.

              EEN  LAATSTE  WAARSCHUWING.
              ----------------------------------

        Gij zijt door het Gemeentelijk Arbeidsbureau aangewezen om in
een der Nederlandsche werkkampen in Drente onder leiding van den Neder-
landschen Rijksdienst voor Werkverruiming te gaan arbeiden. Gij moet
daartoe Zaterdagochtend per trein vertrekken.

        Wij geven U nogmaals  voor het laatst den dringenden raad dit
onvermijdelijke bevel op te volgen. De allerernstigste maatregelen
tegenover U zijn te duchten, indien ge U aan dit bevel onttrekt.
Wij doen een herhaald beroep op U - en hebben daarbij Uw hoogste eigen
belang op het oog - om op den vastgestelden tijd aanwezig te zijn.
Wij herhalen: het gaat om den gewonen werkverruimingsarbeid in de gewone
Nederlandsche arbeidskampen onder de gewone Nederlandsche leiding.

                        De Voorzitters van den Joodschen Raad

                                A. Asscher

                                Prof.Dr. C. Cohen.
```

```
JEWISH COUNCIL OF AMSTERDAM
                                  Amsterdam, 8 January [Thursday] 1942
Nieuwe Keizersgracht 58
Tel: 55003,  55136,  54970

Afd. III  A.Z.
              ONE  LAST  WARNING.
              -----------------------------------

    You have been selected by the Municipal Labor Office to go
to work in one of the Dutch Labor camps in the province of
Drente under the direction of the Dutch Labor Council. You
must therefore leave by train on Saturday morning.

    We give you again, for the last time, urgent advice to imme-
diately follow this order. If you do not do this, the most
severe punishment will occur. We repeat again, that you must
give this — for your own good — your most urgent priority to be
present at the indicated time. We repeat, that this is about
normal work provision in normal Dutch labor camps under normal
Dutch supervision.
              The Chairmen of the Jewish Council

                        A. Asscher
                        Prof. Dr. C.[D] Cohen
```

1. Flip's poem to Truus that she recited some 70 years later.

Het is uit tussen de trommel en de fluit
En weg is mijn bruid.
Ze was die avond erg stil,
Het is niet meer dat ze wil,
Ah fijn, er is vast een ander op til.

Its over between the drum and the flute
And gone away is my bride.
The evening was still,
It is not what she will,
Ah fine, there is another at her side.

DUTCH WORK CAMPS

During the depression prior to World War II, the Dutch government contracted the *Heide Maatschappij* (Moor Corporation) to operate work camps for the unemployed. The men dug canals, laid roads, and worked on land improvement. They were paid a small wage, had freedom of movement, and had leave at the end of every two weeks. In December 1941, the men in the camps were sent home, and in January 1942, were replaced by Jews who had been made unemployed by German laws. The Jews were paid lower wages, given less food, had restricted movement, and were allowed no leave. Board, lodging, and health insurance were deducted from their wages.

Flip was prohibited from attending school and from working. Perhaps he complied with the Jewish Council's summons because it was work, and they assured him that it was "in normal Dutch labor camps under normal Dutch supervision", or perhaps he feared that non-compliance would result in the "most severe punishment," which implied that his parents might be arrested and sent to a concentration camp. Shortly after his arrival at Molengoot work camp, Flip wrote to his parents, and he continued to write to them and to his friends almost every day.

Flip's letters are unedited. The omissions, strikeouts, spelling errors, incorrect days, dates, or years are left just as he wrote them.

Flip's mother, Seline Rozetta Salomonson-Slier was born March 14, 1890, in Denekamp, 20 miles southeast of Hardenberg, three miles from the German border.

[25 April 1942 Saturday]

Dear Father and Mother,

Have arrived in the camp. Fairly comfortable. Reasonable bed, 3 blankets. Clean. Good atmosphere, decent people. We have very little freedom. In Overijssel [a province] we are allowed to leave the camp for an hour now and then. In Drente [neighboring province just north of Overijssel] it is forbidden.

Send me a windbreaker as soon as possible.   <u>Clogs</u>   Camp knife.

↑

Urgently needed

Little to eat. It's possible that soon it will be forbidden to receive packages. Don't let this go any further, none of this is certain. Had a good journey. Greet everyone from me. A kiss from *Flip.*   Be brave.

Cannot tell you anything more.
Fond regards and a kiss from *Flip*

If you have any food, send it. There are 8 of us in one room.

The camp leader made a speech, not encouraging, but he hopes to see us back in A[msterdam] soon.

The first page of Flip's first letter home

Hardenberg, 25 April 1942 [Saturday]

Dear Father and Mother,

After a really pleasant journey with a nice bunch of people,[1] we arrived here in Molengoot. The accommodation is much better than I expected. We all have separate beds with three blankets and clean straw mattresses. Everything is quite neat. Good toilets, washrooms, and good barracks. My bed is next to Nico Groen's.[2] That's good company for me. In Hardenberg we were able to throw our cases onto a cart. That cost us a dubbeltje.[3] After a half-hour walk we arrived in the camp. I am with the same people as on the train. There are eight people to a room. After we had been here for an hour we all went to the canteen. It is a large hall with books, chess and checker games, and billiard tables. We listened to a speech in which we were told that unfortunately we would not get enough to eat. We were also warned not to protest or anything *Also the sp[eaker] said he hoped he would quickly see us back in A[msterdam]. This got great applause.* like that and what the punishments would be. Then we had our first bread and butter meal. Six slices of bread ~~and~~ for one meal and 1¼ ounces of butter for the whole week. We were all still pretty well fed so it was enough. 2 hours later we each got a tasty plate of red cabbage with real fat and meat. So for tonight I have had enough. Only, the coffee tastes like dishwater. Of course I can't say anything about the work yet. That we must wait and see. We are 150 men here. I think they are mostly decent people.

This evening we had a lot of fun and laughed a lot. I think our barrack will turn out quite pleasant as long as the food is decent. Pa, will you send my clogs as soon as possible? Also my raincoat, camp knife, envelopes, windbreaker. Also send the yellow filter[4] for my camera. *Mending wool, shoes (brown).* Also send a box of cookies. It's possible that soon nothing will be allowed to be sent. Compared with the camps in Drente, we still have some freedom. We may, now and then, have an hour free, that is, out of the camp. *1 or 2 times in 14 days* We just collected bread. It is very little, hardly more than half a loaf for two days. That will never be enough. But, for now I still have some. For the time being I won't have to be hungry.

Enough writing for tonight. If you send me something now and again I will manage. Also, I will get used to this camp life. If only they leave us alone. Now, more tomorrow.

It is now Sunday morning [26 April]. I slept well last night. Yesterday evening we were all in the canteen. It is a big hall, with chess, checkers, billiards, and books. You can also buy different things like coffee, lemonade, toilet paper, wax paper, writing paper, and stamps. I'll take a photo of it. Tomorrow we start work. We formed our own work group. None of us has family at home that depends on our wages, so we can take it fairly easy. It is a pity that there is so little freedom here. Also you are not allowed to visit us.

You can probably talk to us on Sundays. How, I'll write and tell you later. This morning I have already eaten almost half of my bread for 2 days. Can you also send my slippers?

I'll stop now. Give everyone greetings and a kiss from me. Ma, be strong. Everything will be all right. Best regards and a kiss from

Flip.

Hardenberg
Camp Molengoot
(Overijssel.) Room 7

1. Among the "nice bunch of people" at Molengoot was Bernard Cohen. He was born in Amsterdam on February 13, 1923, to Isaac and Vrouwtje Zwart-Cohen. In May 1942, he escaped from Molengoot (see p. 164, note 39 A) and went to The Hague where he worked as a courier, carrying food stamps to help people in hiding. He is listed on the Dutch Honor Roll in The Hague. The Roll (*Honorlist*) names about 18,000 Dutch people who died fighting the Germans or the Japanese in World War II. They include members of the resistance, the Merchant Service, and the Army and Navy.

2. Nico Groen, was Flip's closest friend in the camp. Nico lived on Oosterpark street, two streets north of Vrolik street. They were both typography apprentices. There is no record of any Nico Groen in the Netherlands.

3. dubbeltje = 10 Dutch cents

4. A yellow filter allows less blue light to pass through, hence, the sky appears darker, and the increased contrast shows off the clouds.

1. We think the "Sjaak" that Harry mentions is Isaäc Creveld, born November 19, 1923.

Mantinge. 26. 4. '42 [Sunday April 26, 1942]

Dear Fam. Slier,

I received your letter Friday evening and from it learn that Flip must go on Saturday. That really upsets me, but there is nothing to do about it. He is in the same camp as Nico Groen, so it is nice that he knows someone who is there already. I can understand that one is not rejected on account of flat feet, but in any case the effort has been made to stay out of the camp. But we are not the only ones. So many have to go to Germany. I expect to receive a note from Flip shortly, and then we can keep in touch with each other, but I hope that it will soon be normal again. I hope that we can come home soon on leave, great leave! Did Flip take some foodstuff along? I hope so. I specifically wrote to him that he has to take food along because we are not allowed to receive food in our packages. Only clean laundry every 2 weeks. Also, no one is allowed to leave or visit the camps anymore. This, since yesterday, is the German regulation for all the camps. At the moment all is okay with me; only the work is hard, but I take it easy and say, "If I do not get there now, I will get there tomorrow." In fact, we all say that here because you can't work on the little bit of food. I have not gone home even once. Now I will finish because I still have to write a lot today. I hope to be in Amsterdam soon, and, of course, Flip as well, and that we can continue our daily lives again in the old way. That is my wish and also Flip's.

Greetings and best and strong wishes
also from Sjaak[1] Creveld

Chin up, you hear!

Eventually this

storm will also pass.

Left to right: Flip; Dick van der Schaaf; Appie (Abraham) Reis; Harry Elzas; and Maupie (Michael) Vogel in 1939

Map of the Netherlands showing towns in red,● camps in black ●

[POSTCARD]   26 April '42 [Sunday]

Dear Father and Mother,

My first workday is behind me. It was extremely hard. They say that they can make no distinction between hard or easy labor. We work with Christians and get along very well with them. But our group has separate work. We are the only ones who work with Christians. We have to fill carts with sand and push them along ourselves.[1] It takes about 10 minutes to a quarter of an hour to push each one away. We filled about 10 carts. It doesn't seem like much, but it is incredibly tiring. I had the good luck to find a pair of great clogs. My shoes were almost murdered today. Can you also send some <u>goggles</u>? So much sand blows into our eyes here that our eyes will certainly be ruined if it continues to blow like this. Again, please send mending wool, raincoat, windbreaker, and if possible, "<u>overalls</u>." I will send my clothing coupons.[2] Yellow filter.

This morning we had porridge. It was simply skim milk with almost nothing in it. The hot meal is tasty, but there is so little that you are still hungry after you've finished it. I went to see the cook, but he says there is nothing he can do. We have a fine group of boys who are honest and loyal to each other. We do a little foraging around [buying food illicitly from the local farmers] but don't mention that to anybody. If I can ever come home on leave, I'll tell you about it.

If you have anything extra, you can send it without a problem. I am very careful, but the ration is so little that everything is finished very soon, though I haven't touched my butter yet. And I still have more than 1½ loaves of bread and I am very thrifty. We must get up at ~~om~~ 5:30 and by 5:45 get our food and at 7 leave for work. I'll write again.

[signature]

I'm writing this two days later

1. The carts or wheelbarrows are shown below.

2. The Germans imposed rationing on the Dutch. Nothing could be bought without ration cards (*below*) and coupons for *brood* (bread), *boter* (butter), *vleesch* (meat), *aardappelen* (potatoes), *zeep* (soap), and *textiel* (clothing) and everything else. The stamp 'ONGELDIG' on the blue and red block of coupons means not valid.

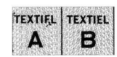

Workers with their barrows. *Left to right:* ? name; Flip; Nico Groen; ?; ?; ?

MOLENGOOT WORK CAMP REMEMBERED

Egbert de Lange from Mariënberg was twenty-two years old when he arrived in Camp Molengoot. This camp served as housing for the unemployed who were then put to work digging drainage canals for the Moor Corporation. Mr. de Lange worked as assistant cook under the supervision of cook/manager C. Abspoel.

In March 1941, when de Lange had only been working in the camp for one week, the first residents arrived. They were unemployed people from The Hague and Scheveningen. They would work for three weeks, get one weekend off, and then spend another three weeks digging. In December 1941, they were given a longer vacation period because it was no longer possible to perform work outside. The men were supposed to return in mid-January. The kitchen crew had prepared 180 liters of pea soup, but nobody showed up. They didn't return until one and a half months later. The people sent from Scheveningen and The Hague worked there until about the end of March 1942, when they had to give up their places to Jews.

"This group [of Jews] consisted mostly of business people, especially owners of clothing stores . . . but there were also some younger people among them. They had to do the same work as the people from Scheveningen, but they were given less food to perform this heavy physical labor. We were simply given fewer provisions for these people," de Lange stated, "but sometimes we were able to remedy the situation. For example, we secretly purchased potatoes as supplements, which were paid for by the Jews themselves." But it gradually became more difficult to prepare a decent meal for the workers because, after a few months, the rations were even more restricted. Camp Molengoot was a true labor camp, very different from a transit camp like Westerbork.

The Jews were reasonably free; they could, for example, leave the camp and cycle to Hardenberg. "To do so, they would use the service bicycles. The same bicycles were also used at times to

Egbert de Lange in 1999

escape, or to look for a place to go underground. We received a letter from one person after he had disappeared. He wrote that he had cycled to Almelo and the bicycle was parked in the bicycle lock-up. He enclosed the parking stub. There were also Jews who asked for permission to leave the camp (and who were given permission) because they wanted to join their spouses who were in Westerbork. This 'freedom' of the Jews could also be seen in other ways. There were in fact no guards at the camp and Germans came rarely or never. And some men received visits from their wives. They would arrive in Hardenberg by train during the morning, meet with their husbands outside of the camp and return again by train in the evening.

"The Jews also did not have to do exercises. Abspoel, the cook and manager, did go to Camp Erika, in Ommen, for a week once in order to learn how to make the Jews do exercises, but nothing much came of it."

Officially de Lange worked in the camp for the Government Job Creation Department, but the work that was performed by the unemployed and later by the Jews, was done for the Moor Corporation, which also handled compensation for the Jews. The organization [Moor] did not exert any influence on life in the camp, according to de Lange. "Not on meals either. Those [Christian] workers from Scheveningen and The Hague were given substantial meals, even a double ration because it was such heavy labor. But the Jews were given a lot less. Soup with bread in the morning, and bread, milk and coffee later during the day. There would be a warm meal in the evening, but there was never enough. Except for vegetables, there were plenty of those." The Jewish workers remained in the camp until October 1942. A company of Germans came to the camp one evening, supposedly in transit. The next morning, they took all the Jews with them to Westerbork. They were allowed to pack their things after breakfast, and then they were taken away under guard. "Their reaction was very resigned when they were told that they were going to Westerbork," de Lange recalled.

"We had 24 rooms in the camp, each for eight people, but they were not all full. The group of 20 German soldiers had to guard about 150 Jews on their walk to the station in Hardenberg."

One month after the departure of the Jews, evacuees were housed in the barracks. By that time, de Lange had been transferred to Camp Balderhaar, which was managed by a member of the Dutch National Socialist Movement. "He was a rather unpleasant person, so I was glad that I could go back to Molengoot after a while." At the time, there were some women and children from the west of the Netherlands in Camp Molengoot. They had to be evacuated because the Germans were in the process of building the Atlantic Embankment. "They were not very social, those families who spent the entire year of 1943 in Molengoot. They did hardly anything at all. From time to time, a social worker would visit, or a kindergarten teacher, and sometimes a nurse, sister Binnenmars from Emmen. But no one else. The camp was placed under the management of the Agency for Evacuation Camps in Overijssel. The commander was someone from Ommen, but he did not concern himself with the families."

De Lange disappeared from Camp Molengoot as a result of an allied bomber that crashed in Baalder in February 1944. The airplane's pilot had parachuted out and landed very close to the camp. The Employment Service at Ommerweg, headed by commander Von Papen, wanted to arrest the pilot, but he managed to escape. The management of the camp demonstrated a form of resistance at that point: the Employment Service were unable to place a call from inside the camp in order to try and get auxiliary forces. But the next day, the Sicherheitsdienst (SD) came to visit. Manager Sluijter and other people involved, such as Hendrik Jan Grootoonk and Jan Hendrik Pullen, were arrested. On the following day de Lange was taken to Arnhem, supposedly for interrogation. The "interrogation" lasted about six weeks, from the end of February until the middle of April. The Germans thought the men arrested had helped the pilot to escape. "But we had not done anything; we had just been standing there," de Lange recounted.

After Arnhem, he was taken to Camp Amersfoort where he remained until September. The next stop was Zwolle where work had to be done on trenches. "We were lodged at the club house. All the benches had been removed, and straw had been placed everywhere on the floor. I stayed there until the end of December. At that point, I supposedly went away to pick up some winter clothing. But, despite the fact that I had signed a statement saying that I would return (if not, they would arrest my family) they never saw me again in Zwolle. In February 1945, I went back to Camp Molengoot because it was a safe place for people who had gone underground." In July of that year, de Lange left the camp for good because he was going to work in Vledder at a former work camp.[4]

Interview with Egbert de Lange by Roel Gritter

Postcard of Molengoot camp. The building at the front left is the canteen.

Cantine Rijkswerkkamp „Molengoot" Hardenberg.

1. Bora (Debora) Prijs (*left*) and Bep (Elisabeth) de Vries, who were first cousins, wearing their AJC uniforms

2. Flip's paternal grandparents, Philip Slier and Betje Benjamins-Slier. Philip died in 1936. Betje died in Westerbork camp on February 17, 1943. When news of her death was received after the war by her only surviving son, Jack (Izaak) in South Africa, he said, "I can understand the Germans arresting my brothers, but what harm could an 81-year-old woman have done to the Germans?" Flip's maternal grandparents died before World War II.

Hardenberg 28 April '42 [Tuesday]

Dear Father and Mother,

I am waiting for your letter but have not received anything yet. I got mail from Bep,[1] Aunt Jo [Joanna Samas], and Grandma![2] The first two days were not easy. Mornings up at five-thirty, five-forty-five get/food, at six-thirty go to work to begin at seven. In the morning there is a strong, freezing wind that penetrates all my clothes and makes me ice-cold. The sand blows in my clothes, my nose, my mouth, and eyes. And then on top of that, the cold hands, I can say that the early morning hours are torture for me. We are building a road, and that is why we have to fill and push the carts. It is very hard work. Even if we don't work hard, we are exhausted. But I am not made of doll's poop, and I will get through this. Please buy me a pair of gloves and send them <u>express</u>. I need them badly. If I can just have them first, I will be happy for the present, and also the other things I wrote and asked for. Bread coupons I could use as well.

Hot meals are painfully small, but we forage around for some from the farmers. There are good people here. When I come home, I will tell you about it. If I get really hungry I will let you know. Though a little package is always welcome because we don't have too much.

Now about something else. I hear that they are still calling people up. It is really terrible. I hope that you, Pa, stay away from this rotten mess. It is true you get hardened here. It's a consolation that we have a decent camp and work and sleep together with decent people. We do a lot together. However, I don't share everything. I still have three eggs, one for each day. We even have fried eggs here, but the boys don't want me to write about that. Don't let others read it, cross it out first, or all of Amsterdam will know in no time. And that mustn't happen. The others are all very united and do everything together, but I don't. Also, I am not crazy. Tonight we are going to make tea; tomorrow we will cook potatoes. Don't let anyone read this. I don't know if it could do harm. Send me my package soon. If it has been sent, send the gloves express. I now think a lot about home, especially when I am "working."

I'll stop now and will write more soon. A kiss from *Flip*
and give everybody my warmest greetings. Maybe you can visit me, but it has to be on the sly. It is strictly forbidden to have visitors at the camp. But then I do it at my own risk.

Now best regards and a kiss from *Flip.*

Keep yourselves well. I am fit and healthy.
Let Bep de Vries also read this letter.

Once I have washed myself in the evening, everything feels all right again.

The Reich Commander
The Security Police and the SD　　　THE HAGUE
For the Occupied Dutch Territory　　　29.4.1942
IV B B. Nr. 1o36/41

To the
Commissioner for Justice and Administration,
Dr. Dr.　W i m m e r,

T h e　H a g u e

Re. : The introduction of the Jewish star.
Whereas—

The Jewish Council was notified today at 16.00 that
within three days all Jews in this country must be identi-
fiable by the Jewish star. Regarding particulars of this
conversation, the leader of the Central Office for jewish
Emigration hereby relays the following information:

"As requested, on 29.4.42 [April 29, 1942] at 4 PM, the
two presidents of the jewish advisory, A) Asscher -B)
Cohen, were summoned to appear at the Central Office
for jewish Emigration. There, SS Captain Aus der Fünten
first informed them that this form of identification (the
Jewish star) would be implemented. They were told that
the notification of the measure would appear in that
evening's papers and that the decree would come into
force in three days' time. Upon hearing this news,
Asscher and Cohen were speechless. They apparently
had not expected this measure. Then they declared that
they, namely Asscher and Cohen, did not find this a
pleasant measure to relay to the Jewish people, but that
they personally would be proud to wear the Jewish star,
which would make them free men of the Netherlands.
Further, Cohen asked why the color of the star needed to
be yellow; for the Jews, this was the color of humiliation.
SS Captain Aus der Fünten replied that the color had
been chosen for its clarity and that the star was also the
same color in Germany. Thus, 569,355 stars were to be
placed at the disposal of the Jewish Council. The
distribution of these stars would be handled by the
Jewish Council, but they considered 3 days to be too
short a time to do this. It was then pointed out to them
that this time limit was not open to negotiation. Next,
they asked if the Jewish Council could place a notification
of the measure in the daily press. This was rejected.
After this, Cohen then declared it to be an awful measure,
Asscher said, literally: "It will not last long, one to two
months, until the war is over, and we are free!" In
general, it can be said that the Jewish Council tried to
strongly protest the introduction of the star. Cohen thus
expressed himself as follows, "You must be able to
understand our feelings, Herr Captain, it is a terrible day
in the history of the Jews in the Netherlands!"

[W. Harster was Dr. Wilhelm Harster,
Hanns Rauter's head of the Secret Police]

DER BEFEHLSHABER
DER SICHERHEITSPOLIZEI UND DES SD
FÜR DIE BESETZTEN NIEDERLÄNDISCHEN GEBIETE　　　DEN HAAG,　den 29.4.42

IV B B.Nr.1o36/41

An den
Generalkommissar für Justiz und Verwaltung,
Dr.Dr.　W i m m e r,

D e n　H a a g

Betr.: Einführung des Judensterns.
Vorg.: ---

Dem Judenrat wurde heute Nachmittag 16 Uhr eröffnet,dass er
innerhalb der nächsten 3 Tage die Kennzeichnung sämtlicher
Juden mit dem Judenstern durchzuführen habe.Über die Einzel-
heiten dieses Vorganges teilt der Leiter der Zentralstelle für
jüdische Auswanderung folgendes mit:

"Auftragsgemäss wurden am 29.4.42 um 16 Uhr die Vorsitzenden
des jüdischen Rates, A.) A s s c h e r - B.)　C o h e n
zur Zentralstelle für jüdische Auswanderung bestellt. Durch
SS-Hauptsturmführer Aus der Fünten wurde ihnen eröffnet,dass
die Kennzeichnung (Judenstern) durchzuführen sei.Es wurde
darauf hingewiesen,dass in der heutigen Abendpresse die Veröffentlichung erscheint und 3 Tage nach der Bekanntgabe in
Kraft tritt. Nach dieser Mitteilung waren Asscher sowie Cohen
völlig sprachlos. Man hat scheinbar nicht mit dieser Massnahme
gerechnet.Dann erklärten sie,nämlich Asscher und Cohen,dass
es keine angenehme Mitteilung für die Judenschaft sei,sie per-
und würden somit Ehrenbürger der Niederlande. Weiter fragte
Cohen, warum die Farbe des Sternes gerade gelb sei. Es sei
ja die Farbe der Erniedrigung für das Judentum. SS-Hauptsturmführer Aus der Fünten antwortete darauf, dass diese Farbe der
Deutlichkeit halber gewählt worden sei und der Stern auch in
Deutschland dieselbe Farbe habe.Dann wurden dem Judenrat die
Sterne zur Verfügung gestellt(569 355 Stück).Die Verteilung
der Sterne wurde dem Judenrat übertragen,worauf dieser jedoch
die Einwendung machte,die Durchführung innerhalb 3 Tagen sei
zu kurz.Es wurde darauf hingewiesen, dass dieser Termin unbe-
dingt einzuhalten sei.Weiter wurde gefragt,ob seitens des Ju-
denrats eine Veröffentlichung in der Tagespresse erscheinen
dürfe. Dieses wurde abgelehnt.Nachdem Cohen äusserte,es sei
doch eine furchtbare Massnahme,sagte Asscher wörtlich:
Es wird nicht lange dauern, ein-zwei Monate ,bis der Krieg
abgelaufen ist,und wir sind frei! Insgesamt kann gesagt werden, dass der Judenrat versuchte, scharf gegen die Einführung
des Sterns zu protestieren. So äusserte sich Cohen wie folgt:
"Sie werden unsere Gefühle verstehen,Herr Hauptsturmführer,
es ist ein schrecklicher Tag in der Geschichte der Juden in
Holland! '

The Netherlands is the only country in Europe that has never
expelled, ghettoed, nor legally discriminated against Jews, thus
Dutch Jews felt as Dutch as non-Jews did. When the Germans
introduced laws and regulations to separate, humiliate, rob, and
expel them, they were so skillful that at each stage the Jews were
shocked, as Asscher and Cohen were *(above)* at the Jewish star
proposal that had been introduced into Germany on September
1, 1941. The yellow star, the ban on donating blood, the
prohibition of football, fishing, and libraries; changing the
spelling of "Jew" to "jew" were clever ways to induce humiliation
and make the case that Jews were different—in defiance of the
Pauline assertion that: "There is no difference between the Jew
and the gentile." In defiance of the Germans, that verse
continued to be so printed in almost all Dutch Bibles,[A] (and see
page 179).

1. Vriezenveen was the birthplace of Flip's mother's father and other relatives. It was 15 miles south of Molengoot.

2. In Flip's day, when metal type was used for printing, the letters were held in an oblong tray or case that resembled long flat sailing galleys. The printer would then print a proof of the set type, called a galley proof, for the editor to read and check for mistakes.

The cases in which typesetters stored all letters were stacked in a box with the capital letter case on top and the small letter case below, hence the terms "upper case" and "lower case" letters.

3. *Back*: "Liesje's Lou" Louis Slier, born December 19, 1912. He was the son of Flip's uncle, Jonas Slier and Liesje (Anna) Plas-Slier. *Front, left to right*: Debora Slier; Betje Benjamins-Slier; Duifje Slier; and Philip Slier, Lou's aunts and grandparents.

Hardenberg. 29 April 1942 [Wednesday]

Dear Father and Mother,

I received the package and your letter in good health. I am not as tired as I was in the beginning. I am getting used to it, although it is not easy. Ma must not cry or fret. I am convinced that we shall get through. This morning the ditches were full of ice, that's how cold it was, and a strong northeast wind is blowing. But I have already written about that. Sitting here now, I feel fit as a fiddle. I have washed my legs and face and ears and eyes. I don't let myself get dirty. You write that I should go to the doctor, but there isn't one here.

You can't imagine how happy I am with my package. I don't need the clogs anymore, *now* somebody else can make good use of them. If I had worn my old shoes one day longer, I would have had to throw them away. I am wearing the windbreaker now. It fits beautifully; thank Riek [Hendrika Schaap] very much. It is wonderful. I am also happy with the slippers and the flute and the syrup and everything else. Too bad I haven't got gloves yet. My hands are absolutely raw from the cold. Tomorrow I'll take socks with me to wear on my hands. I don't need a camp knife immediately, and you don't have to send my yellow filter. What a dirty trick that they can't send Harry packages anymore. All they want to do is harass the jews.

When I am no longer allowed to receive packages, send them to Friesenveen [sic] [the Dutch pronounce "v" like "f"].[1] Perhaps they will be able to give them to me. I will write about the de Bruin family in a separate letter [see opposite page]. Also thank you for the postage stamps. I am enclosing the clothing coupons. We are not allowed to go to Hardenberg. We can't even leave the camp. We are locked up here like slaves. My galley[2] is still at the Verdoner printing works.

If Liesje's Lou[3] had to do the work we do for 1 day, he would collapse. Let him stay in A[msterdam]. It is no joke here.

But again I will get through it. If anything happens here, I will be gone in no time. You can count on that. Well, Pa and Ma, keep strong. If Pa is called up, bluff, do whatever it takes.

A hearty kiss from

I can make good use of a pair of old socks [to wear] in the clogs.

I am really happy with it.

Send by <u>express</u> a thick pair of ~~gloves as quickly as possible~~. Again thank you for the package.

daaaag[4]

4. The word for goodbye in Dutch is "*dag*," which literally means "day." It is similar to our "good day" or "g'day." The Dutch often extend and inflect the farewell, thus: *daaag, daaaag* or *dáááááág*.

1. Ru de Bruin's café, bookstore, and publishing house is the second building from the left.

The first edition of Ru de Bruin's weekly paper (*above*), and Ru (*foreground below*) with the locals.

RU DE BRUIN

Ru (Rudolf Emanuel) de Bruin (*bottom left*) was born in Hardenberg on May 29, 1887. His wife, Rosalchen Salomonson, was born 22 miles to the east in Nordhorn, Germany, on September 1, 1889. Flip's mother Seline Salomonson-Slier and Rosalchen were cousins, whose mothers and fathers were related in several ways. Ru de Bruin, who had Cohen and Salomonson grandparents, was a journalist, editor, printer, and publisher of a weekly paper he founded, *De Vechtstreek*. He owned the Café de Bruin[1] where many cultural activities took place. He and his son, Lion, were active members of a theater society named Thalia. Ru was a founding member of a brass band "*Kunst na Arbeid*" that still performs today. He was a well-known figure in Hardenberg and the surrounding villages. When the Germans invaded the Netherlands, he was a member of the Hardenberg town council, an alderman, and deputy mayor. When Jews were dismissed from the civil service in November 1940, he too was dismissed. Ru and his wife had four children:

Rosetta, born September 5, 1916

Lion Emanuel, born March 29, 1918

Mennie (Emanuel), born October 20, 1921

Alex Sallie, born November 26, 1927

who attended the public primary school in Hardenberg and high school in Coevorden.

On December 17, 1941, Ru's newspaper and printing business were closed and sealed by the *Sicherheitspolizei* (Security police). Willem Snel, Ru's erstwhile business partner, commented in 1949 that "de Bruin did not want to go into hiding because he did not want to put someone else in grave danger." In April 1943, de Bruin and his wife were sent to Vught, and as the train pulled away, Ru de Bruin shouted through the train's open window, "We will come back . . ." But they never did.[A]

Through his contact with the resistance, Mannes Meijer, a friend and neighbor of the de Bruins, managed to get a place for Lion de Bruin on a boat going to Sweden. But Lion refused to go because there was no room for his brother Mennie. Soon after, the boys were sent with six other Jews from Hardenberg to Camp Linde and from there to Westerbork. Meijer offered to hide Alex Sallie, Ru de Bruin's youngest son, but Ru refused the offer as he felt it was too dangerous for the Meijer family. When Alex was arrested, his father would not allow him to take along a photo of the Meijer family because it might have put them at risk.[B]

1. Aunt Duifje Slier, Flip's father's youngest sister, was born July 13, 1891. She was a dressmaker who lived with her sister Debora, and their mother, at 291 Vrolik Street.

3. Flip's family lived in the Transvaal district of east Amsterdam, where most people were poor and to whom May Day was significant.[A] The annual income of those living in the Jewish area of Amsterdam was approximately half that of the rest of the city. The unemployment rate was higher among Jews, particularly among diamond workers. Flip's Uncle Jack said, "For a diamond worker it was either feast or famine, but usually famine. It was a rotten occupation." He added that his tall, ginger-haired father used to work for a local Catholic burial society when he had no work and as he was a diamond worker, that happened often. Flip's uncles Jack and Andries both immigrated to South Africa to find work.

Amsterdam Jews gave little support to communism, yet many were socialists to whom May Day symbolized the hope that there would soon be work for all. On the first May Day speech in Hyde Park, London in 1890, Karl Marx's daughter Eleanor had said, "The unemployed, both at the top and at the bottom of society will be got rid of." Four years earlier, the American Federation of Labor had declared a national strike to demand an eight-hour workday and chose May 1 as the day to celebrate victory.

[POSTCARD]

Hardenb. 1 May '42 [Friday]

Dear Father and Mother,

I received your parcel with the gloves, goggles, wooden sole shoes, *etc.* I am very happy with it. Thank Aunt Duif[1] a lot. Bep I will thank myself and give her a kiss. I now have other work, but it is also very hard. Whatever you do, do not come here. It can have serious consequences for us. One camp has already been threatened with being moved to Germany because 2 men left their jobs for a few minutes. Also we are not allowed to buy anything from the farmers anymore. But we scheme and get around the rules. Harry has written that the best thing you can do is send me food.

You can't complain that you don't hear from me, can you?

If anything bad happens, I will see to it that I get away. I will not let them take me to Germany. But I don't worry about that. Today we received one guilder of pocket money and our yellow stars[2]. Don't they look beautiful. I never celebrated May 1st[3] like this before. It was tough when I got up this morning. But chin up.

ALLES KOMT TERECHT.

FLIP

[Everything will be all right]

2. By May 3, 1942, all Dutch Jews over the age of six were required to wear the yellow Jewish star at all times. A mock Hebrew style of letters was used to spell the word "*jood*" (Jew). Everyone was allotted four stars, which cost sixteen cents and one clothing coupon. The stars were printed on cotton cloth and had to be sewn to the left breast of all outer garments. Failure to wear a star was punished initially by a fine of 1,000 guilders (an amount that few had) and six months in jail. Later the penalty was punishment camp followed by deportation.

The Germans maintained that it was easy to spot a Jew—although easier if they wore a bright yellow star, the size of a saucer, with the word "jew" marked in black in the middle.

When Hanns Rauter, the head of the SS in the Netherlands made a visit to Vught concentration camp, he sat down next to a blonde woman, whose star was hidden by her hair because her head was bowed as required by German discipline.

"How long have you been working here?"

"Seven months."

"I suppose you have hidden a Jew."

"No, you see, I'm Jewish myself!"

Rauter could not get away quickly enough after making such a blunder.[B]

Hardenberg, 3 May 1942 [Sunday]

Dear Pa and Ma,

At the same time as your letter arrived, I received a package from Aunt Juul,[1] Uncle Karel, and Barend and his wife.[2] How they spoiled me! Half a cheese, 4 meatballs, almost ½ a pound of butter, 2 packets of rye bread,[3] and 4 eggs. How I will feast. The four meatballs I will share with the boys. They share a great deal too; that improves our moods. Last night, for the first time, I ate all that I wanted to. I thought I was going to be sick. We were having sauerkraut and potatoes. Several people didn't like that. So they called us over, because we are mostly boys in our group, and gave us a pan that was still half full of sauerkraut. I ate until I was full. Yesterday I managed to get 32 eggs for the boys, 4 for each of us at 20 ct [cents] per egg. How we enjoyed them. I also got cigarettes in the canteen. Those I am saving. The devil will dance for a cigarette here in Twente.[4]

We have ordered rye bread again, 7 pounds at 40 ct per pound. So for the time being I have no complaints. Don't let anyone else read this; it is a great risk for us if the wrong people find out. Here in Twente the farmers have been threatened that they will lose their farms if they sell food to the jews. But they [the Germans] can't stop it completely. We also walk around here with yellow stars, but that can be overcome. I have received everything that you sent me. Perhaps I forgot to write that to you. I spend almost all my free time writing letters, but I do that with pleasure. From Karel and Dick and Lilly,[5] I received May Day greetings, drawn on a card. Very beautiful. Many thoughts went through my head when I received it. I have just had a good meal. Cabbage, potatoes, a good piece of meat, and gravy. On Sundays we always get an extra portion. Also the Primus stove is a joy for us [see p. 57].

We still fry eggs, in secret of course. We now have other work, digging a canal on the moor. So now it is shoveling and trundling. Wednesday we receive our wages. It will not be much. We earn 29 ct per 18 wheelbarrows. That is just about one guilder[6] per day. But for this week we get a standard wage, so it will be a little more. I haven't had to use the goggles. Luckily the wind isn't blowing so hard. I have used the gloves; though they will probably be ruined because they are not suitable for this work; one needs leather mittens. Ma, please send a few pairs of very old socks, it doesn't matter if they are worn out. I would also like a pair of work shoes, but not Pa's, because his are much too big. Please see what you can find.

There is no point in taking that medical certificate to the doctor; that really would do no good, and besides, there isn't even a doctor in the camp. You have to walk for ¾ of an hour to get to a doctor, and even so, you still don't get permission. Now something about the visit you want to pay me. I still can't say anything in particular yet. It is officially forbidden. But even so, today some wives came. Nothing has been said about that yet. Let's wait a little longer and see. But if you should come to our camp (you certainly wouldn't be allowed inside), you would have to talk to me at the fence. But if you come during the week (don't bring anyone else, only you two).

Then you could see me at work as you walk eastward from the camp, to the right of the little house with the red roof. That you will see right away. But I can probably only talk to you and be with you during my breaks. That is in the morning 9 to 9:15 and from 12 to 12:30 and from 3 to 3:15. Write to me beforehand if you are coming and what day; then I can try to plan it. If something unexpected happens, I'll write to you at once. It will probably be forbidden. Now I stop again. Give everyone regards. I'll send a postcard to the Bleekveld and Pekel[7] [Peekel] families. Now keep a stiff upper lip. I do too. A big kiss from

Flip

Tot ziens in Mokem[8]

daaag!!!

Thank Aunt Duif heartily for me and give everyone my regards.

1. Aunt Juul, Juliette Anna Salomonson-Schaap, was Flip's mother's sister. She married Koopman (Karel) Schaap, a butcher whom Flip and Karel visited in 1939.

2. Koopman's brother Barend was born in 1894 in Vriezenveen. He married Hendrika Gerritdina Eshuis, born 1912 in Vriezenveen.

3. Country baked rye bread

4. In July 1943, a packet cost ƒ22.50.-

5. *Left to right*: Dick van der Schaaf; Flip; Lily (Liel) van der Berg; and Karel van der Schaaf. Karel, Dick and Lily were Christian neighborhood friends and members of the AJC.

6. The abbreviation for a guilder or florin is ƒ or fl. Guilders are no longer used, but one would be equivalent to 60¢ U.S. in 2007.

7. The Bleekveld and Peekel families lived in the same building as Flip. The Peekels lived on the ground floor; the Bleekvelds, on the second floor; and Flip on the third floor.

Aron Peekel was born January 13, 1899. His daughter Betty was born June 10, 1925. Barend Bleekveld was born on December 20, 1903. His wife, Sara Brandon was born June 25, 1905.[4]

8. *Tot ziens* means "till we meet again" or "see you soon." *Mokum* is Dutch Yiddish for Amsterdam from the Hebrew *makom* meaning "place" or "place where I live."

1. We believe that the poem Flip was referring to is *Bij de Onbekende Soldaat* (*By the Unknown Soldier*) by Garmt Stuiveling (1907-1985). He was a well-known Dutch poet and a man of letters and a good friend of the AJC.[A]

2. Harry Pos was a popular singer who sang on VARA, a Dutch labour party radio station (*logo below*).

A survivor who was in the Blechhammer camp, a sub-camp of Auschwitz, watched three Jews being hanged for a minor misdemeanor: "We all had to watch . . . Later in the evening we had to go to a concert as usual and listen as Harry Pos stood and sang, while outside the bodies dangled."[B]

The pre-war VARA broadcasting station logo.

3. "we lazed around." (*Photo below right*).

4. The *rijksdaalder*, the largest Dutch coin, had a denomination of 2½ guilders and was common currency until the introduction of the euro. It is now a collector's piece and is valued at about $25.

It is not clear whether Flip received a paper *rijksdaalder* note or the coins below.

A 1931 *rijksdaalder*

5. "National Socialism has created a new type of political criminal: criminals who had not committed a crime."[C] —Vasily Grossman

[POSTCARD]

Hardenb. 4 May '42 [Monday]

Dear Father and Mother,

Again a few words to reassure you. Today we again worked very hard and I came home dead tired. But I quickly washed myself all over and now feel refreshed again. I also washed 2 pairs of socks and a towel. But next week I will send my dirty washing home. We work hard because of the cold. If we stand still for five minutes, we shiver. And then there is the terrible hunger. But that I can cure with something good and a few slices of bread. And afterwards there is the hot meal.

Last night we had fun putting on a show. I did that poem about the *Unknown Soldier*.[1] It was well received. I had a good time. Harry Pos[2] is also in the camp. He used to be with VARA. He sings beautifully. He sang some jewish songs.

Best regards and a **kiss** from

Flip

dáàag!!!

Hardenberg, 5 May '42 [Tuesday]

Dear Father and Mother,

I received your letter in good health. I am fine. This morning we worked hard, but this afternoon we lazed around.[3] I received your package. That was wonderful for me. You can well understand that I am often very hungry. Today I bought a pound of rye bread and ate it in two sittings. That took care of the hunger. I also received the *rijksdaalder*[4] in my letter. Now I can buy eggs and rye bread when it is necessary. I am sure you haven't received my last letter yet, I know that from what you wrote. Sometimes the letters seem to take several days.

Don't worry that I first wrote that you should not come. Indeed we are not criminals,[5]

Flip and his workmates

but we are as good as prisoners. Don't forget that. Yes, in my earlier letter ~~skek~~ you read one thing or another, if you've received it by now. I will try to get a few hours free on Sunday, but I'll write about that later. We are really not allowed visitors. In Drente they have threatened to put fences around the camp if the visiting doesn't stop. And that too mustn't happen to us. We don't want to lose the little freedom we have. One must understand these are not normal times. We are just jews.

We have a good cook who helps us in all kinds of ways. But he too is dependent on the "Authorities." You must <u>not</u> let anyone else read my letters. What I write about here is nobody else's business. Everyone gets a note in person from me. Soetendorp[1] [a rabbi that the Jewish Council used] has emphasized that we must beware of traitors, and I must not ignore his warnings. Now something else, as soon as I have the opportunity, I will go to the doctor, but it is almost not worth trying. People who are much worse off than me have been sent back to work with threats. I'll never be declared unfit here. Besides, it isn't quite as bad anymore. I am toughening up, and luckily it's not so icy cold in the morning any more, though at 7 o'clock it's still freezing.

I read that a man here was allowed to leave the camp with his daughter and go to the village. It can't be true. We get one-hour leave, and it is impossible to go to the village in that time. If he did do it, it was on the sly and he put the whole camp in danger, and that is a responsibility I won't take. I already wrote that maybe you can visit me inconspicuously at my work; I'll write to you as soon as possible, by express, and tell you what hours I might have free when I know something about free time.

Thank Uncle Max [believed to be Flip's nickname for Uncle Joseph][2] and Uncle Eduard for the money and also Uncle Bram. [Abraham Samas married Flip's mother's sister, Johanna Sophie Salomonson.] I will write to all of them myself. Once again, do not let anyone read my letters because you know they will immediately talk, and that mustn't happen.

I am saving the can of food Aunt Jo sent me for when I really need it. Then I will really enjoy it. For the moment I have enough to put on my bread. I am still busy on my first pot of syrup. I eat a lot of cheese and also eggs. So I needn't be hungry, right? I hope I never need the vitamins. And for the time being, I don't need them.

Now, Ma and Pa, until Sunday or a day in the week, I will let you know.
A big kiss and
warm greetings from

Flip

Häijg

I also wrote to Barend and
will send him a postcard.

[Postscript added Wednesday the 6th]

Today (Wednesday), I received my wages:
It was $f7.62$, plus $f1$ for Friday that's $f8.62$.
Next week it will probably not be as much.
I also got a letter from Henk [Schenk].

I reopened this letter <u>myself.</u>

1. In June 1942, a doctor was asked to go with Soetendorp on a home visit. "We had the horrible task of telling the parents of a young man who had been arrested after the February strike, and had been taken to Mauthausen, that their child was dead. . . . He introduced himself as Jacob Soetendorp. Nobody can describe what we experienced together. If one accepts that only God can understand this sorrow, we can also understand that He will never show His face to a human being. *NESHOMME* [a big heart]. After this Soetendorp never played any role in my life. But I will tell everyone as long as I live that this man did an impossible job in an unsurpassable manner. What *neshomme!*"A

2. Joseph Slier, born April 9, 1885, with his son Philip, born in 1922. His wife, (*below*) Cato (Catherina) Vleeschhouwer, was born June 28, 1898. They had two other sons, David Leo, born 1926, and Henri, born 1929, and a daughter Elisabeth Anna, born 1930.

1. Henk (Hendrik J.) Schenk, born July 19, 1918, was a Christian fellow member of the AJC. He was awarded the Resistance Cross.

2. The chief administrator in many of the work camps was the cook.

3. David Blits and Bora Prijs, on their wedding day. She said, "We do what we have to do now, and after the war David and me, we will go on together forever."**4**

Bora lived at 150 Vrolik Street, David at 36. She was a saleslady and he was a diamond worker. He had one brother, Simon, a warehouse clerk, who died in Sobibor on July 16, 1943. Bora's father and her young brother Wim (Sally) survived the war, but her mother Sientje, and other brother, Samuel, did not survive.

Bora Prijs and David Blits' signatures in Jules and Chelly Schelvis' wedding guest book

Hardenberg, 7 - 5 - '42 [May 7, Thursday]

Dear Parents,

This afternoon I received your letter and I read that Pa is planning to come. I find that wonderful. I'll probably have an hour free on Sunday, and then we can talk to each other. Great that I am getting work shoes because I really need them. Today I saw the doctor and complained about my feet and that the work exhausts me and I can't tolerate the wooden clogs. He said that I had better get used to it. I then asked if he could get work shoes for me. He said that he would try, but there's not much chance. So today I wore my black shoes again, what a difference. This evening I wasn't so tired and work was much easier. So you see, you can get used to anything. We are also getting less potatoes here, thus everything is reduced. But we buy extra. I had eggs in addition to my dinner. They cost 21 ct each, cooked. Expensive, but better than being hungry, right? I also buy cheese for the others, but I don't need it myself, luckily, because it would add up to too much.

How good that Henk Schenk[1] is free. But we will be free, too. I sent Bep de Vries a soap coupon because my letter to you had already been posted. She will bring it to you.

Pa, you write that I should be careful not to catch cold, but that's not possible here. When you sit on the toilet here, a small breeze blows you away. But luckily the weather is now a little better.

So you are coming, but please come as inconspicuously as possible because that's best. The cook[2] will probably turn a blind eye. Now Pa and Ma, I'll end expecting you on Sunday. I'll see how it goes. So I end with a couple of hearty kisses from

Blits[3] also wrote to me. He says that they are still not allowed to receive any packages, and while I still can, you should send. He says that then I can build up a little reserve. Maybe he is right. But we will see. Again, a kiss from

From van der Brave I received a letter with ten 7½ ct stamps.[4]

1940 7½ cent stamp

1924 7½ cent stamp

1924 3 cent overprint 7½ cent stamp

4. Three types of 7½ cent stamps. In 1940, just prior to the outbreak of war, the Netherlands issued a new series of stamps depicting Queen Wilhelmina. The Germans withdrew the Dutch stamps. Knowing that stamps depicting Hitler would not be accepted, they reissued the impersonal 1924 stamps shown above. The Germans removed portraits and statues featuring members of the Dutch royal family and all royal emblems, including coins which were replaced by zinc coins displaying Nazi symbols. Many Dutch women wore the Dutch silver *dubbeltjes* (10-cent coins), featuring the Queen, as self-made ornaments to express their defiance of the Germans.

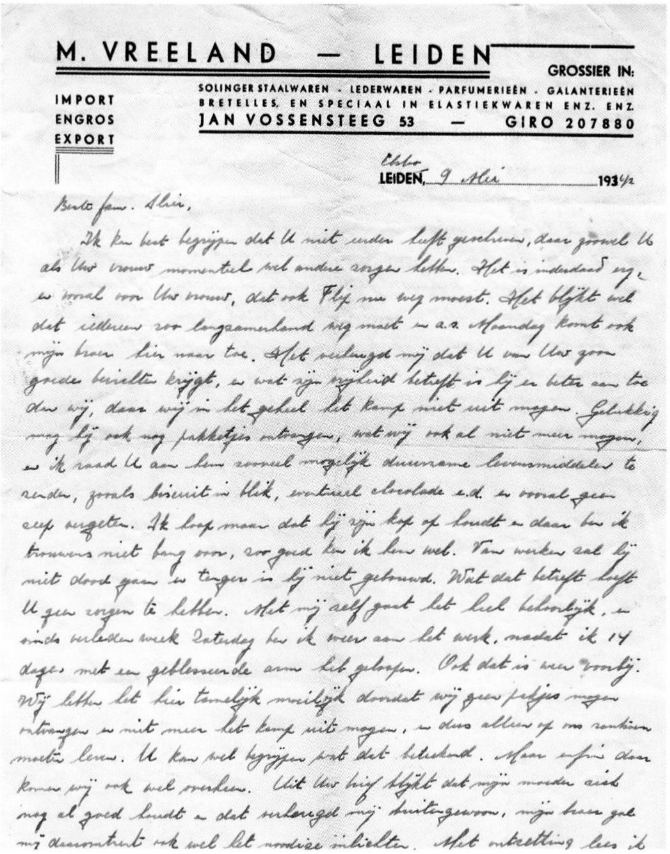

A letter to Flip's parents, probably from Flip's friend David Blits in Elsloo camp. David used to live on Vrolik Street, where their respective parents were neighbors.

1. The only adult named Siep listed by the Digital Monument[4] is Siepora Presser of 32 Tugelaweg, one street away from Vrolik Street. She worked at the Hollandia-Kattenburg clothing factory until November 11, 1942, when all the Jews in the factory were arrested.

Elsloo, 9 May 1942

Dear Fam. Slier,

I can well understand why you did not write before. You and your wife have other concerns right now. It is indeed bad, especially for your wife, now that Flip also had to go away. It appears that slowly everyone is disappearing. On Monday my brother will also come here. I am happy that you have had good reports from your son. As far as freedom is concerned, he is better off than we are because we are not allowed to leave the camp at all. Luckily he is still allowed to receive packages, which we are not allowed anymore, and I advise you to send him as much as possible of durable foodstuffs like cookies in tins and chocolates and especially don't forget soap. I hope he keeps his chin up, and of that I am not afraid, I know him well. He will not die from hard labor, and he is well built so you need not have any concern about that. I am keeping reasonably well. I walked around with an injured arm for 14 days; now that is past and I have been working again since last Saturday. Things are fairly difficult here because we are not allowed to receive food parcels and not allowed to leave the camp; therefore, we have to live on the rations; you can understand what that means. But, in short, we will also get past that.

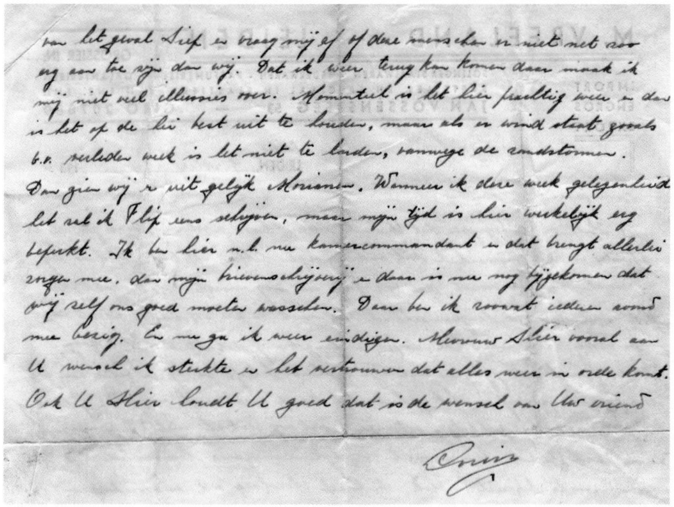

In your letter I read that my mother is still holding up quite well and that pleases me greatly; my brother sent me the same news. I read with horror about the strange affair of Siep[1] and asked myself if those people are not just as badly off as we are. That I will come back, about that I have no illusion. But I'm not thinking about this kind of thing for the time being.

It is beautiful weather and it's quite tolerable here, but if the wind blows, it is not bearable because of the sand storms. Then we all look like Mulattoes. When I have the opportunity, I will write to Flip again this week, but my time here is very limited. Here I am the room commander, and that brings all kinds of concerns with it, and then my letter writing and the fact that we have to wash ourselves thoroughly, and almost every evening I am busy with that. Now I am going to stop; again especially for you, Mrs. Slier, I wish you strength and confidence that everything will be all right and also you, [Mr.] Slier; that is the wish of all your friends.

Davi (David)

2. The doctor may have believed that "orders are orders," as Flip reported, but there were exceptions. When Dr. Adelaide Hautval, a doctor from Vichy, France, objected to the mistreatment of Jews in 1942, she was sent to Birkenau and later to Auschwitz. There she hid patients with typhus, saving them from certain death. She treated Jewish patients with compassion, saying, "Here we are all under sentence of death. Let us behave like human beings as long as we are alive." When ordered to assist Mengele's[4] assistant in experiments on prisoners, she refused and spoke out against them. For that, she was sent to Ravensbrück concentration camp. Dr. Hautval survived the war.

In 1941, when Dutch doctors were pressured to join the NSB (see page 45), 5,000 of the 6,500 doctors resigned from their medical organization in protest. After further pressure on the doctors, 3,500 wrote to the head of their organization saying they would not follow the orders of Seyss-Inquart.[B]

Dr. A. Lehmann reported that at camp Vught, Ben Bril, who as a 15-year-old flyweight boxer represented the Netherlands in the 1928 Olympic Games, ". . . was the only man I saw, or even heard of, during two and a half years of concentration camp life, who dared to disobey a formal SS order. Indeed who flatly refused, and what is more, in the presence of the entire high command and all the prisoners on parade. This was the order to pick up a whip made from a bull's penis and to flog another prisoner with it." Bril was deported from Vught to Bergen-Belsen. Both he and his wife survived the war.[C]

Hardenberg, 10 May 1942 [Sunday]

Dear Father and Mother,

Last night I received your letter just before our evening entertainment began and I read it hurriedly. Once again it was a very jolly evening with all kinds of turns.

I read that Pa's plan is to come to me on Tuesday or Wednesday. Well, that's possible. Yesterday and today there were also several [visitors]. But it's best to come at 4 o'clock. We stop work at quarter to five. If you can arrive then, where I work, Pa, the location is east of the camp, on the right of a little house with a red roof.[1] (Just follow the road and you will get there); then we can happily walk back to the camp together. I really don't think you need a travel permit. There are so many people who have done this.

I have not received the package yet, but it will probably come tomorrow. How strange that Lientje van Emden keeps on coming. What did I do to deserve that? Nevertheless, I'll send her a postcard. Now, again, about the doctor. There was a man in our room who was rheumatic. He was totally stiff. And the doctor said, "You have to work until you drop. Orders are orders."[2] But for the rest I can adjust pretty well, even though now and again I inwardly boil with rage because we are just like prisoners.

But still, our camp is one of the best and freest.

Luckily you don't have any shortages yet. Now, luckily I don't either yet. ¾ of a pound of butter went rancid on me so I am eating it as quickly as possible. Things like that you can't keep. I put it in water with salt and it will do. As long as we can still buy stuff, we don't suffer. Only it costs a lot of money. And a package now and then is a great help (for as long as it is allowed).

Now, Pa and Ma, I stop with warmest greetings
and a big kiss from

Greetings from all
the boys in the room!

1. Flip is on the left and to his left is "the little house with the red roof."

Hardenberg 13 May 1942 [Wednesday]

Dear Father and Mother,

Today we are free, and so now I have the time to write some letters. The shoes fit very well. They are wonderfully roomy, but not too wide. I can also make good use of the knee socks. Ma, a big kiss for all the trouble you took for me. I will eat the brown beans this afternoon; that will be good. Ma will certainly be more cheerful, huh, now that Pa has visited me.

On the days we don't work, we only get coffee in the morning. If we don't get paid, the day costs us ƒ2.60. Yesterday I received my "wages": ƒ4.71. A lot, huh? But at least I again have some free eggs and something good to eat. So you see, one day [off] costs more than I earn in three days. But who cares?

I wrote a letter to Aunt Jo,[1] Uncle Bram and Uncle Alfred, and I also thanked Mrs. van Geldere.[2] But why must I do that again? In my happiness I've forgotten. Now, Pa and Ma, I must end again with

a big kiss

Flip

Yesterday we went home at 3 o'clock because of rain. If only it would rain a lot, we would earn more than when we work.

daaag

tot ziens in Mokum.

1. Aunt Jo (Johanna) Sophie Salomonson-Samas, Flip's mother's sister. She was born October 6, 1888, and married Uncle Bram (Abraham) Samas, who was a baker, on Professor Tulp Street, Amsterdam. He was born November 21, 1884. He and Aunt Jo had two children, Salomo, born May 1, 1918, a typographer, and Philip, a baker, born June 25, 1920. Philip was one of the hostages arrested in the first mass arrest of Jews in 1941. He was killed at Mauthausen on October 3, 1941.

2. Mrs. Eva van Geldere, whom Flip thanked, had four daughters and two sons. Her daughter Willy (Wilhelmina Magdalena) (*above*) is standing in front of (*left to right*): sister Sientje (married to Joop Stodel); Klara, a friend; and Schoontje Frinkel, who married Arthur Philips' brother Philipp. In 1953, when Flip's cousin, Deborah Slier (*below*), stayed with Willy she told her that when the police came to arrest her mother, she wept, begging them to take her as well. They refused because she was not on their list. Whether their refusal was an example of conscientiousness or conscience is unclear. Willy and her brother Jules were hidden by the Vink family; they were the only van Gelderes to survive.

Wedding photo, August 19, 1942. *Front row, left to right*: name?; name?; name?; probably Grietje Slier Philips—Arthur's mother (his father had been taken to Erica camp two weeks earlier); Willy (Wilhelmina Magdalena) van Geldere, the bride; Arthur (Abraham) Philips, the groom; Mrs. Eva van Geldere; Seintje van Geldere Stodel; and behind them Seintje's husband, Joop (Joseph) Stodel.

NEDERLANDERS

VOOR UW EER EN GEWETEN OP !- TEGEN HET BOLSJEWISME DE WAFFEN SS ROEPT U !

About 10,000 Dutch volunteers fought on the eastern front in the German army. Dutch soldiers were a large part of a 12,000-strong infantry division that fought against the Allies at Arnhem in 1944. More Dutch soldiers died fighting the Allies than died fighting the Germans. In all of German-occupied western Europe, the Netherlands had the highest membership of the Nazi Party (early in the occupation), and the highest percentage of Jews killed. However, it also had the highest percentage of people who received the Yad Vashem medal for helping Jews. The medal was awarded to 1 person in 2,000 in the Netherlands, 1 in 4,000 in Poland, 1 in 160,000 in Germany and 1 in 470,000 in Bulgaria where no Jews were lost.[B]

It is likely that fewer medals are awarded to countries who saved the most people because of political considerations.

Hardenberg 19 - 5 - '42 [May 19, Tuesday]

Dear Pa and Ma,

This afternoon I received the letter, Ma. You ask if Karel, Dick, and Lily could find a place to sleep around here. They can always do that at one farm or another. The people here are very hospitable. I would love to see them. When I find accommodation I will write to them. And if Ma wants to visit me once, it would be great. You can sleep at the Salomonsons or the de Bruins. And if you are not allowed to travel on a Sunday, just go without a star. In the meantime you have probably found the health insurance stamps.

Tomorrow I will write to Bleekveld. If my letters don't arrive immediately, perhaps it is just a small delay.

About candy and cigarettes I have heard nothing. As soon as I know something I will write about it. Can Pa still buy that shag [tobacco]? Let him do it. It will never be wasted. And it will cost more all the time.

The address of Daaf is: Room 10, De Vecht
Dalfsen.

I have just come from the de Bruins, where I visited for a quarter of an hour; I had a glass of milk and a couple of slices of bread. I ordered a loaf of rye bread; at least I asked if they could get one for me. Now that was good. But she said a 4-5 pound loaf could well cost f2. I said to go ahead.

As I spend a lot of money here, could you possibly send me a little every week? I eat a lot of cheese now. That's an excellent extra. I also still buy eggs. Tomorrow I get f5.22. But I have already spent it. Salomonson came to see me this week, but I cannot visit him. He lives too far away. I got mandolin strings from him and also half a loaf of bread.

Nice, huh? Today we worked hard again. Much harder than when Pa was here. That's because a couple of guys went crazy. I am not interested in killing myself working. And for that rotten little bit of food. I can't imagine not being able to buy some food on the side. I have still not been really hungry. If you can send me durable stuff, please do. I have not yet used anything of what you sent me. I still have it all. The sausage, the syrup, the jam, honey, etc., etc.

So you see I don't eat everything as soon as it arrives. When the time comes (and it is definitely coming) that nothing more can be sent, I will still have something.

This evening I got 6 letters. One from Lies van Emden, from Jo van Wessel, from Henk, from Henny, and one from Harry [the sixth was from Flip's parents]. So I have enough mail.

Now Pa and Ma, I stop again with a big
kiss from

[signature]

Dany

I am fine.
Send me a towel, saccharin,[A] or sugar
I don't think I need anything more.

Saturday 23 May 1942

Dear Pa and Ma,

I am sending this letter express, so you will receive it today. Nowadays we quit at 10:15 so there is little time to write. Last night I was too tired and went to bed at 9 o'clock. This week, as you probably heard, we had a meeting in the canteen. Rules have been tightened. Naturally again things happened for which the whole camp has to suffer. Just because of the stupidity of some people.

Sometimes when you had visitors you were allowed to leave the camp for three hours. Now it is not allowed. Also visits are strongly discouraged, and so I immediately cancelled the visit of Karel van der Schaaf, Dick, and Lily. But I followed this with a letter that they, being non-jews, can probably come.

Also the NSB people have taken offense because there are so many jews in Hardenberg.[1] We can't be too careful.

Also the greens[2] were here again and complained about so many [of us being] sick. Otherwise everything is good. I received a package from Aunt Juul and Uncle Karel with great contents: cheese, butter, and eggs. The butter was especially welcome because I had none left. They also sent candy and a jar of jam. From de Bruin I received a whole loaf of rye bread[3] and from Salomonson a few pieces of delicious butter cake. Everything was brought to me. I also received the photos. I need a lot of them. You pay for them Pa, and then I can have them pay here and send you back the money that I receive.

I received a letter from Uncle Alfred and Aunt Jenny[4] who wrote that they have reserved a package for me. So that is also great. Again this week I won't have to be hungry. I bought some more eggs and a bottle of tomato juice.

We worked hard this week and again earned nothing. But it will be even less in the future. Also the supplement [money sent to dependent wives] was reduced during the month. So then the women in Amsterdam will receive even less.

At the moment the weather here is miserable. Not Pentecostal[5] weather at all, but there is nothing we can do about it. This week two men who are married to Christian women went home. What luck, huh? Now, Pa and Ma, best regards from

and a big kiss

1. The NSB, an acronym for the *Nationaal-Socialistische Beweging*, a Dutch Fascist Party, seen marching in the photo (*below left*). Even though the NSB did not consider anti-Semitism important, and had 20 Jewish members, the NSB objected to the 38 Jews and two half-Jews in 13 families in Hardenberg.[A] Anton Mussert, their leader, maintained friendly personal relations with Jews which did little good for them or him. The Nazis did not trust him and the Dutch executed him in The Hague for treason on May 7, 1946.

2. The "Greens" (*Ordnungspolizei*), were a branch of German police, dressed in green, who were widely feared for their brutality.

3. Dutch rye bread from Groningen

4. Aunt Jenny (Jeanie Muriel Gestetner) was born in Lienden July 24, 1903. She worked as under-chef at the five-bed Jewish wing of the Joles Hospital in Haarlem. She married Flip's mother's brother, Alfred Salomonson. Their children were Martha Sophie and Philip, born on October 27, 1934, and February 22, 1943.

5. Pentecost (Whitsun) fell at the end of May. In 1942, Easter fell on April 5.

1. In 1936, Nol (Arnold Simeon) van Wesel and Max (Salomon Meijer) Kannewasser worked at de Bijenkorf, an Amsterdam department store, but at night, as Johnny and Jones, they wrote and performed jazz songs satirizing current events with a mixture of Jewish and Amsterdam humor. *Mijnheer Dinges Weet Niet Wat Swing Is* ("Mr. What's-his-name Doesn't Know What Swing Is") was their most popular song and can be heard on the web.[4] On October 9, 1943, Johnny and Jones and their wives were sent to Westerbork where they worked at the airplane demolition plant and at night gave concerts. Without their wives, they were allowed to visit other camps and go to Amsterdam where they recorded "Westerbork Serenade" and *Tussen de Barakken Kreeg Ik Het te Pakken* ("It Struck Me Between the Barracks"). On September 4, 1944, they were deported to Theresienstadt, then Sachsenhausen, then Ohrdruf, and finally Bergen-Belsen.

Johnny (Arnold Nol) van Wesel, born Aug 3, 1918, died at Bergen-Belsen April 15, 1945.

Jones (Salomon Meijer) Kannewasser born Sept. 24, 1916, died Bergen-Belsen Mar 20, 1945.

Hardenberg 24 May 1942 [Sunday]

Dear Pa and Ma,

Yesterday Karel, Lily, and Dick were here with me and I spent a great afternoon and evening with them. I had an hour free and we ate together and had a great time. I received the packages and am very happy with them. Again it's a great addition to my rations. Aunt Juul also sent me another package with butter, cheese, eggs, a jar of jam, and candy. Really great. Also I appreciate the candy from the girls. That is always great. Yesterday Rosette de Bruin [Ru de Bruin's daughter], who works for Aunt Jenny, came to see me and brought me some things. She is a very nice girl, and today she is coming back with Martha [Aunt Jenny's eight-year-old daughter]. She told me that what she had brought, they did not want themselves. (Very confidential. We talked to each other for a long time). It was a box of fudge and a tin of sandwich paste and a piece of homemade cake (ugh!). Also a jar of jam she had to buy for me here in Hardenberg. Well they can keep it as far as I am concerned. She does not like staying with them. From the de Bruin family I received a whole loaf of rye bread. So I can manage for a while.

I am again sending a package of laundry home and the wrapping paper so you can use it again. Don't buy any more saccharin for me. This week I bought a few packages from a farmer. I made a big pudding for the boys on Saturday. They loved it. I treated Dick, Karel, and Lily to some eggs. It was worth it for me, sure.

We just had an afternoon of varied entertainment with Johnny and Jones[1] and Prof. Ben Ali Libi.[2] It was really nice. I don't remember if I already wrote you the reason why I did not want Dick, Karel and Lily to come here. But that was because something happened in the camp. Somebody abused his permission to go on leave, and then there was a man who wanted to send cheeses and other rubbish home. Not exactly crimes, but you know everything is closely watched here. This week I was talking with the girl who works in the canteen, but the cook refused to allow that. I suppose we look like criminals. We are also forbidden to talk to the people and girls from the village. But we don't pay any attention to that.

Now Pa and Ma, I'll stop again. When there is more news I will write.

Best regards and a kiss from

Is Ma still under treatment from the doctor? Please don't worry about me being here. I don't. The night before last we played ghost. I died laughing, and then they came and threw water on Dave's bed and last night Dave and Joop threw water again in Room 10.

2. *(Left)* Professor Ben Ali Libi (Michel Velleman) born Jan 5, 1895, was a very popular conjurer who had entertained Prince Hendrik and the German ex-emperor Wilhelm, but did not lose the common touch. He performed for the Roman-Catholic Institute for the Deaf and Dumb and the Jewish Mental hospital at Apeldoorn. The famous Dutch poet, Wilem Wilmink, wrote a poem in his honor. He died at Sobibor July 2, 1943.

Hardenberg 27 May 1942 [Wednesday]

Dear Pa and Ma,

I just received your letter and am writing back immediately. As I had expected the pay rate has been lowered, so now we have to again work harder to get the same wages. Today we spoke to the boss, and he said that 2 years ago there were people here from Amsterdam who earned one hundred percent more than we do and they did not have to pay for board. So you see how we are put down.

You must have been pleased when you heard from Karel and Dick ~~that~~ that everything here is all right. I received the "ƒ10 *gulden*" [literally means a paper or a coin with the value of 10 guilders][1] and have already bought a small cheese for an emergency or for when I can't get anything more. I am not totally broke yet, but must buy extra food every week and that costs a lot. I already wrote to the Bleekveld family. First, I wrote to all the people who sent me letters. Thank them heartily for the guilders.

Yes, I did treat Dik, ^Lily^ and Karel [Dick and Karel] but it was worth it.

I am not writing to Uncle Alfred and Aunt Jenny anymore. I don't think I need to. They have tons of money, and refuse to part with one cent. Ma, don't be upset about me being here. Maybe that's why you itch. Of course, I am not here for fun and we have to work harder now. For instance, today we had to work all day. But as long as I have enough to eat, it is making me strong and healthy. Sometimes I get food from the other rooms. Last night I got a triple portion, and tonight I got a plate of brown beans from another room and a whole pot of food for all of us. Good, huh? So you see, Ma, it's going very well, and if it weren't so, I would write about that also. I got a letter enclosing a guilder from Uncle Jonas and Aunt Annie.[2] How do they know I can buy food from the farmers? I hope you don't tell them. As soon as it is known, it can only hurt us. So, mouth shut about the things I write.

The medical coupons for two weeks are enclosed.

No, the cake from Aunt Jenny was not spoilt, but it had no taste at all. Ma, you see, I was ahead of you in sending back the bottle. I also enclosed the clogs. I am using the pudding dish, but as soon as I have an empty jam jar, I will send it.

Did you receive a postcard from Appie [Reis]?[3] The girls haven't received a proper letter from him either. Uncle Bram visited me, and I got ƒ2 from him.

So, I had a fair amount of visitors.

Now, Ma and Pa, I stop again with best
regards and a kiss from

Flip.

Haag.

Golden guilder
(*Gouden tientje*)

1. Flip said he received the "ƒ10 golden" the ten golden guilder coin (*below*).

2. Uncle Jonas, Flip's father's brother, (*above*) was born March 22, 1886. He had a stall in the Nieuwmarkt street market in Amsterdam as did his son Louis. He married Liesje (Anna) Plas (*below*).

3. Appie (Abraham) Reis was two years older than Flip, and lived two streets away (Tugelaweg). His photo is on page 67.

1. Bep (Elisabeth) de Vries

Hardenberg 3 June 1942 [Wednesday]

Dear Pa and Ma,

I just received your letter and I am glad to hear all is well. Everything is also fine with me. Monday and Tuesday we again worked very hard, but this afternoon we hardly did anything and let ourselves bake to a nice brown. Last week we earned ƒ5.09 and today ƒ5.25. So you see that will get us through. Although there have been several inspections and we were told our wages are going to be reduced, it hasn't happened. Why, I don't know.

Why don't you save my letters? There's no harm in that. They know very well how the jews feel. We are careful with that fellow at work, he won't learn anything from us.

I already wrote a second letter to Mrs. Michaels [probably a Jewish Council employee]. How great that Harry was home. I would like to come, too. But we still have a lot to lose, so I will wait a while. Maybe pretty soon I will be home for good. Perhaps I am more optimistic than you, Pa. I see an end to it. But more about that later.

From Lientje I received another letter and a bread coupon. That's worth a kiss, huh! Yes, I already heard that she is dating that van Dresden boy.

You ask who is my favorite? Well, it's Bep.[1] I thought you knew that already.

The main reason we work so hard is that we want to hold onto everything we still have.

And then with the money we can buy eggs, cheese, and bread and that is good extra food, otherwise I would be too hungry.

Left to right: top row: Wim Tokkie; Arie Bakker; Flip; Stella Aluin; Lena van Bienen; *middle row:* Fia Broekman; Henny de Lange; *bottom row:* Truus Sant; Jetty Kaas; Bep de Vries. Flip's parents asked Flip who his girlfriend was, because it had been Truus Sant (*below left),* to whom they had objected because she was Christian. Flip could now give the safer answer, "Well, it's Bep," (Elisabeth) de Vries (*below right*; *summer, 1940, and above left, 1942*). Bep's identity card (*left*) was issued by the Jewish Council, March 29, 1941. It had a Star of David on the other side.

Pa, write and tell me if you have handed anything in [this refers to the German theft of all Jewish assets]. No, I hope? Just like with everything else. They don't check anyway.

And about that money, I don't worry about it. We can live and that will straighten out.

Last night I got up at a quarter to two; the boy with the cracked wrist woke us. He has workmen's compensation and has to go to Zwolle to be examined.

First swarms of airplanes[1] flew over and then in the distance we heard the sound of bombs falling. The ground seemed to tremble. The bombardment lasted 1½ hours, and I was scared at the thought that I could be sitting in the middle of it. It went on and on. Not a half-minute's break. Again a lot of sorrow was sown. But they earned it.

Pa, you can safely keep the letters. Put them in a corner somewhere, nobody will notice.

On Saturday I am going to the doctor about my stomach. It seems swollen. The boys laugh about it and ask which month I am in. But for the rest it doesn't bother me. Maybe it has been this way for a long time, that's also possible. I have not had another day as nice as today. We all thoroughly enjoyed the sun and are all red and tanned. I was just called because an ice cream man was at the gate and I ate a delicious ice cream. It tasted pretty good.

Now I will stop again and hope that I get a package tomorrow. I am anxiously looking forward to it. Oh yes, I made a package with food, 2 cans of stew, a tin of milk, some sardines, salmon, and a tin of biscuits that I got from Aunt Rosalie[2] all tied together so that I can grab it and throw it over my shoulder. Handy, huh?

You can now be satisfied with a long letter, and I end with a big kiss from
That's all so far.

Flip.

Pa, would you buy a few packages of <u>Esbit</u>[3] with a little stove for me from Pimontel in Utr.[echt] Street. It doesn't cost much and I can make good use of it.

I also need a fork.

Now I will stop again and end with very best wishes
and a kiss from your loving

Flip

Houd moed! Houd moed![4]
De zon straalt ons reeds tegemoet.
Met zijn mooie gouden stralen
Waarmee wij vrede zullen binnenhalen.

Flip.

Avro "Lancaster" heavy bomber

1. On the night of May 31, 1942, Britain's Royal Air Force launched the first of a series of 1,000 bomber raids on Germany. The first target was Cologne. 1,046 planes took off; 59 aircraft were lost. The second raid was on June 2, and the target was Essen, less than 100 miles from Molengoot. 956 planes took off; 31 aircraft were lost. On June 25, there was a third raid against Bremen. 1,006 planes took off; 49 aircraft were lost. There were many smaller bombing raids in-between. The Dutch could see the British bombers on their way to and from Germany.

The value of these large bombing raids has never been established, though Albert Speer, German Minister for Armament Production, later wrote that after the July 24, 1943, raid against Hamburg that left 20 square miles of the city burning for nine days: "I informed Hitler that armament production was collapsing and threw in the further warning that series of attacks of this sort, extended to six more major cities, would bring Germany's armament production to a total halt."[4]

2. Rosalie Johanna Salomonson was Flip's mother's eldest sister, born in Denekamp in 1887. She worked as a domestic servant for Eduard and Betsie Andries at 42 Honthorst Street in Amsterdam.

3. Esbit is an acronym for Erich Schumm's Brennstoff (fuel) In Tabletten (tablets), a light weight solid fuel. Chemically it is hexamine. When burned, a ½ ounce tablet will boil one pint of water in nine minutes.

4. Stay strong! Stay strong!
That our days may be long
The sun's golden rays
Herald peaceful days.

HEYDRICH DE MOORDENAAR

1. This drawing of Reinhard Heydrich *(above),* by an American artist and labeled Heydrich the Murderer, is from an RAF leaflet, Wervelwind *(Whirlwind),* that was dropped over the Netherlands between July 13 and October 3, 1942. Heydrich was second in command of the SS and Gestapo, and what was Czechoslovakia. With the collaboration of the Czech government-in-exile, Britain trained two Czechs, Jan Kubis and Josef Gabcik, who attacked Heydrich in his Mercedes near Prague on May 27; he died on June 4. In reprisal, Hitler demanded the execution of 30,000 Czechs but to avoid too great a dent in the labor force, compromised at 5,000. The Germans executed 1,331 Czechs, 52 German Jews from Berlin, and sent 3,000 Jews from Theresienstadt camp (50 miles north of Prague) to death camps.

On June 10, German troops surrounded Lidice, a village 12 miles northwest of Prague that had no connection with the assassination. All the men (191) and seven women were shot, and 184 women were sent to Ravensbrück concentration camp; 143 survived. All the children (105) were sent to Gneisenau concentration camp; 17 survived. The village was then bulldozed and utterly obliterated. The Germans also murdered 252 people related to the Lidice villagers. In every country they occupied, the Germans killed ten, or a thousand, or more for the death of one German. When one German was killed by the Dutch resistance on September 30, 1944, in the village of Putten (30 miles east of Amsterdam), the Germans burned 87 houses to the ground and sent 600 men aged 18 to 50 years old to concentration camps; of whom, 48 survived. In Poland there were hundreds of Lidices; in Greece there were 879.[A]

Hardenberg 4 June 1942 [Thursday]

Dear Parents,

I just received your package and am very happy with it. Everything arrived in good shape.

I was busy for a long time picking the wrapping from Mom's candy. It tastes delicious. Also my clean laundry is very welcome. My clothes are literally stinking again. Several people fainted today from the heat. The sun also affected me. We are getting really brown. It was almost impossible to work today. So hot.

In the night we were up again. We could almost touch the bombers with our hands. That gives me courage. I also received a letter from Harry again, in which he recounted his adventures.

Aunt Juul also sent me a letter. I enclose it with this one. Crazy letter, don't you think? I have never hinted at packages, never a word about it. I only wrote a cheerful letter and said that she must not worry about everything that is happening, because when we are free again, everything will be fine again. And no more.

Should I write to her again? What must I now reply?

Now, Pa and Mom, I end again with a big

kiss from

I sold the photos for 7½ ct each.

Amsterdam •   • Putten

Hardenberg 7 June '42 [Sunday]

Dear Parents,

I just received your letter because we also always get mail here on Sundays. Yes, that little letter from Aunt Juul is peculiar, but she'll get over it. Maybe there is a lot of misery in store for us, but there is a chance that it will be over before winter, and then I can come home to stay. That is what I meant. Here you don't get medically discharged; for that you have to be half dead. This week I went back to camp because I was overheated. On arrival I was called by a member of the contact commission. That is someone appointed by the cook to represent our interests. He said I had better not go back to my room because the doctor has to make a report on every sick person. So I went to the woods and lazed around from 1 until 5 o'clock. So I had a nice easy afternoon. In this heat the work doesn't go so fast when nothing can happen. Apart from that, earnings are indeed minimal, and you have to consider they deduct *f*7 ½ for room and board and wage taxes and health insurance.

As far as Bep is concerned, don't worry about it. We are still young. However here in 6 weeks you age years, but that you understand well. Don't take it too seriously, you hear.

I have absolutely no trouble with my stomach; it was just a little swollen. That may be because of my unusual diet. I noticed that a number of people here have it. I again found bread at 50 ct a pound, expensive for rye bread, but not nearly as expensive as in the city. Sometimes I get it much cheaper. But that is how it goes. There are boys here who never have anything, but they also do nothing about it. You have to have a talent for it.

The package was really great. I know it is extremely hard to get anything in Amsterdam. The [chocolate] truffles were delicious and the hard candies tasted great too. At least all three of us still eat well. When I come home again healthy, this will also have had its good side. I suppose my being away makes a difference to your meal preparations at home. Yes, it is awful that people have to stand in line for hours to obtain a little food. Have you heard anything from Mrs. Michaels? I keep on hoping and will send her another letter.

Ma, you must have been surprised when you saw Harry at the tram stop. Sometimes I feel the urge to take a little trip. But it is just not possible. I am not without money at the moment. I still have more than ƒ30.-

I ate the little sausage. It was great. The cervelaat sausage is also finished too. It started to get moldy, so I ate it.

Does Harry write regularly to Bep? I write so much that often I just don't feel like writing anymore.

Last night we had a water ballet. We took pails of water to our room and then threw the water into the other rooms. Some people got soaked to the skin. On Saturday nights we always do something like that. We always have fun.

Today someone had a birthday and he ordered a large cake. So again a party in the room. I hear that Mr. Salomonson[1] is at the gate so I'll end with

a big kiss from

[signature]

It is now afternoon and I was with the Salomonsons. I had a wonderful treat of chicken soup with a fine pair of drumsticks. I also had rhubarb and salad. This morning I got some bread from him. So again, today I wasn't hungry. Yesterday we had potatoes with the meal and whole milk, a portion for everyone for 22 ct.

Now I'll stop again. Warmest greetings and a big kiss from *[signature]*

Wednesday I'll send my washing. It is really filthy. So then let it soak for a few days in water. *[signature]*

I reopened this letter. We just had roll call for the first time. 2 boys are gone and they took everything with them.

> They have already been caught at the station
> The idiots did it completely wrong.

Back (left to right): Friedrich Salomonson; Ru de Bruin; Rosalchen Salomonson-de Bruin; Hillie Dekker (housemaid); Diny Snijder (shop assistant). *Middle*: Esther Philips-Salomonson (Friedrich's wife). *Front*: Lion Salomonson; Mennie (Emanuel) de Bruin; Lion de Bruin; Hanni Bertel Salomonson; Alex de Bruin. Photo taken in 1938 in the garden at the back of Ru's printing press.

1. Friedrich Salomonson, his wife, and their two sons left Germany in November 1938 (after *Kristallnacht*) and settled in Hardenberg. He was the brother of Ru de Bruin's wife, Rosalchen. There were several paths of relationship between him and Flip, making him as close as an uncle. Friedrich must have told the de Bruins what William Shirer later summarized:

> . . . by the summer of 1936, the Jews had been excluded either by law or by Nazi terror—the latter often preceded the former—from public and private employment to such an extent that at least half of them were without means of livelihood. In the first years of the Third Reich, 1933, they had been excluded from public office, the civil service, journalism, radio, farming, teaching, the theater, the films; in 1934 they were kicked out of the stock exchanges, and though the ban on their practicing the professions of law or medicine or engaging in business did not come legally until 1938, they were in practice removed from these fields by the time the first four-year period of Nazi rule had come to an end . . . Moreover, they were denied not only most of the amenities of life but often even the necessities. In many a town, the Jew found it difficult if not impossible to purchase food. Over the doors of the grocery and butcher shops, the bakeries and the dairies, were signs, 'Jews Not Admitted.' In many communities Jews could not procure milk even for their young children. Pharmacies would not sell them drugs or medicine. Hotels would not give them a night's lodging. And always wherever they went, were the taunting signs 'Jews Strictly Forbidden in This Town' or 'Jews Enter This Place at Their Own Risk.'[4]

1. Sourballs were candies made from sugar and lemon juice. As they were a bit sticky, they were sprinkled with powdered sugar. Alice van Keulen recalls that after the war, at Passover, they used to be sold in little tins.

2. Flip (Philipp) Philips, above (*center left*), was born August 23, 1922. His brother Arthur (Abraham) (*middle right*) was born August 2, 1920, and his twin siblings, Betje and Elie, were born November 11, 1928. Debora Slier (Aunt Bora) is standing behind the children while their mother, Grietje (Flip's aunt), who was married to Eduard Philips, is peeping from behind the curtain.

Hardenberg 10 June 1942 [Wednesday]

Dear Parents,

This evening I received your letter with the *f*10 and the certificate. Many thanks and a big kiss for it. I can make good use of it. In the afternoon we now have a great pan of potatoes with milk mixed in. That costs ± 25 ct, and today I mixed in a beaten egg. So for 50 ct we had a feast.

I doubt that Mrs. Michaels can get me free. Anyway, we don't have to worry about food. This evening we had spinach with potatoes. Not a very large portion, but I ate my fill. We made coffee with whole milk and whipped cream. Delicious.

One thing you could send me is a coffee cake and sourballs.[1] I am sure you need everything you have for yourselves. I know what it's like in Amsterdam now.

Did Flip [a cousin][2] earn *f*13 in Bethlem?[3]

Here someone was sick for three days, and they deducted *f*3.60, and on top of that *f*5½ will be taken for rent. Now we don't work so hard anymore, it makes no difference anyway. Today I received *f*5.21. It is always around *f*5. We don't give a damn anymore. At first we thought we were going to get leave, but none of us think that will ever happen now.

I don't think we have to worry about the money in the savings bank, we will get that back.

Are you really the chef again Ma? They can't do without you, can they?

I'll send my packet of dirty laundry Saturday because we must first have it checked and also pack it under supervision.

Of the people who tried to escape, three were caught, and one came back from A[msterdam] today. He wasn't punished, only his hour break has been cancelled.

With the de Bruin and Salomonson families all is well, I must give you their greetings. On Sunday the Salomonsons said that I must call them uncle and aunt.

I am not writing much because I have a number of other things to do and some letters to answer.

So, Ma and Pa, the next will be longer.

Best regards from the boys
and a big kiss from

3. We have been unable to find any reference to Bethlem camp other than this one by Flip and one by J. Presser in his book *Ondergang*. Presser states that 54 men were told to report there,[4] but it is not known how many did show up aside from Flip's cousin, Philipp Philips. He signed his name "Philip" on a birthday card (*left*) to his Uncle Jack. Arthur signed it "Athur" and they wrote in German as the family was living in the Rhineland.

[POSTCARD]   [Postmarked June 12 1942 Friday]

Dear Pa and Ma,

   I am asking for some things that I need, and I hope you will include them in my package. Toothpaste, shoe polish, fountain pen ink, and if you can, saccharin. I have enough sugar.

   I lost two chess games, although I don't play badly. It's just that I haven't played for such a long time. Yesterday I bought some nice eggs and a piece of cheese.

   We can't complain about food. I still fill my stomach.

   Best regards and a big kiss

           from

Flip's June 12, 1942 postcard

I will probably get your letter tomorrow.

NIEUWE EDITIE: 2e JAARGANG No. 10 - 12 JUNI 1942 (27 SIWAN 5702)

Het Joodsche Weekblad

UITGAVE VAN DEN JOODSCHEN RAAD VOOR AMSTERDAM

ONDER VERANTWOORDELYKHEID VAN A. ASSCHER EN PROF.DR.D.COHEN

Verbod van inkoop van groente bij niet-Joodsche winkeliers

De Duitsche autoriteiten deelen ons mede, dat Joden hun groente voortaan uitsluitend in Joodsche zaken en op de voor Joden aangewezen markten mogen koopen. Bestellingen bij niet-Joodsche zaken voor levering van groente zijn verboden. Deze regeling betreft voorloopig alleen Amsterdam.

Aangifte van rijwielen, voertuigen enz.

Ingevolge de Verordening van 23 Mei 1942 moeten Joden paarden, voer- en vaartuigen, waaronder ook rijwielen, aangeven. Formulieren hiervoor zijn van a.s. Maandag af te verkrijgen bij alle bureaux van den Joodschen Raad voor Amsterdam, tegen den prijs van 5 ct. per stuk.
   Deze formulieren moeten ingevuld vóór 30 Juni a.s. worden ingezonden bij de Zentralstelle für jüdische Auswanderung, Adama van Scheltemaplein 1, Amsterdam-Z.

In verband met vele aanvragen wordt erop gewezen, dat, naar ons gebleken is, de bepalingen van de Anordnung van 15 September 1941 aldus moeten worden opgevat, dat voor Joden elke vorm van sport in het openbaar, o.m. roeien, kanoën, zwemmen, tennissen, voetballen, visschen, e.d., als verboden moet worden beschouwd.

De Jodenster

De Duitsche autoriteiten maken er ons opmerkzaam op, dat voortaan alle Joden, die de Jodenster niet vastgenaaid op hun kleeding dragen, ter verantwoording zullen worden geroepen. Vasthechten van de ster met spelden of gedeeltelijk opnaaien geldt niet als juiste naleving der verordening.
   Verder wordt de opmerkzaamheid er op gevestigd, dat het Joodsche deel van hen, die in gemengd huwelijk leven, verplicht is, bovenstaand kenteeken te dragen.

New Edition: 2 Volume No 10 - 12 June 1942 (27 Siwan 5702)

The Jewish Weekly

EDITED BY THE JEWISH COUNCIL OF AMSTERDAM

UNDER THE DIRECTORSHIP OF A. ASSCHER AND PROF. DR. D. COHEN

Buying Vegetables at Non-Jewish Stores is Prohibited

The German authorities have advised us that Jews may from now on only buy vegetables in Jewish stores and at the markets designated for Jews. Orders at non-Jewish stores for delivery of vegetables are prohibited. This arrangement applies only to Amsterdam for the time being.

Reporting of Bicycles, Vehicles, etc.

Pursuant to the Ordinance of May 23, 1942, Jews must report horses, vehicles, and vessels, including bicycles. Forms for this purpose may be obtained as of this coming Monday at all offices of the Jewish Council for Amsterdam, at a price of 5 cents each. These forms must be filled out and sent before June 30th to the Central Office for Jewish Emigration, Adama van Scheltemaplein 1, Amsterdam-Z.

In connection with many requests, it is pointed out that as far as we can determine, the rules of the decree of September 15, 1941, should be interpreted such that for Jews, any form of public sport, such as rowing, canoeing, swimming, tennis, soccer, fishing, etc., must be considered forbidden.

The Jewish Star

The German authorities have pointed out to us that henceforth, all Jews who have not sewn the star completely onto their clothing will be called to task. Following the decree, affixing the star with pins or sewing it on only partially is invalid and incorrect.

Furthermore it is pointed out that Jews living in mixed marriages are obliged to wear the above-mentioned badge.

The sign (*above*) reads "Renkum Municipality [near Arnhem] Warning notice restricted for Jews"; (below) on the road to Doorn near Utrecht: MUNICIPALITY OF DOORN JEWS ~~NOT~~ WANTED

"The Jewish district" in Amsterdam was clearly marked. It differed from other German-established ghettos in that the entrances did not have armed guards. The sign (below) reads: "Jewish canal".

Hardenberg 13 June '42 [Saturday]

Dear Pa and Ma,

I just received your package and letter and find it really great. I have already finished the lobster. It was wonderfully delicious.

I also gave Nico a little piece. We really feasted on it. We often share with each other. You have really spoiled me again. It is wonderful to get something so special. I still have a few sour balls you sent me earlier, so I won't eat the new ones right away. The pieces of cake will also taste good. I can't send my package until Monday, it has to be checked first and there isn't always a chance to have that done. I again received a nice package with some butter, two pieces of cheese, ½ a loaf of bread and a small piece of rye bread from Aunt Juul and Uncle Karel, so for the time being I won't be hungry. I will send them a nice thank you letter. Did you receive my postcard? It was written in a hurry because I wanted to go to bed.

I am sending this letter by express so you will have it tomorrow.

Today we had potatoes with whole milk again. Delicious, a whole portion with an egg for 20 ct and a handshake. After that we had the camp dinner, but ate very little of it. Still it wasn't bad. I bet people in Amsterdam would be happy to pay a guilder for such a helping.

We complained about the porridge, and now it is better. They took out the potato flour and the powdered milk. I hear the food situation in A[msterdam] is still terrible. Are jews no longer allowed to buy meat and vegetables in Christian shops? I heard something like that here. Now, I don't know much anymore. Everything is good and I'm healthy.

I stop with a big kiss and thanks

by

give greetings to all.

For a short while the Jewish area of Amsterdam was fenced in.

1. Joop is probably Samson Leijden van Amstel, a baker, born January 8, 1922, of Jodenbree Street. His father was Jacob Leijden van Amstel.

As early as September 1940, Jews were banned from shopping in certain markets, stores, and many streets. In June 1942, a regulation was introduced that forbade Jews from shopping in Christian shops. The sign in the butcher shop says "No Entry for Jews." Signs like these were posted everywhere.

Hardenberg 14 June 1942 [Sunday]

Dear Father and Mother,

This morning I received your letter, again I was the only one who had mail. The boys all said just imagine if you too got no mail. I have absolutely no trouble with my stomach. Luckily, because there are some who have painful cramps.

Last night Joop van Amstel[1] threw up again, and there was blood in the vomit. Nico and Ap have the same problem off and on. They have been sick several times. I went and told the cook that Joop vomited blood, and he said that sometimes he had the same problem himself.

I have sent a package of dirty laundry; it is really dirty. Send it back in a package next week or send it by mail. There is also a little letter in the package. The tomatoes are delicious, really something you need as extra food. I'll see if I can buy some in the village. Everything you listed was in the package.

Ma, why don't you go into the Christian shops; what do you care as long as you have food?

Pa, must we now hand in our bikes? I heard that again. Rather give them away, or try to park them with somebody else. Ma, that small suitcase is good for sending stuff in. Write to Appie and say that he must send it back, he knows all about taking but not about returning. Write to me soon, and tell me how it went at the Handelsblad. I am really anxious to know.

Now, Pa and Ma, *tot ziens* and a
kiss from

"Jews not wanted"

The letter (*below*) authorizes the posting of "Jews forbidden" signs in Vriezenveen.

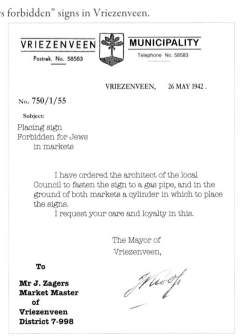

In June 1942, the Germans instructed the Dutch Railways to extend the railway track from Hooghalen, about five miles from Westerbork camp, into the camp itself. The railway line was completed in November 1942, and there-after deportations were out of sight of the general Dutch population.

[POSTCARD]   Hardenberg, 17 June [1942 Wednesday]

Dear Father and Ma,

I received your letter and now quickly write a postcard back because tonight we had another meeting in the canteen. I will tell you the particulars in a letter tomorrow evening. Luckily Pa is still working, that is a big relief for me. Could you possibly get me some kerosene, try to get one liter. Everybody in the room will chip in. Today we worked almost all day in the rain. We can only take shelter if it pours. It makes you miserable, if not sick. You have to be really healthy. The stomach is the result of always [having] the same food. Not everybody can take it. It doesn't bother me. Tomorrow I'll write more. Will you quickly send me socks?

Dear Pa and Ma,

Greetings and a kiss

from your

Flip

Hardenberg,
Molengoot

Right: people boarding a train at Westerbork for Poland.

Hardenberg 18 June 1942 [Thursday]

1. *Bottom of page*: Molengoot barack

Dear Parents,

Now again a letter from me. As you read in my _{post} card, it was a great relief for me to read that Pa is still working and still receives the same salary. I am very happy about that. Here it is already bad enough. But if things should change, keep your chin up. I do too. Last night we again had a meeting. They talked about running away and there were warnings again that we might be guarded by Germans. We must wait and see. The boss said today that if we don't make 15 ct an hour, there will be no bonus. This week we made 15 ct an hour for the first time. I earned ƒ7.58 but for that we have to work hard now and then. But then the time goes faster, and that is worth something.

I get along well with the people here. Yes, in the afternoon we get boiled potatoes with whole milk. That usually costs 40 or 35 ct. Then I have a whole pan of potatoes with ¾ of a liter of milk. Today I also had an egg with it. That made it 62 ct. But that's better than nothing. There is nothing else to buy. I know about the situation in A[msterdam].

You can send the bike to the following address/ᴵᶠ ⁿᵉᶜᵉˢˢᵃʳʸ· I arranged this with a very reliable laborer. His name and address is: A. Kremer, De Koppel A161, Hardenberg. If you send my bicycle there, it will be safe. But if it's not necessary, you don't have to do it.

I don't know which books I loaned, but I think I got them back long ago. Send me the titles.

Yesterday we worked all day in the rain again. Only if it rains really hard are we allowed in the barrack.[1] When I came <u>home</u>, I was ice cold and shivering. Then I washed, put on fresh clothes, and we boiled milk on the Primus[2] and everyone drank a glass of wonderful coffee.

So we muddle through, and I can now say that with hard work and good food, I will probably grow stronger. In the beginning we sometimes had muscle cramps because of the enormous exertion. That hurt a lot, but now that's passed and we are used to it. The right side of the canal[3] is finished, we are now working on the left. The ground there is stone hard, and we often have to use pickaxes.

Pa, can you send me some of this writing paper? There is still a packet of it at home.

I will stop now. Don't look at the handwriting, because this is not my 1st letter, and I have more to write; I also had several letters from Tonny. You know, that girl from the print shop.

Now, dear Pa and Ma, big kiss from

Flip.

2. Primus stove of the 1940s.

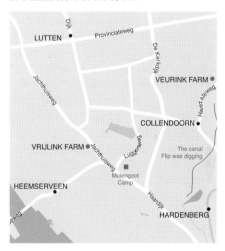

3. Map showing Molengoot camp, the canal that Flip was digging, and the surrounding area.

The only Molengoot barrack still standing, as it is today. It is used for farm storage.

1. Flip's friends, Lena van Bienen (*right*) and Jetty Kaas (*left*), were members of the AJC.

2. Aunt Bora (Debora Slier) sent a card (*below*) to her favorite brother Jack in South Africa on July 9, 1922. Her silhouette is on the other side and is shown on the opposite page.

Dear Brother,
I send my heartfelt thanks for the 5 guilders that you sent me, I will use it to buy a coat. Luckily everyone is healthy. Mother is also progressing well, she gets electric steam baths for her rheumatism. Louis comes to us again for a 5 week holiday, he will still be here this Sunday. Last week we had three extra sleeping here because we had a birthday for Annie's mother who turned 60. [Annie was Anna Plas whose mother was Vrouwtje Sons, born 4 Feb 1862]. Further, I have no more news. Greetings from Z. O. L. A kiss from Mother

3. It is probable that Sally Kesnig was Saul Kesnig, born May 20, 1906.

Hardenberg 19 June '42 [Friday]

Dear Parents,

I feel I wrote such a short letter last night, so now I am writing again.

First of all, our team is being split up. The weak ones are out, and the strong ones will form another team. Nico, Ab, and I have been assigned to the strong group. Now perhaps we will be able to earn more than the average $f5$. We must work anyway and the day passes much faster, and I can spend a bit more. Tonight we again had tolerable food, namely cabbage stalks with potatoes, but it tasted OK. Also this afternoon we had potatoes again. Six of us had to share, so it wasn't very much. But I mixed an egg in with mine; they are 28 ct now, so my meals cost about 50 ct per day. Well, I was happy to sign up for that during my stay here. I read in Lena's[1] letter that the potato ration in A[msterdam] has been cut to 1 kg. Where does that lead? It gets worse and worse, yet I believe I will be home for my birthday [December 4th], or even sooner. I think the signs are fairly good. I have now been here for almost two months. It is almost unbelievable how fast the time has passed and yet every day is too long for us.

We now have a sickbay here with different things. It is about time. This week an acquaintance of Aunt Bora's,[2] Sally Kesnig,[3] was not well. He had an attack of a sort of sciatica; he was as stiff as a board and could not bear to be touched. When they fetched a ladder with blankets and pillows from the camp and put him on it the ladder, he screamed with pain. Queer business, I thought. Anyway, we achieved one thing with that, now we have a stretcher, bandages, etc. Joop van Amstel must stay in bed. I told you about his weight-reducing cure, he stopped and then began to eat twice as much and, of course, his stomach protested. Now, he is somewhat undernourished. Just as Pa said, he now gets special meals.

By the time you get this letter, [tomorrow] Dick will be [here] with me. We again have leave so I may go out of the camp. I get one hour free now and then because there are so few visitors. So I am with him continually.

This week Nico and I managed to get a kilo of molasses. It cost $f1.10$, so that is a jar each for 55 ct.

As I already wrote, Herts from Groningen was here to warn us against running away and he also said we must work harder. We do work hard, but killing ourselves is

asking too much. We asked questions about leave, increasing our rations, and tobacco coupons. All of this, according to Herts, is brought to the attention of the authorities, but he himself does not believe it will do any good. So I am not counting on it. What good luck for Harry[1] that he does not have to push a wheelbarrow anymore, that is not going to happen to me.

It seems that I feel stronger every day. But that is not surprising with the hard work I do, and for the time being I am managing to get enough extra food so you don't have to worry about me. I may be able to buy some bread for you for f1.- should I do that? But remember, <u>only</u> for you, mouth shut, naturally. I think you have to pay much more for it now in the city.

Two boys from our room left. They didn't like it; well, I don't care. Nico is my best friend here, and we are together all the time. We help each other with everything. That is really great.

This morning they threw half a pail of skim milk over me. We always throw it away. Now you mustn't think we live in luxury here, but as long as we can rustle up whole milk, we can do that. Can you send me a small strainer, preferably a coarse one? It is for the porridge; then I can sift the grits out of the pan and don't have to drink skim milk with it. We always get the runs from it.

I took photographs again and will get them back soon. If there are any really good ones, of course I will send them; there is a beautiful nature photo of a farmhouse with an old tree in front. I am curious to see how it comes out, the others are only of people.

Ma, do you remember ~~a~~ the young man who was with me, that dark, neat-looking man, who said he would keep an eye on me? Well, he has also left our room. Good, he acted as though he was the director himself. Not a nice person at all in the end. We also have an old man in our room, he is 45, but is much older than Pa [52], he looks at least 65. He never washes and this evening I saw his feet. Pitch black, a lovely sight. You can't understand how he can feel comfortable like that.

Concerning my bike I have already written to you, you can safely send it to the address of that man. De Bruin also knows him very well.

Now, Pa and Ma, this has again been a long letter. I hope you are satisfied with it. I end with my best greetings and a big kiss from your

I will write a letter again on Sunday and tell you how things went with Dick.

[Dated from postmark: assumed Saturday, June 20, 1942]

Dear Pa and Ma,

I got the package from Dik [Dick] and again find it wonderful. You have again sent me all kinds of good food.

I am making this letter short because Dick is standing and waiting at the gate. I will shortly write a very long letter and send a parcel back. Anyway I am very happy with everything you sent.

Now dear Pa and Ma, I hope that this is the last parcel that you will have to send me. Hearty greeting and a kiss from

Silhouette of Aunt Bora

1. This Ex Libris label came from one of the books that Harry Elzas gave to Jo van der Schaaf (Karel's brother) for safekeeping. The book was "*De gronden der staatsinrichting van Nederland*" (The Basics of Constitutional Law of the Netherlands), by A. Feenstra, 1931. In contrast to Dutch law, German law was not related to the constitution, nor to morality, guilt, or proportionality. For example, in Belgrade, sheltering Jews or accepting for safekeeping objects of value of any description "shall be punished by death."[4] Rauter promised that Aryans who helped Jews would have their goods confiscated, and be sent to concentration camp.

1. *Right*: AJC members in uniform wearing their blue shirts and lanyards. They often wore red neck-scarves. The boys wore brown corduroy shorts. *Left to right*: name?; Jo van der Glas; Dien Metz; Karel van der Schaaf; Chelly (Rachel) Borzykowski; and Bora Prijs. This is a pre-German occupation photograph. Dien Metz married Jo van der Schaaf, the eldest of the three van der Schaaf brothers.

Chelly Borzykowski married Jules Schelvis on December 18, 1941.

We do not yet know the fate of Jo van der Glas.

2. Miep was probably Miep Lampie, who lived at 62 Vrolik Street. She was born on November 20, 1930, and died in Sobibor with her parents and three siblings on April 9, 1943.

Hardenberg [undated; mailed June 21, 1942 Sunday]

Dear Pa and Ma,

It is now Sunday afternoon. Dick has already left. Yesterday I had a great day. He came during dinner and of course I went to him immediately and got the packages. Boy, oh boy, how you have spoiled me again with everything.

Everything is clean and tidy again and also there is a new shirt. Just like an AJC[1] shirt. I think it's beautiful! Everything arrived safely and in good condition. The little fish are already eaten. I gave one to Nico, we feasted on them. I know how hard it is to get everything, so I appreciate it doubly. I can make good use of the sugar. The only thing I haven't got is butter, but I can buy that here. For the time being I don't need any more money. I now have more than ƒ60.- If I need more, and I hope I won't, I'll write. From Bep I also got a lot of stuff. Tomatoes, candy, licorice, Frujetta [fruit candy], and a pair of very nice shoes with wooden soles.

Also, I received candy from the girls and Miep.[2]

I had a great afternoon and evening with Dick. We visited the de Bruins and had a couple of cups of coffee there. He left this morning.

Now what else. Friday night Nico and I had a real Friday night [Sabbath dinner]. There was some milk left over and the others had gone to bed, so we heated up the milk, opened a packet of cocoa and had a few delicious cups. To finish we feasted on a nice little piece of the cheese that I got from Aunt Juul.

This week 2 English and 2 German planes came down in flames. All of us were up. Last night again swarms of planes came again, of course they fly much lower here than over Amsterdam, so it sounds much louder.

I will be able to do something with the tobacco as it gets scarcer.

The other is also good. I have still not heard anything from Aunt Juul or Uncle Karel.

I'll stop now and end with a big kiss from

I'll write another letter this evening.

Hardenberg, 25 June 1942 [Thursday]

Dear Pa and Ma,

This evening I received your letter and am writing back again. How are you now Pa? Are you already better? I hope so. Everything is fine with me. I have become as black as an African in the last few days, and I still have enough to eat. This week I will spend more than I usually do on food, that is, about ƒ10.- well above my earnings. I have earned ƒ7.57 plus ƒ1.- if I look at it as pocket money, it is not too bad. It must be absolutely terrible in Amsterdam now; all the boys get letters about it. Here we sometimes have food left over, and every time we have to throw it out, we think about Amsterdam where it is so hard to get. Yes, sometimes in the evening, when I make a cup of hot chocolate, I think of home. But so far I am managing and you must also do so. In any event it is reassuring for you to know that I have few needs. This week Nico and I went out again and, of course, did not return with empty bags. On Tuesday we got a jar of artificial honey, and on Wednesday, a loaf of rye bread, and today again, butter!! and bread. So you see you don't have to worry about me, and that's good.

Yes, it's great that Dick[1] was with me again and it was good to be able to unburden my feelings. I will try to buy b[read] for you. I sent Bep a roll of film to be developed. You will get to see it. I got really beautiful photos from the store in the village, but they are all of people. There are some really terrific ones, which the people loved. I also sent Bep a few which you will see when they arrive.

This afternoon we had a nice little meal with a farmer. A plate of potatoes and some beans with delicious fat for 12 ½ ct and on top of that two kilos of potatoes cooked separately in their skins. They are not as tasty but we don't care; what you get per week, we get double in one day, but . . . we had to go to a lot of trouble to get that, believe me! Ma, I have never used that little bag from Aunt Bora,[2] I prefer to keep my money in my pocket, then they can't steal it, and I can keep my eye on it all the time.

The boys would really like to get some tobacco. Especially Nico, but don't give away your ration! They all get some, and I regularly buy cigarettes for the boys for ƒ2.- and you may not get them in the city for that price.

Dear Pa and Ma, I end again with a big kiss and greetings

by *Flip.*

tot ziens,

very soon *!! ??*

1. Dick van der Schaaf and Flip

2. "Aunt Bora" (Debora Slier). She sent this photo of herself to her brother Jack in South Africa in 1926 on her 30th birthday.

A POGROM

On June 26, 1942, Szmul Zygielbojm, a member of the Polish government-in-exile, broadcast in Yiddish on the BBC a report prepared by the Jewish Socialist Party in Poland. It described the Nazis' extermination of the Jews of Europe, including details of gassing. Zygielbojm read out a letter from a woman in a ghetto to her sister: "My hands are shaking. I cannot write. Our minutes are numbered. The Lord knows whether we will see one another again. I write and weep. My children are whimpering. They want to live. We bless you." Zygielbojm added, "It would actually be shameful to go on living, to belong to the human race if steps are not taken to halt the greatest crime in history." He could not persuade any government to intervene in any direct way on behalf of the Jews. On May 10, 1943, Arthur Goldberg told him that the US had rejected his request to bomb Auschwitz and the Warsaw ghetto.[A] On May 12, Zygielbojm committed suicide in London with an explanation: "The responsibility for this crime of murdering the entire Jewish community of Poland falls in the first instance on the perpetrators, but indirectly also it weighs on the whole of humanity, the peoples and the governments of the Allied States, which have so far made no effort towards a concrete action for the purpose of curtailing this crime. By passive observation of this murder of defenseless millions and of the maltreatment of children, women, and old men, these countries have become the criminal's accomplices." *The New York Times* published his letter—three weeks later.[B]

In 1942, Jan Karski was a 28-year-old Roman Catholic Polish diplomat who was smuggled into the Warsaw ghetto disguised as a Jew, and then smuggled into Belzec disguised as a guard. He duly escaped to England and the US with documents and a good memory. He informed Anthony Eden, H.G. Wells, rabbis and archbishops, the US defense secretary, President Roosevelt, and the Supreme Court Justice Felix Frankfurter, who responded: "I don't believe you." Karski: "Do you think I am lying?" Frankfurter: "No, but I simply cannot believe you."[C]

Karski reported that Roosevelt asked him many searching questions about conditions in the ghettos and the Polish resistance, and asked how come Poland was the only occupied country without a Quisling. Throughout the war, Karski tried to persuade good men to refrain from doing nothing.[D]

A German police officer shooting naked Jewish women and children who were still alive after a mass execution of Jews from the Mizocz ghetto in the Ukraine.

```
JEWS IN POLAND ALMOST COMPLETELY ANNIHILATED STOP READ REPORTS
DEPORTATION TEN THOUSAND JEWS FOR DEATH STOP IN BELZEC FORCED TO
DIG THEIR OWN GRAVE MASS SUICIDE HUNDREDS CHILDREN THROWN ALIVE
INTO GUTTERS DEATH CAMPS IN BELZEC TREBLINKA DISTRICT MALKINIA
THOUSANDS DEAD NOT BURIED IN SOBIBOR DISTRICT WLODAWSKI MASS
GRAVES MURDER PREGNANT WOMEN STOP NAKED JEWS DRAGGED INTO DEATH
CHAMBERS GESTAPO MEN ASK PAYMENT FOR QUICKER KILLING HUNTING
FUGITIVES STOP THOUSANDS DAILY VICTIMS THROUGHOUT POLAND STOP
BELIEVE THE UNBELIEVABLE STOP
```

Szmul Zygielbojm

On December 2, 1942, at Stratton House, Piccadilly, London, Karski met Zygielbojm and told him what he knew of the Warsaw ghetto and the plight of the Jews and passed on the Bund leaders' messages, including their intention to go down fighting if the Polish resistance would give them weapons. On the same day, Zygielbojm and his colleague Ignaty Schwarzbart sent the cable (*above*) to the World Jewish Congress in New York.[E]

Jan Karski

MASS MURDER

The Crime.

In Germany up to 1939 there were roughly 200,000 Jews. All except 40,000 have been done to death or deported.

In Austria at most 15,000 Jews survive out of 75,000.

In Bohemia and Moravia also only 15,000 survive. (Previously there were 80,000)

In Slovakia over 70,000 out of 90,000 have been deported.

In Poland more than 600,000 Jews have died a violent death.

In Holland and Belgium out of 180,000 only one-third survive.

In France nearly 50,000 were deported to the East and countless Jews were murdered.

In Yugoslavia out of roughly 100,000 not less than 96,000 have been killed, deported or imprisoned.

In Greece all Jews between 18 and 45 are condemned to slave works; an uncertain number were murdered.

In Roumania there were 900,000 Jews: now there are scarcely 250,000

In Latvia one quarter of the Jewish population has been murdered. The rest are doing forced labour or starving in the ghettos.

In Norway all the Jews, over 2,000, were arrested and deported.

One must reckon that far more than 1,000,000 European Jews have already been exterminated.

The United Nations on 17th December 1942 published a Joint Declaration signed, among others by representatives of Great Britain, America and the Soviet Union. It stated:

From all the occupied countries Jews are being transported, in conditions of appalling horror and brutality, to Eastern Europe. In Poland, which has been made the principal Nazi slaughter-house, the ghettos established by the German invaders are being systematically emptied of all Jews except a few highly skilled workers required for war industries. None of those taken away are ever heard of again. The able-bodied are slowly worked to death in labour camps. The infirm are left to die of starvation or are deliberately massacred in mass executions. The number of victims of these bloody cruelties is reckoned in many hundreds of thousands of entirely innocent men, women, and children.

"The above-mentioned Governments declare that such events can only strengthen the resolve of all freedom-loving peoples to overthrow the barbarous Hitlerite tyranny. They reaffirm their solemn resolution to ensure that those responsible for these crimes shall not escape retribution."

"The destruction of a foreign people is not in contradiction to the laws of life if it is completely fulfilled."

SS. Brigadefuehrer Dr. K.W. Best, "Zeitschrift fuer Politik", June 1942.

MASSENMORD

DAS VERBRECHEN

IN DEUTSCHLAND gab es bis 1939 etwa 200 000 Juden. Von ihnen sind bis auf 40 000 alle zugrunde-gegangen oder deportiert.

IN ÖSTERREICH leben von 75 000 Juden höchstens noch 15 000.

IN DER TSCHECHOSLOWAKEI wurden 137 000 Juden festgenommen.

IN POLEN sind mehr als 600 000 Juden eines unnatürlichen Todes gestorben.

IN HOLLAND UND BELGIEN blieb von 180 000 nur ein Drittel übrig.

IN FRANKREICH wurden nahezu 50 000 nach dem Osten verschleppt und unzählige ermordet.

IN JUGOSLAWIEN wurden von rund 85 000 nicht weniger als 84 000 getötet, verschleppt oder einge-kerkert.

IN RUMÄNIEN gab es 900 000 Juden. Jetzt leben dort kaum mehr 250 000.

IN GRIECHENLAND müssen alle Juden zwischen 18 und 45 Sklavenar-beit verrichten. Viele wurden ermordet.

IN LETTLAND ist ein Viertel der jüdischen Bevölkerung getötet worden. Die übrigen sind Zwangsarbeiter oder verhun-gern in den Ghettos.

IN NORWEGEN wurden sämtliche Juden, soweit das norwegische Volk sie nicht verborgen hat, verhaftet und verschleppt.

Man muss annehmen, dass weit mehr als eine Million europäischer Juden bereits ausgerottet worden ist.

DAS URTEIL DER WELT

Die Vereinten Nationen haben am 17. Dezember 1942 eine gemein-same Erklärung veröffentlicht, die u.a. von den Vertretern Gross-britanniens, Amerikas und der Sowjet-Union unterzeichnet ist. In ihr heisst es:

Aus allen von den Deutschen besetzten Ländern werden die Juden unter den brutalsten und grauenhaftesten Bedingungen nach Osteuropa verschleppt. In Polen, das die Nazis zu ihrem grössten Schlachthaus gemacht haben, werden die Juden aus den von den Eindringlingen errich-teten Ghettos herausgeholt, ausgenommen die wenigen Fach-arbeiter, die für die Rüstungs-industrie verwendbar sind. Von keinem der Verschleppten hat man je wieder etwas gehört. Die Arbeitsfähigen werden in Zwangsarbeitslagern langsam zu Tode geschunden, die Alten und Gebrechlichen dem Hungertod ausgesetzt oder in Massen hinge-richtet. Den mit kaltem Blut begangenen Grausamkeiten sind Hunderttausende völlig unschul-diger Männer, Frauen und Kinder zum Opfer gefallen.

Diese bestialische Methode plan-mässig betriebener Ausrottung bestärkt nur alle freiheitslie-benden Völker in ihrer Entschlos-senheit, mit der Hitlerbarbarei endgültig aufzuräumen. Die unterzeichneten Regierungen bekräftigen noch einmal aufs Feierlichste: Keiner, der für diese Verbrechen verantwortlich ist, wird der Strafe entgehen.

The Allies were coy about informing their own peoples of the fate of the Jews. Except for Charlie Chaplin's film *The Great Dictator,* movies, radio, and the press downplayed the subject. "America's most influential journalist, Walter Lippmann, proclaimed Hitler as the authentic voice of a genuinely civilized people and declared that Hitler's anti-Semitism was unimportant."[A]

The New York Times's masthead, "All The News That's Fit To Print," was misleading. Sixty years later, its editor apologized for "the staggering, staining failure of *The New York Times* to depict Hitler's methodical extermination of the Jews of Europe . . . Only once was their fate the subject of a lead editorial . . . No article about the Jews' plight ever qualified as *The Times*'s leading story of the day, or as a major event of a week or year."[B] Laurel Leff, a professor of Journalism at Northeastern University, researched the wartime coverage of the Jews by *The New York Times.* She discovered that you could have read *The Times'* front page in 1939 and 1940 without knowing that millions of Jews were being sent to Poland, impris-oned in ghettos, and dying of disease and starvation by the tens of thousands.[C] Marvin Kalb, Lecturer in Public Policy at Harvard, noted that "In *The Times,* the murder of millions of Jews was treated as minor-league stuff, kept at a proper distance from the authentic news of the time. For example, on July 2, 1944, *The Times* published what it called "authoritative information" to the effect that 400,000 Hungarian Jews had been deported to their deaths, and another 350,000 were earmarked for similar action. This news was published as four inches of copy on page 12."[A] However the Allies informed the Germans explicitly, for example the leaflet (*above*) that was first drafted in English (*above, left*) by the British Political Intelligence Department, was dropped over Germany in early 1943. The photographs (*below*) were dropped over Germany between October 15, 1942 and March 27, 1943,

They are captioned: "The SS amuses itself by pulling out the hair of a Jewish man's beard. The number of people murdered and starved in eastern Europe is in the hundreds of thousands." And: "A starving Jewish child from the Warsaw ghetto. A similar fate awaits 4,000 French children whose parents have been deported to the east because the Gestapo cancelled their exemption papers."

SS amüsiert sich. — Einem Juden werden die Barthaare ausgerissen. Die Zahl der in Osteuropa ermordeten und verhungerten Juden geht in die Hunderttausende.

1. *Wervelwind* was dropped on Holland between July 13 and October 3, 1942.

Only one edition of the pamphlet (*below*) was dropped on the Netherlands by the RAF sometime between March 10 and April 13, 1942. *Vrij Nederland* was then a resistance paper that appeared irregularly. Today it is a weekly opinion paper in which Elma Verhey first wrote about Flip's letters and the forced labor camps in the Netherlands. She drew attention to the camps and to those responsible for running and profiting from them.

Hardenberg, 27 June 1942 [Saturday]

Dear Pa and Ma,

First I will report on the meal we had this afternoon. As usual we went to the camp at quarter past 10. We had again collected potatoes and milk from the farmer, and at half past eleven we made a wonderful little meal from that with an egg and a tomato mixed in. And then we had soup from the kitchen. It looked more like porridge than soup. It was mostly barley, also meat, heart, and little pieces of sweetbread. In a word, we beans etc. have never eaten so well, really what you'd call nourishing. This week, I think I earned more than all the other weeks. I will easily earn about ƒ10,- and that will again cover all the expenses I have had.

Yesterday Nico and I were at a farmer's, and we were there for almost an hour. When we left, they gave us each a loaf of bread. I am sending it with this letter because I have enough for myself. Today I bought bread, and yesterday Nico and I together bought six pounds of rye bread for ƒ3 and again some butter. And when I don't have any more, I'll go after it, and as you know, never without results. Yesterday we found leaflets[1] that were dropped by Johnny Englishman. Very interesting. We found lots of them.

Thursday and yesterday we ate at that farmer about whom I wrote to you already, but we didn't like it at all. It was potatoes boiled in the skin. We talked to the wife and told her that we didn't like that, so now we can go there on Monday during our break and get a warm meal. We'll see what happens.

I will do my best to get potato coupons for you. I haven't got the photos yet; I'll get them tomorrow. They forgot to fetch them. Our work gang has also been split up and now the boss has put together a gang of all strong boys. He says I am the best in the group, but I don't care. Now that the weak ones are out, we can earn more money. It is always good to earn a few ct, this week with the pocket money I get ƒ8.58. Now dear Pa and Ma, I'll stop again with greetings a speedy *tot ziens*, from

The Kraut Mirror booklet of cartoons (*right*) was dropped on the Netherlands Sept. 13-14, 1942

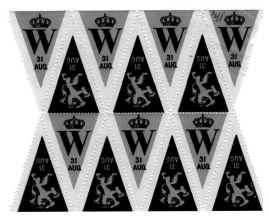

Dropped during the night of August 27-28, 1941.

RAF PAMPHLETS

The head of British Bomber Command, Sir Arthur Harris, did not share the prevailing view that disseminating information was a useful weapon of war. He considered dropping millions of leaflets to be utterly useless except as a supply of toilet paper. The leaflet at the top of page 63 had at least one effect. It induced the Germans to dig up the mass graves and burn the corpses.[A]

In 1941 the RAF dropped gifts and tons of tea in little bags over 22 towns in the Netherlands. On Queen Wilhelmina's birthday, the RAF dropped thousands of cigarettes as well as sheets of the "V" stamps shown on the left ("V" for victory and "W" for Wilhelmina). It also dropped a pamphlet, *"Toespraak van H.M. de Koningen."* (*left*), a speech given on February 21, 1942, by the Dutch Queen. Another speech made on May 22, 1942, was carried in *De Wervelwind* (Whirlwind) (*opposite page, top left*).

On Saint Nicholas day, December 6, 1941, 16,000 packets of toffees in colorful wrappings (shown on page 67) were dropped. The RAF also dropped coffee, Easter eggs, cigarette papers, books of matches, soap, needles and thread, and fake bank notes; and in 1943, V-shaped candies.

Every day during the last year of the war, the RAF dropped a four-page newspaper on Germany, initially 200,000 copies a day, and by May 1945, a million copies a day.

The examples of Allied propaganda, shown on pp. 16, 18, 63-65, 67, did not create or foster myths. They rely more on humor than hatred; whereas German propaganda was infused with hatred and mythology. Since mythology and murder vary directly, it would be expected that as the Nazis intended to murder millions, they would ease the process by propagating myths. In the minds of Nazi leaders and millions of Germans, winning the war became synonymous with the extermination of the Jews who were deemed to have the power to direct Roosevelt, Stalin and Churchill's conduct of the war, yet in reality lacked even the power to remove the quota restriction at Harvard and other universities.[B]

The newssheet, *Luchtpost* No. 9 (*left),* is dated 1941. It was dropped in December, but it could not be the one which Flip found on June 29 (page 66), as it carried no date. Moreover, a newssheet would not have withstood the weather for six months.

Hardenberg 29 June 1942 [Monday]

Dear Pa and Ma,

Tonight I received your letter with the enclosed form which I am returning, signed. You might as well turn it in; anyway you have lost it (for the time being?) and then you won't have any trouble with it. But can't you get *f* 250.- from it? Well, just decide what you want to do.

I am glad you are well again, Pa, and that everything is back to normal. That is also the best.

Lucky that you were sent ration coupons again. I am sure you can make use of mine too. Tomorrow I will buy rye bread again, that is also very nourishing. Saturday night they mixed up all our beds. What a mess we had. The beds were all put in front of the door. We had a lot of work to do to straighten it all out again.

This morning at work we had a big laugh too. The whole of Waterlooplein[1] was together, and all the street vendors were together. Saartje Scheefsnoet,[2] Nebig, Montezinos, etc., etc. Everybody yelling to everyone.

It was great weather again today. I found another leaflet dated Dec. 1, 1941. It is even nicer than all the others.[3]

Dear Pa and Mom, I stop again
  with a kiss from

P.S. Will you send me a fork?

1. Since 1886, there had been a market on Waterlooplein (*below*). Until the German occupation, most of the stalls were run by Jews. At first the Germans closed the market to all but Jews. Later, they made it illegal for Jews to be outdoor-market traders, thus making all traders unemployed and therefore eligible for labor camps.

2. Saartje Scheefsnoet ("Sara Crooked Snout") who sold fruit in the market, along with Nebig and Montezinos, were well-known characters. Jozef Vomberg pointed out that these names are a reminder that Napoleon had annexed the Netherlands in 1811. He required everyone to have a surname. Many people chose nicknames, confusing names and funny names to show mocking compliance as they did not expect Napoleon to last long.

3. The leaflet was most probably like the cartoon booklet (page 64) or the Stalingrad booklet (page 124), both of which were small with many pages. Despite Flip providing the exact date, it could not be found at the collections at the RAF museum at Hendon, at the Imperial War Museum in London, or at NIOD, and it even eluded Hans Moonen (page 182, 183), whose collection is the most extensive.

SECRET

POLITICAL INTELLIGENCE DEPARTMENT
OF THE FOREIGN OFFICE,
2, FITZMAURICE PLACE,
LONDON, W.1

EH(R)533

18th November, 1941

Dear Squadron Leader,

          Here is a very special request which we would be most grateful if you could ask Bomber Command to consider.

          It is the custom in Holland on St. Nicholas Day (5th December) to distribute sweets. The legend is that St. Nicholas himself (our Santa Claus) comes from Spain "par avion", accompanied by his negro servant, Zwarte Piet. St. Nicholas looks after the good children by distributing sweets and other presents to them, and Zwarte Piet, who is armed with a large stick, looks after the bad ones. This distributing of sweets or "strooien" of sweets is a long-standing custom in Holland. The sweets are always individually wrapped and the wrappers have little traditional verses printed on them.

          The proposal is that a small quantity of sweets should be dropped by the R.A.F. about this period, and for this occasion the traditional verses, which are printed on the wrappers, can be slightly altered to have some political sense and also to include, instead of the name St. Nicholas, the name R.A.F.

          It is suggested that quite a plain kind of sweet, say acid drops, could be used, packed in 2 oz. lots in paper bags. Probably a ton of sweets i.e. 16,000 2 oz. bags would be ample. The little bags would be packed in convenient sized cartons, one end of the carton being made so simple to open that the crews could easily pour its contents through the chute.

          The Department is extremely keen on this idea and we do hope that the R.A.F. will consider it favourably.

          Yours sincerely,

Squadron Leader C.F.Hall,   (See over)

*Left: T*he British Foreign Office, with help from the Dutch Government-in-exile, tried to help the Dutch to keep their spirits up. On the candy box cover (*below),* Mussolini is bagged and Hitler is whacked by Black Peter, St. Nicholas' assistant while the St. Nicholas song that everyone knows is parodied. The candy was dropped around December 1, 1941.

SURPRISE VOOR HITLER

ZIE de maan schijnt door de boomen,
     Makker, hoort het wild geraas.
De R.A.F. is weer gekomen,
Die is in de lucht de baas!
Vol verwachting klopt ons hart,
Wie de koek krijgt, wie de gard.
Hitler heeft den strijd gestart,
Maar aan 't eind krijgt hij de gard!

Afzender: St. Nicolaas,
per adres de R.A.F.

SURPRISE FOR HITLER

See the moon shine through the elms
Comrades stop your hue and cry!
The R.A.F. overwhelms,
They are the masters of the sky.
We are anxious to enquire
Who gets candy, who the skewer.
Germany who began this fire
Will end with one Führer fewer.

Sender: St. Nicholas
care of the R.A.F.

Flip's friends at a Saint Nicholas[4] day party, 1941. *Left to right; Back row*: Appie (Abraham) Reis; Maupie (Michael) Vogel; Jetty (Henrietta) Kaas; Lena (Lea) van Bienen; Nico Groen?; Hennie (Heintje) de Lange; Flip's mother. *Front row*: Bep (Elisabeth) de Vries; Dick van der Schaaf; Karel van der Schaaf; Harry Elzas.

A very loose translation to capture the rhyme and light-heartedness of the original.

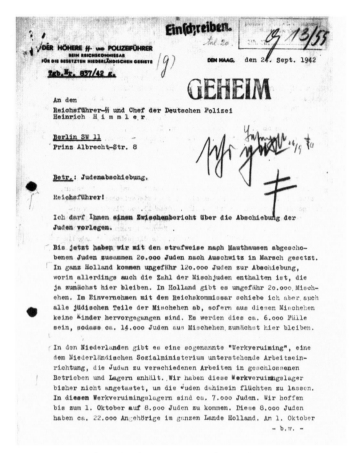

The letter above (*translated on opposite page*), dated September 24, 1942, from Hanns Rauter to Heinrich Himmler, head of the SS in Berlin, describes his solution to the "Jewish problem" that he had begun to implement on July 4, 1942.

Jews who have been arrested being transported on Amsterdam city trams, which are guarded by German soldiers, to an assembly point on the first step to deportation. This was quite unusual, as normally the Jews were transported from the Hollandsche Schouwburg (the theater that was used as a collection post) to the Central Station on city trams after midnight, out of sight of the general population.

The letter above gives details of the way the Jewish problem was being solved in the Netherlands. The problem was a myth. About one percent of the population of the Netherlands were Dutch Jews. There was very little anti-Semitism. They did not pose any religious, political, territorial, or economic threat to anyone. Hitler claimed they wanted to take over the world, something that he intended to do himself.

FROM THE HIGHEST SS AND CHIEF OF POLICE
under the Reich's Commissioner
FOR THE OCCUPIED DUTCH TERRITORY   The Hague,   24, Sept. 1942
Tgb, Nr, 837/42 g.

SECRET

To
General and Chief of the German Police
Heinrich Himmler

Berlin SW 11
Prince Albrecht-Str. 8

Re: Deportation of the Jews

General!

I am honored to submit to you an interim report concerning the deportation of the Jews.

Until now, we have transported 2,000 Jews to Auschwitz, including those Jews who were first sent to Mauthausen as punishment. From all of the Netherlands, around 120,000 Jews will be deported; this number includes those Jews in mixed marriages, who will remain here for the time being. In the Netherlands, there are approximately 20,000 mixed marriage cases. In agreement with the Reich's Commissioner, I will transport all jewish partners from the mixed marriages without children. These amount to 6,000 people, so for the time being, around 14,000 people from mixed marriages will remain here.

In the Netherlands, there is a so-called "employ-ment creation" program, which falls under the Dutch Ministry of Social Affairs and which employs Jews in private companies and camps. Until now, we have left these employment creation camps alone so that the Jews can find refuge there. There are about 7,000 Jews in these camps. By October 1, we hope to increase this number to 8,000. These 8,000 Jews have approximately 22,000 dependents throughout all of the Netherlands. On October 1, these camps will be quickly occupied, and, on the same day, these dependents will be arrested and taken to the newly created Jewish camps of Westerbork, near Assen, and Vught, near 's-Hertogenbosch. Instead of 2 trains, I will try to arrange 3 trains per week. I hope that by Christmas, we will be rid of these 30,000 Jews, so that, in this way, 50,000 Jews (half of the total amount) will have been eliminated from the Netherlands. For a few weeks now, the Population Registries throughout the country have been mak-ing preliminary arrangements for the determina-tion of mixed marriages as well as for the pro-duction of evidence that the Aryan partners of these mixed marriages are actually Aryan. These 13,000 mixed marriage Jews will receive a note on their Jewish identity cards permitting them to remain in the Netherlands. This will also be the case for armaments workers who are absolutely need-ed by the German army. They amount to 6,000, plus their dependents for a total of 21,000. Also included in this number are the diamond workers in Amsterdam, certain art dealers, and NSB Jews (20).

On October 15, Jewry will be outlawed in the Netherlands. This means that this will begin with large police actions. Not only the German and Dutch police, but also the NSDAP, party branches, the NSB, the German army and so on, will be mobi-lized. Every Jew, no matter where he is found in the Netherlands, will be sent to one of the large Jewish camps. Thus, there can be no Jew who does not have privileged status allowed to remain in the Netherlands. At the same time, I will publish a decree stating that Aryans who have helped Jews escape across the border, to hide, or to falsify identification documents, will have their posses-sions confiscated, and the culprits will be sent to a concentration camp. All of this is to pre-vent the flight of Jews, which has already been seen in large numbers.

In the meantime, the catholic Jews, out of all the christian Jews, have been deported because the five bishops, led by Archbishop de Jong in Utrecht, have not kept to the original agreement. The protestant Jews are still here, and it has indeed been successful in exploding the united front between Catholic and Protestant Churches. At a conference of bishops, Archbishop de Jong declared that he would never enter into a united front with the Protestants and Calvinists. The storm of protest that erupted when the evacuation began quickly subsided and has now died off. The hundred new units of the Dutch police are doing good work on the Jewish question, arresting hun-dreds of Jews by day and by night. The only dan-ger arising at this time is the situation that now and then a policeman seizes and enriches him-self with Jewish property. I have ordered these cases to be tried by the ST and Police Courts in front of the assembled police units.

The Westerbork Jewish camp is already entirely ready; the Vught Jewish camp will be fully ready around the 10-15 of October.

    Heil Hitler!

    Your obedient servant,

    [Rauter SS]

SELLINGERBEETSE CAMP

1. The fate of the eight boys who ran away is not known. They were in Sellingerbeetse camp that was nearly 4 miles from Sellingen, a mile from the German border, and 32 miles north of Hardenberg. It was one of the first (built in 1942) labor camps for Jewish men. It was one of the largest (over 300 inmates), yet one of the least known. Even the Dutch National Institute of War Documentation (NIOD) had no information about the camp in 2005.

Hardenberg, 4 July [Saturday]

Dear Pa and Ma,

I got your letter this morning and read that Dick will come here this evening or tomorrow to arrange a few things. It is now half past 7, and he is not here yet. I think I can't expect him until tomorrow. In many ways I think we are better off here than in A[msterdam]. Imagine, if I were home now, then there would be no food at all, while here I have more than enough and have to work hard, but luckily have no problems. In the camp, so far, we have been allowed to walk around freely after eight o'clock. I already heard about the eight boys from Sellingen.[1] I heard they were runaways. Yes, it all seems pretty hopeless, but we have to keep our heads cool and wait and see. There was a great deal of tension here when we heard all the news. But chin up! The time will come. Our time*!!*

This morning I received a package from Bep with a box of peppermints, a roll of licorice, a roll of sour balls, envelopes, cherries, and tomatoes. Really great. She has treated me well again. Oh yes, there was also a roll of film with the photos. Nico's father and brother-in-law visited today.

Packages may be sent.

———

It is now Sunday afternoon. Dick came yesterday at quarter to eleven. I was still sitting outside with Nico[2] and his father and brother-in-law when he arrived with a huge backpack. We sat and chatted for another half hour, and Dick then gave me the money. Yes, dear Pa and Ma, I hope I will never ever have to use it and that we will be together again shortly. I also read the letter at once and read that sometimes you don't get my letters immediately. De Bruins must have physicals tomorrow (all three), him and his two sons. So everyone goes; nobody is spared.

Sending packages is still allowed, but I am really glad that Dick came personally.

My shoes are completely rotten. They were not the best; only the sole is still good. Nico says that Ma must go to his aunt. She knows where they sell excellent shoes with wooden soles. And they are not expensive. Will you do that, Ma? You can simply go to Nico's house. I hope I won't still be here this winter, but you never know.

How the weather has changed again huh? It happened so suddenly this week. Nice and warm in the mornings and rain in the afternoon.

Now, Pa and Ma, I can't think of anything else except warmest greetings and a big kiss from

Flip

2. Sitting on the left with a shovel is Simon Loonstijn; on his left is Kiek van Kleef. Sitting in front with a shovel is Nico Groen; on his left is Flip. The names of the other men are not known.

Hardenberg, 5 July 1942 [Sunday]

Dear Pa and Ma,

Dick has gone, and of course, as you know, he gave me the money, and today I had a great time with him. He will have already told you that I am healthy and look well and am not hungry. This evening we again ate delicious potato salad with tomatoes and cucumber; luckily they can't take that away from me.

Later this evening we were in the canteen and officially heard there that we will be sent to G[ermany] systematically to work there.

So Dick did not come for nothing today. I am writing this because I don't want to keep any secrets from you, but on condition that you won't get nervous or upset. For the time being I am not worrying, so you shouldn't either, and it won't happen in the next few months. So chin up!!! In 2 months a lot can still happen. You know my point of view. I am not going.[1] Now again something else.

I put the tobacco in my suitcase and I may be able to please a lot of people with it eventually. The mood here is still very good. People don't take things too much to heart, so I don't either.

The little fish were delicious. I still have one, and that I have saved for tonight. Also the sausage I will eat in good health, and also the coffee cake. I am enclosing a few ration coupons again; I hope they will arrive. They are from Mr. Salomonson.[2] He also has to have a physical tomorrow. Well Pa and Ma I'll stop and trust you not to worry yet. Where there is life, there is hope, and I end with a big kiss from

Flip.

The end is in sight.
All we have to do is survive*!*
And that we'll undoubtedly do*!!*

Also a soap coupon and a sugar coupon.
The cheese coupon is from me and cost 10 ct.

Flip and his friend inside are probably laughing at the little joke on the sign they have taped to the barrack window; it reads:
VILLA EETLUST (APPETITE VILLA)

1. By writing "I'm not going," Flip was restating his intention to escape and to go into hiding, an echo of "If something happens here, I will be gone in no time" (April 29) and "I will see to it that I get away. I will not let them take me to Germany" (May 1). Flip's attitude was not widely shared, especially at this early period.

When Jews went into hiding, their names were published in the Police Gazette along with those of wanted criminals. (*Below*) Jozef Vomberg's family is included in the list put out by the Zutphen police.

2. Friedrich Salomonson was Rosalchen Salomonson de Bruin's brother.

The Police Gazette for November 23, 1943 advertising for Josef Vomberg and his family and many others.

2703. The C of P [Chief of Police] in **Zutphen** requests to locate and bring in the following persons of jewish blood, who are suspected of having changed residence without having obtained the necessary permission:
Israel Hans NEUGARTEN, born July 28, 1920 in Huls;
Simon ZWAAP, born March 30, 1893 in Amsterdam;
Simon COHEN, born March 1, 1909 in Zutphen;
Geertruida KOPPEL, born Aug. 12, 1888 in Zutphen;
Jacob KNOEK, born Nov. 11, 1914 in Zutphen;
Abraham Salomon NOACH, born Dec. 1, 1903 in Deventer;
Eva ZILVERBERG, born Aug. 16, 1911 in Zutphen;
Sander NOACH, born Oct. 26, 1909 in Zutphen;
Emanuel VOMBERG, born Jan. 19, 1891 in Zutphen;
Elisabeth VAN DIJK, born Aug. 23, 1890 in Oss;
Esther VOMBERG, born May 25, 1931 in Zutphen;
Jozef VOMBERG, born May 27, 1923 in Zutphen;

1. This death notice informed Isaäc Goudeket and Sara Noot-Goudeket who lived near Flip on Majuba Street, that Siegfried, their only son, born February 10, 1920, was taken to Buchenwald where he died in the local hospital of "flu" on May 12, 1941, and was cremated two days later. The father then wrote back requesting his son's ashes. The Germans agreed but never did so. He and his wife died in Auschwitz, September 21, 1942.

2. Within a year most Jewish homes were boarded up and few of Flip's neighbors or friends remained at home. An exception was Jopie (Joshua) Lierens and his wife Juutje (Judith), who lived at 148 Vrolik Street. Because their names were not on any list, they were never summoned to report for deportation nor ever arrested. Throughout the war they never went out because Karel's mother, Hanna Cecelia Meyvogel-van der Schaaf, brought them food.[4]

Hardenberg, 8 July '42 [Wednesday]

Dear Pa and Ma,

Today I had a letter from you again and read that all is still well and that the news did not upset you. Yes, it would be crazy if they allowed us to quietly wait for the end of the war in the camps. I really think that if we were sent to Germany, the greatest terrors would be in store for us, and that is why I am glad you agree with my refusal to go. As you say, Pa, everything must be well thought out, and we (Nico and I) discuss it all the time. I have asked Dick if he can get me a map and a compass. Everything must be done correctly?

I read in Bep's letter that the girls will sleep at home on Saturday night. I wish I were there.

Weren't the coupons great? I am sure you can make good use of them, right? And I certainly wouldn't prefer a kiss from Bep; it is all the same to me. If everything turns out fine, I will have learned a great deal from this time.

De Bruin was rejected, but both his sons passed. About Salomonson, I don't know yet. I also don't know where they must go. Pa, see that you don't go for the physical; you hear, try to get a certificate stating you work for the German Army. They will give it to you. From Dick I received the guilders and I will thank Grandma.

I am writing all this optimistically because I keep my spirits up and hope that this will be over before winter arrives. That could really happen.

Have more death notices come?[1] You see what is waiting for us if we go. I talked confidentially with Nico and told him what you gave me in case of emergency. He wrote home, and his father is seeing to it that he also gets a sum. Half of what I have.

Now I am going to answer Ma's letter. Ma, you write that we should not wait too long, but Nico's father wrote that we must wait till the very last minute. (When you are at Nico's, don't mention any of this to his mother; she knows nothing of it). But we will wait for the right time; the longer we can hang on here, the better for all.

People run away from here daily, on Monday, 2, on Tuesday 2 and again 1 today. So that's 5 altogether.

I heard about the affair of Dick, Lily, and Karel.

And everybody knows that Harry writes such crazy letters. Talk about it with Dick or Bep. Not with the others. I have also already written several things to him and asked questions, but he never gives a straight answer.

I am slowly sending my things home. I don't need the sheet and the shirt, and you don't need to send other clothes, only socks. Will you give the roll of film to Bep, Ma, she will take care of it. Will you also send me a few pictures of myself, maybe two or three?

Ma, you don't have to worry that all families will have to leave A[msterdam]. That can't happen.[2]

Can you still get shoes with wooden soles Ma? please, I can really use them. The ones I have are completely rotten and broken.

I end this letter with a big kiss and

a hug from

Flip.

Be brave and don't take everything to heart!
You don't have to worry about me.

Soap coupon encl.

11
Hardenberg 11 July 1942 [Saturday]

Dear Pa and Ma,

From the letters of various people I heard that Ma is planning to come to me tomorrow. I really don't understand the reason for this. Everything is in good shape here, and we are fine, much too fine for you to risk the great danger of traveling without a star.[1] You mustn't get upset about anything. Why do other people write and tell me that you two are so nervous; I have not ~~sttt~~ written anything to get upset about. The situation is indeed not rosy, but you should not fret yet.

I would be very happy if Ma came to see me, of course, if she dares to take the risk.

At the moment I strongly advise against it. I only wrote that we have to consider the possibility that we will be sent to work in G[ermany] within the foreseeable future, but for the time being there is no talk of it. You agree?

We keep our sense of humor here, and you should do that too. Sometimes we really laugh. This morning some guys were wrestling in front of the shed and someone peed down from the top of the shed. We howled with laughter. There is a great set of guys here. And last week, they spread syrup all over someone, front and back.

I got a few potato coupons for ƒ0.50 and am enclosing them. Well, Pa and Ma, you have to decide what you are going to do. But there is <u>absolutely no</u> reason to worry about me here. I end now with a big kiss and till we meet again soon

from

1. Since April 1941, Jews had not been allowed to travel except with a special permit. The only options open to Flip's parents were not to wear a star and hope that they would not have their papers checked, or to carry false papers and try to pass as non-Jews. In either case, if they were caught, punishment was swift and deportation was immediate.

Below: Receipt for the ten cent fee that was required to apply for a travel permit, which might or might not be granted. It is dated May 1942 and is valid for travel from the 29th to the 30th.

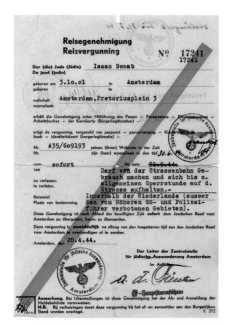

A travel permit issued to a 43-year-old man. It had been renewed for one month. It allowed the bearer to use the streetcars and be on the street during non-curfew hours. On the reverse side are the two further extensions he was granted before being deported.

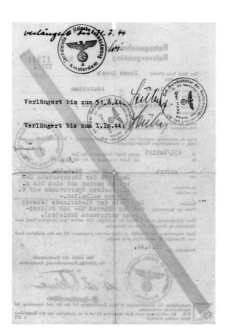

Dutch policeman checking IDs and documents. Having the wrong papers or none at all usually meant instant arrest.

Hardenberg 12 July '42 [Sunday]

Dear Pa and Ma,

This morning I received your letter and also learned that things in Amsterdam are in a sad shape. Men are being called up and even girls from 15 to 40. That bothers me the most. That they touch the women, and even children, that is terrible. There was a terribly depressed mood in the camp. Several local girls and boys from here have been called up, and then suddenly last night there was news of an invasion in France. Such an idiot drives the whole camp crazy; he said that Boulogne and Brittany were occupied. We did not believe it, and at eleven o'clock we went to a farmer[1] to listen to the radio (Nico, Joop, and I). We waited tensely for the eleven-fifty news broadcast, and I assure you that we were greatly disillusioned when we got back to the camp at twelve-thirty. How they cursed that fellow. We had all already said that when the need is at its highest, salvation is near, but no! Pa, I will also now use that small stove and the Esbit. I had not realized before that I can use these things in difficult situations. But it has given me a good idea. Send me a few packages; they work very well; everybody uses them. I don't need money; I still have ƒ40.- aside from the other, of course. You see it shrinks pretty well. Everything here is also now much more expensive. The farmers have to hand in everything. Eggs now cost 30 ct. That is about double from when we first arrived.

The weather is terrible. Saturday and this morning were hellish. Storms and rain, and this week we even had <u>hail</u>.

It is very reassuring for me to know that you are not short of the most important things. If that ever happens, write and tell me, and (if it's possible) I will send you some coupons.

Yes, they want to tear all of Judaism apart and are working hard at it. I already wrote to Bep and told her not to go if she is called up.

We have already talked with a farmer[1] (a good Christian), and if necessary he will be glad to help us to stay in hiding. It is a dirty rotten time.

Ma, I advise you not to come here to me; so far I am fine and you don't need to run any risk. But if you must come, come alone and above all not with that Halverstad woman. ~~Nu ~~

The situation will get worse and worse, and I will consider that. If ~~dd~~ you think it is necessary for me to vamoose, write and tell me.

Nico left 10 minutes ago. He told me in the <u>deepest</u> secrecy.

I don't think it is necessary yet, but when it is, I won't hesitate to beat it.

Dear Ma and Pa, I end

with many kisses and a hug from

I got Nico's clogs.
I have lost my best friend, but . . . grit my teeth
and have faith in the future *!!*

1. Aaltje Seinen Veurink, whose farm abutted the camp. The Veurinks invited the boys to their home in the evening, supplied them with food and listened to the radio with them.

When Flip wrote "That they touch the women, and even children, that is terrible."; it is likely that he was thinking of his friends above. *Left to right*: Bep de Vries; Lena van Bienen; Henny de Lange; Stella Aluin

On July 12, Flip wrote that the thought that bothered him most was "That they touch the women, and even children, that is terrible." The following are examples of the treatment of children.

An eye-witness account of events at the Mizocz ghetto, Ukraine, October 5, 1942:
"My foreman and I went directly to the pits. I heard rifle shots in quick succession from behind one of the earth mounds. The people who had got off the trucks—men, women and children of all ages—had to undress upon the order of an SS man, who carried a riding or dog whip. They had to put down their clothes in fixed places, sorted according to shoes, top clothing and under clothing. I saw a heap of shoes of about 800 to 1,000 pairs, great piles of under-linen and clothing. Without screaming or weeping these people undressed, stood around in family groups, kissed each other, said farewells and waited for a sign from another SS man, who stood near the pit, also with a whip in his hand. During the fifteen minutes that I stood near the pit I heard no complaint or plea for mercy . . . An old woman with snow-white hair was holding a one-year-old child in her arms and singing to it and tickling it. The child was cooing with delight. The parents were looking on with tears in their eyes. The father was holding the hand of a boy about 10-years-old and speaking to him softly; the boy was fighting his tears. The father pointed to the sky, stroked his head and seemed to explain something to him. At that moment the SS man at the pit shouted something to his comrade. The latter counted off about twenty persons and instructed them to go behind the earth mound . . . I well remember a girl, slim and with black hair, who, as she passed close to me, pointed to herself and said: "twenty-three-years-old." I walked around the mound and found myself confronted by a tremendous grave. People were closely wedged together and lying on top of each other so that only their heads were visible. Nearly all had blood running over their shoulders from their heads. Some of the people were still moving. Some were lifting their arms and turning their heads to show that they were still alive. The pit was already two-thirds full. I estimated that it contained about a thousand people. I looked for the man who did the shooting. He was an SS man, who sat at the edge of the narrow end of the pit, his feet dangling into the pit. He had a tommy gun on his knees and was smoking a cigarette."[A]

A man in Rotterdam recorded in his diary, "A woman, her sick husband, and her three-week-old baby were hauled from their home. The woman carried a bag filled with rice for feeding the baby rice water during the transport. The German who had arrested her took away the bag, tore it open, and poured its contents upon the ground."[B]

Wladyslaw Szpilman, the Polish pianist and composer, wrote that on August 5, 1942 [August 6], he happened to see Janusz Korczak[1] and his orphans leaving the Warsaw ghetto. Dr. Korczak was the founder and director of a local progressive orphanage and a champion of children's rights. "It was only with difficulty that he persuaded the Germans to take him too. He had spent long years of his life with children, and now on this last journey, he would not leave them alone . . . He told the orphans that they were going out into the country so they ought to be cheerful. He told them to wear their best clothes and so they came out into the yard, two by two, nicely dressed and in a happy mood.

The little column was led by an SS man who loved children, as Germans do, even those he was about to see on their way to the next world. He took a special liking to a boy of twelve, a violinist who had his instrument under his arm. The SS man told him to go to the head of the procession of children and play—and so they set off.

When I met them in Gesia Street, the smiling children were singing in chorus, the little violinist was playing for them and Korczak was carrying two of the smallest infants, who were beaming too, and telling them some amusing story."[C]

The children were led to the station yard, where other SS men closed off the water supply. They were sent the same day to Treblinka where the ten adults and 192 children were killed.[D]

Walter Mattner, a police secretary, stationed at Mogilev in Belorussia on October 2 and 3, 1941, wrote to his wife boasting that by the tenth truckload of victims, he had calmed down and "was already aiming more calmly and shot accurately at the many women, children and infants . . . The death we gave to them was a nice, quick death . . . Infants were flying in a wide circle through the air and we shot them down still in flight, before they fell into the pit and into the water. Let's get rid of this scum."[E]

1. Dr. Janusz Korczak with some of the children from his orphanage in 1938

1. A contemporary advertisement for Esbit

2. Camp Vledder was 25 miles northwest of Molengoot. Between January and October 1942, 120 Jewish men were held there.

3. Wooden-soled shoes like these were worn during World War II.

Hardenberg, 13 July 1942

MONDAY

Dear Pa and Ma,

We have learned the sad news from Amsterdam. There is such a depressed mood this morning that we didn't do anything the rest of the day. Until now we have been kept completely up to date by telephone.

Pa and Ma, what do you advise me to do? Nico left for Amsterdam yesterday. I hope he found a safe place. I am on my own now, but will not hesitate to make a decision by myself. In every way that I can think of I will try to survive this night that has descended over the jewish people. I cannot write cheerfully, I am too upset, but I still keep my courage up and you must do that too. Now, what I would like best is a letter from you every day, and as long as I can, I will write every night. Send the compass and the map and the Esbit[1] as quickly as possible. Also the knee socks; I don't need anything else. About Ma's visit, I dare not make a decision. It's possible that I'll be gone, but also, of course, that I will still be here. I leave it entirely up to Ma. I would love to see you, Ma, but would not want to see you fall into their hands. I'd rather wait a little longer. Will Bep also be called up? I hope not, but fear it. I think they will call up every jew they can use to "work." Pa, if anything happens, write to me by express or send a telegram.

I heard that the men in Camp Vledder[2] (it is a punishment camp) must leave, but I don't know for sure.

I bought the little leather shoes that were in the package for ƒ4.25 to wear inside my clogs but they were much too small for me.

I now use Nico's wooden-soled shoes[3] and they are very good.

On Wednesday I will send a package with extra things and dirty stuff that I don't need right now. If I need anything I will write.

Now, dear Pa and Ma, I end with a tight embrace and a kiss from
your

Be strong, you hear! Don't despair. I don't either.
Don't worry about me *!*

[Tot ziens in Mokum—See you soon in Amsterdam]

Tuesday Evening 13 [14]
July '42

Dear Pa and Ma,

I can't think of much to write about at the moment. Several people have got the news that they must go to Germany. I don't know if it will happen. Here in our room, the daughter of a man has to go. She is 27 years old. First his son died in Buchenwald, then his daughter died in childbirth and then he had to leave, leaving behind his nervous wreck of a wife. And now this again.

Yesterday and today I got no mail from you. Write to me every night. It is now really necessary. We have to cheer each other up. Today somebody left for Amsterdam. His girlfriend has to go to Upper-Silesia. They are going to get married first. There are several people marrying. Will it do any good? They are together. Pa what do you advise? I wrote to Barend and asked if he has a hiding place for me. Of course, I don't know yet if I will go to him.

Pa and Ma, I have a sense that something is going to happen soon. Will it last another winter? It seems almost impossible to me. Thousands and thousands are dying. But we have to keep our courage up.

Pa, a friend here in the camp asked if you can get him the newspaper from July 8th. Can you take care of that?

I end again and repeat "keep up your courage."
Fondest greetings and a big kiss

from

This special edition of Het Joodsche Weekblad (*The Jewish Weekly),* was published when the German demand for a specific number of people in the July call-up was not obeyed.

New edition: Volume 2 No. 14a
July 10, 1942 (25 TAMOEZ 5702)

The Jewish Weekly

**Published by the Jewish Council of Amsterdam
Under the Directorship of
A. Asscher and Prof. Dr. D. Cohen**

EXTRA EDITION

Amsterdam, July 14, 1942

The "Sicherheitspolizei" [Security police] has informed us as follows:

About 700 Jews have been arrested today in Amsterdam. If the 4000 Jews designated for labor camps in Germany do not depart this week, the 700 prisoners will be deported to a concentration camp in Germany.

The Presidents of the
Jewish Council of Amsterdam
A. ASSCHER
Prof. Dr. D. COHEN

Camp roll call in Buchenwald. The "N" on the jackets stands for *Niederlanden*; "Netherlands."

Hardenberg 15 July 1942 [Wednesday]

Dear Pa and Ma,

I received this morning's letter at work. They bring it so that we can get the news. The news is not good. Everything is gloomy with the raids etc., etc. Here we know about everything. Also, I received the ƒ50,- I now know we are better off here than in Amsterdam. All precautions have been taken here. There is always a guard on duty. Tonight I have guard duty from 1 to 3. People stand in the road, and as soon as anything suspicious happens an alarm goes off. Tonight I got everything ready and went to sleep with my clothes on. Luckily nothing happened.

Nico is now gone. Yes, I miss the good friend I had, but I will manage by myself. Hardly any work is being done. The mood is totally down. For the rest I have no complaints. This afternoon at four-thirty I went to the village. We got there at about 5:15. I bought fresh tomatoes, a bottle of tomatoes [preserved] and other things.

I am again sending a parcel with dirty laundry, shoes, socks, a towel, scarf, and books.

I hope they don't call up Bep. I would find that unbearable. Pa, if something happens, write everything to me. I get to know anyway. Send the package with the map, Esbit, and (just in case) compass. If you can't get a map, I'll probably find one here. Send the package as soon as possible, Pa.

Ma if you want to come with Karel, do so. I would like it very much.

I will remember Brilman's address and use it if necessary.

Dear Pa and Ma, I stop again. Keep your courage up.

A big kiss and greetings from

Flip.

Tot ziens.

Ma are you still coming?
But be careful, you hear.

Men, women, and children who have arrived at Hooghalen are given directions for the five-mile walk to Westerbork camp.

WESTERBORK[A]

In 1939, the Dutch government established Westerbork camp five miles from Hooghalen as a place to house refugees fleeing Hitler's Germany. Although built by the Dutch government, it was paid for by the Relief Committee for Jewish Refugees. Professor David Cohen was president of the Committee. Westerbork camp was in a marshy area in the province of Drente, 80 miles northeast of Amsterdam and 20 miles from Hardenberg. At the time of the German invasion in May 1940, there were about 750 people living in the camp, including 181 from the *SS Saint Louis*.[B] By 1941 there were 1,100. By October 1943 there were 14,000, of whom 3,000 had to sleep on the ground. When the camp was liberated in April 1945 there were about 900 remaining.

A Jewish Council, comprising mainly German Jews, was already established in the camp when the Netherlands was invaded. The Germans ordered the Council to continue to run the camp. When in July 1942, the SS surrounded it with barbed wire, erected seven watchtowers, and patrolled the perimeter, patrols were then assigned to the Jews—the *Joodsche Ordedienst* [Jewish Police Force, known as the OD] who became responsible for maintaining order in the camp. The OD commander was an Austrian Jewish refugee, Arthur Pisk, whose force of 200 men were ". . . drawn from the dregs of Jewish society, rough coarse fellows without refinement, human feelings, or compassion . . . " The camp served as a reservoir to ensure that there were always enough people to fill the trains so that they would run on time and meet the needs of Sobibor and Auschwitz.

The barracks were slightly leaky wooden buildings, 275 feet long, 33 feet wide. Each held about 300 bunk beds, three-high with straw mattresses and pillows. At the end of each dormitory was a washroom with a long sink running down the center with faucets at regular intervals. The latrine was a separate building consisting of a plank with holes above a ditch. There was no privacy in the latrine building, the washrooms, or the sleeping quarters, and there was no place to store the few belongings people still had. A privileged few were given brick houses, whereas those who had been in hiding were placed in barrack 67 [the S-block, S for *Straf:* punishment]. These S-prisoners wore prison uniforms and wooden clogs; they received no soap and little food; they were given hard labor and additional punishments that were increased throughout 1943; and they were assured a place on the next transport to Poland. Most people arriving at Westerbork stayed no more than a week or two, but the prewar residents and those in hospital and the local Jewish Council led by Kurt Schlesinger often remained a long time.

Schlesinger had a cozy relationship with Commandant SS-Obersturmfürher Gemmeker, for whom he drew up the weekly transport lists. Everyone's overwhelming preoccupation was to avoid inclusion on the next transport, which most believed to be a death sentence, except for those on transports to Theresienstadt. Aside from the pervading fear of death, flies, fleas, bad weather, censorship, no privacy or freedom, life was tolerable. Westerbork held Jewish services, had a school, a nursery with Jo Spier murals, a 1,725 bed hospital, a good dispensary, a hairdresser, a canteen, a cabaret and an orchestra.

A dirt road between the barracks

Inside the barrack

Restored Westerbork nursery: murals by Jo Spier

1. Sal or Sallie was Samuel Emanuel de Bruin, born in Hardenberg on May 3, 1889. He married Sophie Abrahamson, born August 30, 1880. Sal and Ru de Bruin were brothers.

2. For Jews, "going to Germany" meant going to Poland. Until 1942, Jews were sent to concentration camps, but beginning in 1942, they were sent to extermination camps. However, as a result of the battle of Stalingrad, the progressive labor shortage gradually induced the Germans to sacrifice principle for practice, and some Jews capable of work were spared for a while; they were first put to work and then put to death.

Germany did not invent slavery, but it did invent the idea of disposable slaves. As long as the supply was plentiful, inferior races were worked to death and replaced.

Despite their public detestation of each other, Stalin and Hitler copied each other's methods, thus both used slaves extensively. There is no settling the point of precedence between a louse and a flea.

Specially printed Westerbork money was given in exchange for guilders but it could only be used in the camp.

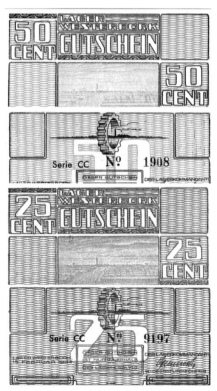

Hardenberg 16 July '42
Thursday evening

Dear Pa and Ma,

This morning I got your letter at work and again read that everything is still rotten in A[msterdam].

Tonight we had guards. I was on from 1 to 3, if anything happens we are warned immediately. The camp is now guarded at night by 12-15 men, and four of them have large whistles. You write that there are no victims in our family yet, but from de Bruin I hear that Sal[1] and his wife must go to G[ermany]. What will that mean?[2] God give strength to the people who have to endure this misery. We must also be strong. Tonight I went to the village again to buy some things. I go into the stores and don't wear a star. Luckily one can get away with that here, and they don't see it

Everything is against us I got a letter from Barend, he can't help me if something happens. He did send me a package with ½ pound of butter, ½ a cheese 40+ [fat content], and some rye bread. Everything here is still good. The de Bruins are not gone yet.

I bought tomatoes again and also rye bread.

If only we can stay here.

In our room there is someone else with the same worries.

Tomorrow I will send a longer letter.

Now, I don't feel like it. I stop again

with a big kiss from your

Felis.

Ma, don't come. Everything is still good here. Kissed by your *Felis.*

and *tot ziens.*

Upon arrival at Westerbork, there was a lengthy registration process (*below*) during which all assets had to be declared.

70 TO 81.7% OF DUTCH JEWS ARE EXPELLED

The first transport left Westerbork on Tuesday, July 16, 1942. The last one left on Wednesday, September 13, 1944. Of the 103 trains from the Netherlands, 68 went to Auschwitz, 9 went to Bergen-Belsen, 19 trains went to Sobibor, and 7 to Theresienstadt. Of the 104,000 people sent east, only 4,532 came back. (page 177)

One short-term Westerbork prisoner was Jo Spier, a fine artist and a well loved person who in 1937 was voted one of the ten most popular men in the Netherlands. He had drawn a cartoon of Hitler, but as Hitler had no sense of humor, Spier was arrested and was sent to prison and then to Westerbork and then to Theresienstadt, where an SS officer sought him out because he had liked the murals that Spier had painted in the Westerbork children's hospital nursery (page 79). "When I made them I had no idea that I was in the process of saving my father's life." The SS officer told Jo Spier that he had arranged for his father to be brought from Westerbork to Theresienstadt. Six months later his father arrived on a transport from Bergen-Belsen. When thanked, the officer said, "So, for once in my life, I have done something decent."*A*

One long term Westerbork prisoner was Philip Mechanicus, author and journalist on the editorial staff of *Algemeen Handelsblad.* For at least 9 months from May 28, 1943, he kept a diary that gives an honest, accurate and sympathetic account of camp life in which the transports were the focal point. He commented several times on their destination, for example: "Yesterday it was decided to close down the camp and send the Jews to the east, to Auschwitz, Theresienstadt and central Germany."*B* (September 4th, 1943). Several times he described the way people reacted to the news that they were on the list: "I know for certain that when I'm sent to Poland, and I'm going off on Tuesday, I won't survive it." (July 18th). "Last night a sixty-five-year-old woman in my hut committed suicide. Her application for Theresienstadt had been turned down. Her daughter had said she was willing to accompany her voluntarily. She wanted to save her daughter from making that sacrifice." (September 13th). And several times he described the weekly loading of the trains. The last transport from Westerbook to Sobibor—2,209 people—left on Tuesday 21st July, 1943:

Wednesday, July 21st: Every week they say that it is a terrible transport. All transports are terrible. It is heart-rending, again and again, to see mothers and fathers, or mothers alone with their offspring, a yellow card on their chests, or bent elderly folk laden with their last meager possessions, setting out on the journey callously ordained by a hater of mankind. But there is a crescendo in the feeling of horror—this time pregnant women in their seventh or eighth month and week-old infants with scarlet fever were taken, in cattle and goods trucks. . . . July 15th was the date on which the Netherlands had to be virtually clear of Jews, *judenrein*.

July 15th has come and the quota of 90,000 Jews demanded by Hitler has been handed over. In the transport there was also a man (an S-man) with his wife, who had just had a confinement, and a small ailing child. This transport was terrible too, because of the large number of families with young children—mainly people who had pinned their hopes on Palestine, but whose papers had been turned down. It was terrible for these people because their hopes had been reduced to nothing. They included practically all the teachers who took classes at Westerbork. It was terrible for the devout Jews because a number of well-known Dutch rabbis were included in the transport. It was terrible because it was stiflingly hot. From a psychological point of view, it was probably the most wretched transport that has ever left Westerbork for the east. [Not one of the 2,209 survived.]

—Philip Mechanicus

Loading a transport at Westerbork. The number in each wagon was chalked on the outside, (*bottom right*), usually 25 to 100 (the goal was 3.6 people per square meter).

1. Flip continually evaluated the risk of going into hiding for himself, as he did for Henny de Lange (*left*), above with Jetty Kaas (*right*). The risk was increased after the Germans began to offer rewards from five to 40 guilders for turning in a Jew, the price fluctuating with the supply (page 178). But money was not the only incentive. Sometimes it was fear, envy, personal feud, or anti-semitism. Walter B. Maass reported that about 12,000 Jews in hiding were either caught or betrayed, while about 4,000 adults and 4,000 children survived. He added:

> "The enormity of the holocaust in the Netherlands was not due to the attitude of the Christian population. In their majority, they condemned the anti-Jewish measures and tried to render assistance to the victims wherever possible. That there were any Jewish survivors at all must be credited to the work of the Dutch resistance and the courage and humanitarian spirit of individual Christians.[A]"

Hardenberg 17 July '42. Friday evening

Dearest Pa and Ma,

This morning mail again arrived at work and I got your letter. Again several tears were shed around 11 o'clock. If the situation does not change, the regulations will get worse all the time. Now it is said that the camps do not have to go, but I don't believe it. I think we will all get our turn, sooner or later. But all the time we have to hold on to our courage. Ma, don't get upset, you hear me? I hear that the boys who failed their physicals in A[msterdam] are now being sent to Germany. So you can see we don't know what's the right thing to do. At this point, I am happy for myself and for you that I am still here. We still don't really lack anything (as far as hunger etc. is concerned). The mood here is not the greatest, but we get letters from people who went home and married Christian women and they write: if only we were still in Molengoot. To be honest, compared with the situation in A[msterdam], we can't complain. Pa, you mention marriage. Indeed it would not help much. If it would help even a little, I'd be willing, but what is the use? The only thing is that Bep would not be alone. My thoughts are with you and Bep constantly. I would find it awful if the worst happens. But let us trust in the future and in God. As I wrote yesterday, Barend sent me a package. It's great that he takes care of that. They are also having difficulty there. Is Aunt Juul still not well? She shouldn't worry about that miserable money. Perhaps later she can use it as wallpaper. The important thing is that they may stay together and live together.

From Barend I received the answer that he can't help me. Nothing to do about that. I will find my way all right. Don't you find it hard to understand that Nico should have left? There is always time enough to take off. I had already reckoned on leaving this week. I was sorry that I had built up a stockpile of various things. Now I am just going to finish it off because it would be a shame to leave it behind.

Isn't it nice, huh, that the girls come and visit you now and then? I hear from Bep that Henny has taken off; if she could do that, I think she is right.[1] The only thing I can advise is not, not, and again not to go when called up. I think it would be best that you send your letters by express mail, then I can get them the following night, and there aren't two days in between. On Monday I am sending you a surprise. You will see what it is. I just hope you like it.

Dear Pa and Ma be strong. We still have many burdens, but Israel [Jews] will not go under. A big kiss and greetings from

Flip.

Hardenberg 18 July 1942
Saturday evening

Dear Pa and Ma,

This morning I again received your letter. Now you can send somewhat better news from A[msterdam]. I don't know if I can say that about here. The rumor going around is that all single and married men from 18 to 40 have to go (I really believe it). Also that no packages may be sent; that we are going to have guards, and the mail will be censored. Somebody just came in with the news that camp Geestbrugge[1] [sic] was suddenly surrounded at 4 this morning and that all unmarried [men] must go. What do you make of it?

The Christians are also getting more and more afraid. This afternoon I again went to the village to pick up photos. I also did other shopping, and then went to the barber to get a haircut. He said he was sorry, but he didn't dare to cut my hair while I was wearing a star. So I took it off and got a nice cut.

Yes, now the sad news has also reached Jetty [Kaas].[2] I expect it this week from Bep also. It is terrible. I only hope Bleekveld is safe. Have you heard anything from Nico?

Last night while I was writing, Karel arrived, so I stopped. He came from Mantinge and told the same terrible news as the rumors we heard. Harry is gone. When us? I don't know. Last night I visited a farmer, and he now says he does not have the nerve after all. One after the other is dead scared. He'll still keep my bike, I will make use of that. It gets worse and worse.

I'll see what I will do, but I am preparing for the worst. If I take off (and without fail will try that) and they catch me, you can give up on me. But you must keep up your courage. Maybe it will all be over soon. At the moment I can stand a lot. You will hear that from Karel. I look well and have not been sick or anything like that.

I received the package. It was again great.

A few big kisses in thanks for it.

Now I end again with warmest greetings and a big kiss from

Remember, don't let it get you down.
Chin up and be brave.

I will write a letter again tonight.

1. This photo, taken September 6th at Geesbrug, is devoid of young men which is consistent with the rumor that the unmarried men had been taken away in the night two months earlier. The sign literally reads: "Concrete Gang 6. 9. '42," or perhaps "tough team." Geesbrug work camp was a few miles north of Molengoot, close to Nieuweroord. It had a capacity for 240, but at the time held 203 inmates.

2. Photograph taken in 1941 showing (*left to right*): Jetty Kaas; Lena van Bienen; Henny de Lange; and Bep de Vries.

1. The boy was Abraham Roodveldt, a bicycle assembler who was born in Amsterdam on March 23, 1923. He and his family lived at 203 Vrolik Street.

2. Abraham Roodveldt visited his brother-in-law Aron Roeg (his sister Celine's husband) in Hoogeveen (Kremboong camp). Both Celine and Aron were killed in Auschwitz, September 30, 1942.

Abraham Roodveldt's brother, Jozeph (*below*), was on the last transport to Sobibor. He was killed on July 16, 1943. He was 22 years old. His father, Louis, a diamond worker, died in Auschwitz on October 12, 1942. His mother, Rachel, and his 13-year-old sister, also named Rachel, were killed in Auschwitz, October 8, 1942.

Flip sent the telegram (*below*) the day after writing the letter (*above*). "Hs" is an abbreviation for house.

Hardenberg 19 July '42 [Sunday]

Dear Pa and Ma,

This morning at 11 o'clock a boy[1] asked me if he could borrow my bike for a few hours. All week he told us that on Monday [tomorrow] he is going to Amsterdam so that he could go with his girlfriend to Poland or Germany. He asked if he could borrow my bike ~~moetd~~ to pay a last visit to his brother-in-law[2] in Hogeveen[Hoogeveen]. He has not come back. My bike is gone. I am really upset. Once again I have been too nice. I went to the cook who told me Roodveldt did not have a travel permit, though the boys say he did. They say they saw it themselves.

Pa, go to his house and demand a new bike. His address is A. Roodveldt, 2 0 3 Vrolik Street.

I don't see how I could be so idiotic. I am full of nerves now ~~apxxxg~~. A bike that was supposed to help me. Oh, how could I be so dumb. You must forgive me for this rashness and enormous stupidity. I notice that I still think I live in a world where honesty prevails. But several times (though of little importance) I have been had by somebody.

I am not selfish, but you are forced to be by the many scoundrels who try to take advantage by exploiting others.

Dear Pa and Ma, forgive me. The war will end and my bike is gone, but I can't do anything about that.

Go to them and demand another bike or replacement. The boy does not look jewish. I hope he arrives with my bike in good shape.

I must stop now and end with a kiss
from

Flip

> **ROYAL TELEGRAPH**
> VERKORTINGEN VOOR BETAALDE DIENSTAANWIJZINGEN
> D = Dringend   PC = Kennisgeving Ont-   GP = Poste Restante
> RPx = Antwoord betaald   vangst   MP = Eigenhandig
> x (bedrag)   TC = Collationneering   LX = Geluktelegram
> XP = Bode betaald   TR = Telegraaf restant   RM = Overneming
> NOTA. HET RIJK VERGOEDT GEEN SCHADE, VEROORZAAKT DOOR HET IN HET ONGEREEDE RAKEN, DE VERMINKING OF DE VERTRAGING IN DE OVERKOMST VAN EEN TELEGRAM.
> **TELEGRAM**
>
> asd hardenberg 150 21 20/7 1007=
>
> Bike stolen by A. Roodvelt of room 18
> Try to reach 203/hs Vrolyk Street.
> Express on the way — Flip +
>
> Ontvangen te AMSTERDAM (met vermelding van draad, paraaf en tijd).   hdb/mp/tfn/1104
> NOTA Indien letters en cijfers, of breuken en geheele getallen, zijn verbonden door een dubbele streep (══) beteekent dit, dat die teekens één groep vormen, b.v. 3 = B wil zeggen 3B; 1 = ²/₄ 25 stelt voor 1³/₄ 25.   Mod. T 17. L 104   NADRUK IS VI

> **RIJKSTELEGRAAF**
> VERKORTINGEN VOOR BETAALDE DIENSTAANWIJZINGEN
> D = Dringend   PC = Kennisgeving Ont-   GP = Poste Restante
> RPx = Antwoord betaald   vangst   MP = Eigenhandig
> x (bedrag)   TC = Collationneering   LX = Geluktelegram
> XP = Bode betaald   TR = Telegraaf restant   RM = Overneming
> NOTA. HET RIJK VERGOEDT GEEN SCHADE, VEROORZAAKT DOOR HET IN HET ONGEREEDE RAKEN, DE VERMINKING OF DE VERTRAGING IN DE OVERKOMST VAN EEN TELEGRAM.
> **TELEGRAM**
>
> asd hardenberg 150 21 20/7 1007 =
>
> Fiets gestolen door A Roodvelt van kamer 18
> tracht Vrolykstraat 203/hs te achterhalen
> expres onderweg = Flip +
>
> Ontvangen te AMSTERDAM (met vermelding van draad, paraaf en tijd).   hdb/mp/tfn/1104
> NOTA Indien letters en cijfers, of breuken en geheele getallen, zijn verbonden door een dubbele streep (══) beteekent dit, dat die teekens één groep vormen, b.v. 3 = B wil zeggen 3B; 1 = ²/₄ 25 stelt voor 1³/₄ 25.   Mod. T 17. L 1046-'41 - K 985   NADRUK IS VERBODEN.

Hardenberg 20 July 1942
Monday evening

Dear Pa and Ma,

I just received your express mail letters. Two letters together and also two letters from Bep.[1] I will answer your first letter first.

Yes, Ma and Pa, the situation is incredibly tense for us, and also, the statement that the jews from the camps are not going to Germany is not true. Harry and Jacq [Sjaak Creveld] are now also victims. Bep had a letter from Harry in which he wrote that at the last minute he did not have the courage to run away. Yes, the situation is not good. At the blink of an eye, you must make a decision. I too expect to have to make this decision. At the moment I still think I won't go [to Germany]. For myself I hope that I will have the courage and the will-power to try to escape. And indeed, I have not let myself be influenced by Karel when he advised me to leave. Every day I am here is a day gained. Pa, if you have to go to a camp, try to come here to Molengoot. As far as I can tell, it is one of the best camps. That won't last, and I expect this week there will be a call also for you.

Pa and Ma, keep up your courage even if it gets harsher and worse. We will get through all right. Many people here are getting married. For myself, I don't see the use. I and others have discussed it long and hard. How does it help? I am not writing any more about it. I again received everything from Karel. I just have to accept that my bicycle is now gone. I received a good but costly lesson. When the damned war is over, I'll get another bike. I was very depressed about it and minded terribly, but much worse things are happening. The bikes of many local christians have been confiscated; perhaps that would have happened to mine also. If I get into trouble about it, then I know nothing about it. Though the cook hasn't received any message that he [Roodveldt] has been caught. I don't understand that boy. He had a travel permit and was supposed to leave today. I received another nice package from Bep. Now to the next express [letter] in which you write: stay where you are. That was already my plan. I'll stay as long as I can and then see how to manage.

I end again, with

a very fat kiss from

Be brave !!

1. Bep's parents, Louis de Vries and his wife, Hanna Blog-de Vries, lived at 31 Tilanus Street, Amsterdam. Bep's brother Boetie is on the left. Bep is on her mother's lap. Her brother Jonas is on the right. Both parents and Bep survived in hiding thanks to Douwe Douwstra, who was Jonas' friend and colleague at the Apeldoorn Mental Hospital (*Apeldoornsche Bosch*). He found a hiding place for Bep and her parents with the family Bas Douwstra in Zeist, in the province of Utrecht, and also found hiding places in Friesland for Flip's close friends, Karel and his brother Dick van der Schaaf.

Boetie (Samuel) de Vries, Bep's second brother, was a typographer who born on June 2 or 21, 1921. Shortly after he married, he was arrested in the first raid (February 1941) in Amsterdam. According to the family, he was sent to Mauthausen and then to Auschwitz where the death register at the Auschwitz State Museum lists his death as Sept. 30, 1942 (pp. 34518/1942).

Jonas de Vries, Bep's elder brother, born November 6, 1919, was a nurse at Apeldoorn Mental Hospital. On January 21, 1943, the Germans arrested everyone in the hospital: doctors, nurses, patients, and visitors. The psychiatric patients were beaten and thrown onto trucks under the supervision of Aus der Fünten and then taken to the Apeldoorn railway station. Over 800 patients and 50 nurses, herded into cattle cars, went directly through to Auschwitz, where nearly everybody was gassed on arrival. Jonas was selected to work, he died in Warsaw on February 28, 1944.

WHEN DID THEY KNOW IT?[A]

November 1939, William L. Shirer, Diary:[B] "An American friend . . . tells me the Nazi policy is simply to exterminate the Polish Jews."

January 1940, David Low, Cartoon[C] (below): Hitler complimented Low, first by requesting the gift of a few original cartoons, later by banning the London *Evening Standard,* and, as a final tribute, by placing him on the Gestapo's list of people to be executed.

July 1941, the Jewish Telegraphic Agency:[D] (using personal testimony), and the **Bletchley Intelligence Unit,** both in **UK** (using the broken Enigma code) reported the mass murder of Jews in the USSR and eastern Europe.

April 1942, Victor Klemperer, Diary:[E] "Ghastly mass murders of Jews in Kiev. The heads of small children smashed against walls, thousands of men, women, adolescents shot."

June 1942, BBC:[F] Szmul Zygielbojm, a member of the Polish Parliament-in-Exile in London, broadcast a detailed and explicit account of German atrocities, mass murder, and gassing of Jews.

July 1942, Flip feared that "if we were sent to Germany the greatest terrors would be in store for us. . . . Thousands and thousands are dying."

October 1942, Anne Frank, Diary:[G] "Our many Jewish friends and acquaintances are being taken away in droves . . . We assume that most of them are murdered. The English radio speaks of their being gassed."

December 1942, The Allies:[H] Anthony Eden, the British Foreign Secretary, said, "The German authorities . . . are now carrying into effect Hitler's oft repeated intention to exterminate the Jewish people in Europe." Parliament rose and stood in silence. Lloyd George said to Eden: "In all my years in parliament, I have never seen anything like this."[I]

1945, Asscher and Cohen[J] "Of course we did not know what really was the fate of those who had been transported. I was first told about it in the spring of 1945."

1946, Herman Goering,[K] the Nuremberg trial: "The first time I heard of these terrible exterminations was right here."

Hardenberg 21 July '41 [42]

Tuesday

Dear Pa and Ma,

This evening I received your letter and read that you went to see Roodveldt. Tonight it became known that he [Abraham] was arrested and sent to Amersfoort. That is terrible for the boy; the whole family must be in despair. I will write them a letter tonight.

I believe now that it wasn't a case of theft. Luckily, I got over it pretty quickly, and considering that far worse things are happening, I made my peace with it. This too, was an expensive but important lesson. The situation is getting worse and worse so also the possibility of escaping is being made more difficult. Sal and his wife have also been caught again. They were certainly trying to get to Belgium. Work still goes on. Digging and pushing wheelbarrows. Lucky for us. Anything is better than going to Germany. The rumor is that the boys and men who have been taken to Westerbork from the camps are conscripted for service. I hope it's true, but don't believe it.

Dear Pa and Ma, I stop again with a big

kiss from

David Low in the *Evening Standard,* January 20, 1940

LEBENSRAUM FOR THE CONQUERED

Hardenberg, 23 July '42 [Thursday]

Dear Pa and Ma,

This morning at my work I got the letter. Last night I wrote nothing. It got to be too dark, so now I will write a longer one. I had already heard from Bep that you must go for your physical today. Now I am very anxious to know if you passed. Or did you get a deferment?[1] In 6 or 12 weeks a lot can happen. Let's just hope for the best, though from England [the BBC] we don't have good news about the jews. They are all going to Poland. Yes, the question is will they ever come back, but luckily there is a chance it will all be over soon. I also had a letter from Henny. They have to leave tonight. Also, I read that our whole family has been called to go to the camp and to Germany. They keep calling up! Yes, I am glad I did not take off when Karel told me to. Every day here is a day gained. Bep is now working for the [German] army too,[2] so she probably won't have to go. Today again several people left to get married. Loek Halverstad[3] is also married.

Did you like the photo, Ma? I myself didn't think it was too great, but after all, it is only a village photographer.

As I wrote, Roodveldt is in Amersfoort. I already wrote to them.

If you can send me a little piece of soap, Ma, I'd like that. It gets used up very fast here. We are now working in a real pool of mud,[4] and it rains the whole day.

Ma, stay strong, you hear. I will aswell.

I just got another letter; I'll read it first. It's from last night and I read that Pa has a certificate from the doctor that he is totally unsuitable for camp life. If only it would help. It was Lientje Elzas's[5] good luck that she had an attack of appendicitis. At least she is free for the time being.

Yes, Pa, I also hope that soon I will hear you call me "rotten kid." The sooner the better. Now I finally realize how great it was to be free and well taken care of. I sent the shoes back because I still have the black ones, and it would be a shame to leave them behind if I suddenly had to leave. The socks and the roll of film also arrived. The socks fit well, considering they were not too expensive. I don't need warm clothes for the time being; while you work you don't feel the cold, though we have hardly done anything the whole week. But I'd like it if you could get me a pair of gloves. That may be needed for the winter. Don't bother about the price. I can make good use of a pair of fur lined leather ones. Everyone must go to Poland. 20,000 jews from France; 80,000 jews have been sent to P[oland] from Rumania. But . . . we will also come back. For myself I am not afraid. I am more afraid for you than for myself. Besides, the war will probably be over soon. It can't possibly last for another whole year.

Tomorrow night for dinner we'll have chicken with little potatoes, pudding, cucumber salad, lettuce, and tomatoes and of course chicken soup. Good huh? It will be roasted in butter. All I can say, if I should be taken away I'll be able to stand it for a while. I have become strong and sturdy here and have not been short of food yet, and I hope that is so for you also for some time. Now, dear Pa and Ma, I stop again with a hearty kiss from

Fhs.

Be strong and brave *!!!*

1. Initially the Germans employed Jewish doctors to examine men who had been called up for work camps. But the doctors found some who were unfit and failed them. The Germans replaced the Jewish doctors with NSB doctors who found none who were unfit and passed them all.

2. Bep was a cutter and seamstress for a textile company in Amsterdam that supplied the German SD and SS.

3. Loek (Louis) Halverstad, an office clerk, born April 6, 1923, married Klara Pach/Pakh, seamstress, born on January 28, 1924.

4. Working in the mud at Molengoot

5. *From left to right*, three Elzas siblings: Vogeltje (Lientje); Harry (Gerhard); and Maurits

1. Uncle Andries Slier and his wife Anna van Es-Slier had two children, Philip (*below left*), born October 29, 1916, and David André (*below right*), born December 31, 1919. Andries was a diamond polisher who immigrated to South Africa in 1928 to join his brother Jack (Izaak). A year later he returned to Amsterdam as Anna was reluctant to leave her family. In August 1942, Andries was sent to Kremboong camp, about 16 miles from Molengoot.

On October 5, 1942, Andries's son Philip and his 26-year-old wife, Sophie Roselaar, who was 8 months pregnant, were put on the transport to Poland. The train carrying 2,012 men, women, and children stopped in Kosel (Cosel), a complex of camps about 50 miles northeast of Auschwitz. About 500 men were taken from this transport to several sub-camps of Kosel. It is most likely that Philip was among them. The train arrived in Auschwitz on October 7, 1942. Forty men and 58 women were selected for labor in Auschwitz. One day later, 1,414 men, women, and children were killed in the gas chambers, Sophie with her just born or just unborn baby among them. Philip died in Gross-Rosen concentration camp on February 2, 1945, 11 days before the camp was liberated by the Russians.[A]

Andries asked his nephew, Nol Slier, who had good Communist party friends to help find a hiding place for his son David André. An arrangement was made for him to meet a courier at Amsterdam Central Station. He was betrayed and arrested while waiting there. David André died on April 30, 1943, in Sobibor.

Anna van Es-Slier's mother, two sisters, and a brother did not survive. A second brother, André, born February 28, 1901, told his South African nephew Lionel Slier that he lived openly throughout the war in a village outside Amsterdam with his Christian German wife. He explained: "Nobody dreamed that a nice German woman would have married a Jew."[B]

Hardenberg 24 July 1942
Friday night

Dear Pa and Ma,

So I read Pa has been approved for light administrative work. Yes, it was to be expected, if only Ma can just keep herself from being too nervous. Where there is life, there is hope. If this works out, how happy we will be. It's always better than going to Germany, but you probably won't have to go there. And there is the hope that you will be excused.

Pa, you didn't say anything about your bronchitis? But that's all right.

We are saving the chicken for tomorrow. I bought eggs and potatoes, lettuce, tomatoes. Great huh? It's a long time since we ate like this. 6 of us are doing this together, 3 from our room and 3 from another room who are members of our work team.

Every day people run away. A few yesterday and now another 4.

Also daily many leave to go to G[ermany] or to marry Christian women. Several rooms are empty. Perhaps Uncle Bram, Jonas, or Andries[1] will come to this camp. This has been a good camp till now, though we have been warned again. I rustle up food everywhere. Now we have located a new farm with three nice daughters.[2] [The three daughters were Jenny, Judien and Riek (Hendrika) Veurink. Riek and her mother are shown in the photo at the bottom of page 89.] We were there yesterday and today.

I haven't received any letters from Dick. Maybe they got lost, or will still arrive. I also had a letter from the Roodveldt family. They are trying to free him. I hope it works.

Pa, next week will you send a tube of toothpaste, a cake of soap, and if possible, a packet of <u>esbit</u>?

I had a letter from Barend. He says everything is still fine and healthy with his family and asked me if I can still receive packages. Well, that's still allowed, so of course I wrote to him immediately. Does it cost a lot, Pa? If so, you don't have to do it as often, but it's very welcome.

I don't share as much with my roommates as in the beginning. They are too spunkless to make any effort for themselves.

We are still working in the creek. It goes fast now. If Pa comes to visit again (I hope he does soon), he will see how much progress we have made. At first there was a farmer who for 70 ct gave us enough potatoes for two. In A[msterdam] that is cheap, but here it's much too expensive, so we stopped dealing with him. Now we get food from other people.

The laborers here literally work themselves to death in order to make some money. They never rest their butts. They work all day. Three times as hard as we do and what do they earn? 18 whole guilders in such an expensive rotten time as this. But they too prefer that to *f* 40 in Germany.

Now, dear Pa and Ma, I have again told you about this and that and stop now with a big kiss from

Ma, be strong; then everything will be all right again.

Hardenberg, 26 July 1942
Sunday mid-day

Dear Pa and Ma,

Last night after our delicious meal I received your letter. We really stuffed ourselves. I will list the menu. We began with a fried egg as hors d'oeuvres and a tomato. Then a dish of delicious chicken soup with potatoes, cucumber, salad, tomatoes, a boiled egg, berries and, of course, the unforgetable chicken.

Altogether it cost ƒ2.80 per man. It's not cheap, but for this one time it was wonderful. And then the rotten terrible news came that you also passed your physical, Pa; yes, it is their intention to tear all jews apart and to destroy families. I hope you can stay with the *Handelsblad*. Perhaps Biederman will do his best. Should that not happen, Ma should not lose hope; at least Pa does not have to go to Poland, and maybe the whole rotten mess will soon be over. It is exactly as you wrote Pa: as long as there is life, there is hope. About Henny,[1] I knew already. I think it is terrible for her; I am glad that Ma has changed her opinion about her and realizes she is a <u>really</u> <u>decent</u> girl. I hope never to have to make such a big trip. If it does come to that point, I still hope to be able to run away and escape. I am now two weeks up on Nico. I don't know where he is. We have not heard anything more from him; probably he is safe in Amsterdam.

I received the package this morning. I have already eaten one piece of cake to wish you good health and a good ending to all this. The package was not tightly wrapped when it arrived, but nothing was missing. The soap is really great. I hope I don't have to use it all and I will be home soon.

Pa, how can you talk about having leave now? They are crazy with us. We have to be grateful that we are still here. I don't think you will see me back before the end of the war. The cook here has nothing to say and is as scared as a weasel. I think he has to go away for 1 or 2 weeks to learn how he should deal with jews. It seems that he is too soft on us. People are still running away every day; of the 180 there are only 125 left. That includes those who went to G[ermany] and those married to Christian women.[2]

I will keep the address of Blok firmly in my head. Maybe Pa will talk with Blok again so that whenever it is necessary I can go to them.

Now I end again with a big kiss
speedy *tot ziens*
from *Flip*

Chin up*!* Ma*!*

1. *Left to right*: Jetty Kaas; Henny de Lange; and probably Henriette Gerritse, born February 17, 1925, and died at Sobibor on May 14, 1943.

2. As Flip implied, marrying a Christian conferred some protection and more if castrated. Joe Vomberg knew of many whose castration had at least delayed their deportation.

On July 11, 1942, ten Christian churches sent a joint telegram to Seyss-Inquart expressing outrage at the deportation of Jews and urgently requesting them not to proceed. They added that a copy of their telegram would be read from the pulpits of all churches on July 26. The churches further pleaded that Jewish converts be spared. The Germans replied that Jews baptized before 1941 would be exempt from deportation. On July 26, the July 11 telegram was read from the pulpit of Roman Catholic and all Protestant churches except the Dutch Reformed. On August 2, Rauter retaliated; he arrested and deported 92 of the 690 Catholic Jews, explaining to Himmler (page 69), that he was responding to the intransigence of the five bishops led by Archbishop de Jong and "it has been successful in exploding the united front between Catholic and Protestant Churches."

From right to left: a visitor, Mrs Aaltje Veurink, Riek; *onderduiker* and son. The *onderduiker's* husband had been a fisherman, but refused to fish for the Germans.

AMERSFOORT CAMP

1. Amersfoort was controlled by the SS who called it a transit and punishment camp. Prisoners came from everywhere. In August 1941, about 200 communists arrested in Amsterdam were taken to Camp Schoorl—a temporary internment camp for British, French, and Belgian civilians and others—and from there to Amersfoort and then to Dachau. The Amersfoort camp was used to hold resistance fighters, Protestant and Roman Catholic clergy, political prisoners, Gypsies, Jews, Jehovah's Witnesses, homosexuals, black marketeers, and even some Russian POWs. Starvation, torture, and execution were commonplace. Over 35,000 prisoners had been registered by April 1945, when it was liberated.

Philip Mechanicus wrote on May 31, 1943:

"Those folk from Amersfoort and Ellecom and Vught who had been starving, sometimes for months on end, did not eat in the ordinary way— they devoured and gobbled and guzzled the things set before them. They were insatiable . . . Those who had come from concentration camps would argue about which had been worse: Amersfoort or Ellecom. The public took part. Amersfoort was recognized as representing the peak of human misery. The people from Vught who came later, but had lived at Amersfoort first, confirmed this."*A*

Alice van Keulen-Woudstra witnessed an arrest:

"My mother and I were in Denekamp staying with family of my father's mother. While we were there the SS came to arrest my father's uncle. He didn't want to go and four men were needed to take him away while he was fighting and screaming. The whole family was standing outside, crying. It made an enormous impression on me. My mother and I never talked about it.
"At the age of 34, my father, David (Dé) Woudstra, was then the director of the Matzo factory in Enschede. He was betrayed because he was not wearing his yellow star in his own office. He was put in a local police cell, then two days later Arnhem prison, and then Amersfoort and on September 23, 1942 on my birthday, he was sent by train to Mauthausen where he died December 10, 1942."*B*

Right: prisoners in Amersfoort camp

Amsterdam [sic], 27 July 1942
Monday evening

Dear Pa and Ma,

Tonight I received your letter from last night and read that you are not very cheerful. Yes, it can hardly be otherwise, being torn apart by such a bunch of bandits after having lived happily together for so many years.

My only hope still is for an exemption for you, Pa. If you do get it, send me a message by express or telegram. Would being sick help? I don't think so. Dear Pa and Ma, whatever happens, we <u>must</u> be brave until the time comes that we are free again. Ma, stay strong, you hear.

Yesterday and today more people ran away; they keep on doing it. If I run away, I think I can find shelter somewhere, but until it is really necessary I am not going to do it. Every day I am here is a day gained, a day nearer to the end and another day to eat well! Is the Roodveldt son home yet? It is terrible. There [in Amersfoort][1] you are not treated like a human being, but like an animal. Of the four packages of esbit, only one is used up, but I asked for more so I can have some in reserve. The package from Barend was not expensive, *f* 4. for butter, cheese, and bread. If I had to buy that here, I would have to pay much more.

Yes Pa, how I would love it if ✝ you could ~~at~~ visit me once more; some day it will be possible again. Conditions here are the same, in a word, <u>rotten</u>. Now we have been told that we must make 20 ct an hour to get a bonus. Mr. NSB says the food situation here is adequate. "We buy enough from the farmers"? They think we have money like water and that everybody can do that. I have heard nothing from Nico. I stop again with a big kiss from

Filip

Remember, chin up *!*

[POSTCARD]

Hardenberg 28 July '42 [Tuesday]

Dear Pa and Ma,

Tonight just a little letter from me. This evening we had a small meeting again. It was griping about small stuff. They don't have any other worries. I received the package complete and in good shape. The cake was great, and I also think it is great that Ma is so brave. I hope you can both continue to send me packages (at least for the duration of the war). Pa, I do hope we get lucky and that you get your exemption. Tomorrow I will send a longer letter again in which I will write more.

Now dear Pa and Ma,

big kisses and

greetings
from

1. *From top to bottom*: Dick van der Schaaf; Henny de Lange; Flip; Lena (Lea) van Bienen; Appie (Abraham) Reis; Bep de Vries; Harry Elzas; Jetty Kaas; and Maupie (Maurits) Vogel in 1941.

Hardenberg 29 July '42 [Wednesday]

Dear Pa and Ma,

Tonight I did not receive a letter from you and can't think of much to write myself. Getting food is more and more difficult and also more expensive. I hope I will soon receive another package from B[arend]. Today for the first time I have no bread. I'll see that I get some tomorrow, you don't have to send me any, you hear. If one could only get a decent hot meal, but that too is a very small helping now and watered down. In the afternoon we still get some food. Eggs are now 30 ct. Every once in a while I buy something, the ƒ65.- have shrunk to ƒ25.- But that doesn't matter as long as I can support myself. Karel and Dick[1] and Liel are coming to see me next week. Karel by himself, and Dick and Liel together.

Rotten idea, isn't it? But I will be happy to see them.

Can't think of much more and so end with a big kiss from

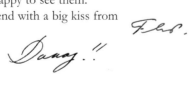

1. Uncle Alfred Sallie Salomonson may be one of the men at camp Vledder (*below*). He escaped, was caught, and was then taken to Scheveningen prison where he somehow avoided a scheduled deportation to Westerbork in 1943. However, while he was being moved from prison in February 1944, he was involved in an accident on Jozef Israelsplein in The Hague (an escape attempt?). He was taken to hospital where he died on February 2, 1944.

2. *Below*: Men held at Camp Vledder

3. It is not obvious why Flip associated Tommies with tennis. The generic Englishman, Tommy Atkins, was an average soldier who played football, not tennis.

Hardenberg 30 July '42 [Thursday]

Dear Pa and Ma,

This morning I got your letter and read that Uncle Alfred[1] must go to Camp Vledder.[2] Well, tomorrow another batch is arriving here.

If Ma can get a travel permit, of course she can visit me here.

I have also heard nothing from Roodveldt. That's not so good. Now his girlfriend has gone away alone, and he sits in a concentration camp. Karel, Dick, and Liel are coming this week. Great huh? Pa, will you give Bep ƒ6.30 for the photos? I'll straighten it out with you later. Is that OK?

Tomorrow new groups will arrive here, again from Amsterdam. Joop's father is also coming here. Has Pa not heard anything yet? Pa, if you get a deferment, send me a telegram because letters usually take two days.

At the moment nothing special is happening here. Do you have the address for Henny and Harry? Maybe I can still reach them, though I am not hopeful. They have probably gone already.

Dear Pa and Ma, I can't think of much else to write, that's why my short letter. I stop with the wish that Ma can visit me soon and a big kiss

from

Be strong.
Chin up
Tot ziens in Mokum

31 July '42
Friday night

Dear Pa and Ma,

Tonight I received three letters from you, one from Wednesday night, Thursday night, and one from this morning.

Now I have the bad news that you are supposed to leave this afternoon, Pa, don't you have an exemption yet? Follow up Pa, and don't leave a stone unturned. If nothing can be done, make sure you don't have to go to Hogeveen [Hoogeveen, Kremboong work camp]. There is still room here, and once you are in that camp, you can't get out. It is a terrible camp; I hear it is very military; you have to march etc., etc. But luckily you haven't left yet, and we can still hope; however, I don't think you will get an exemption. Pa, <u>see</u> that <u>you</u> <u>come</u> <u>here.</u> It is <u>not</u> full yet. This is the best camp. Yes, Pa and Ma, as you see nobody escapes the blows, but we must all keep up our courage.

I have half ended my relationship with Bep. I just didn't feel enough for her. If you want to know more, I'll write. I'm not at all angry with her. But it must have been a blow for her. At first I liked to get visitors; now it's no fun.

Let us but hope that the Tommies will come quickly with their tennis balls.[3] The whole world is anxiously waiting. Then we must again fight for a new life and for a new humanity. Pa, I just heard again that you can apply to come to Molengoot. <u>The cook says: "There is still room."</u> You have to leave anyway.

I am glad Ma is being cared for. This is a great consolation for us. I received the bread coupons. I am delighted because I had nothing left. My slices of cake are now finished too. Tonight at ten o'clock 34 new men are coming here. More victims, but they are always better off here than in Hogeveen.[Hoogeveen].

Probably I will get the package tomorrow. Ma, you try also to get Pa to come here to me; that would set your mind at rest.

Now I end again with a few
big kisses and
see you soon again.

Maybe very soon *!!*

Hardenberg 1 August 1942 [Saturday]

Dear Pa and Ma,

This morning I received your package. Now that was a wonderful package. It really comes in handy. It arrived in good shape and I will feast on it.

I can make good use of the bread because for some time I have been living on my ration and that's not much. Next week there will probably be rye bread again. They are already mowing. Pa, if you urgently request to come to Molengoot, it will most likely be granted. Several people have done that, including Joop v. Amstel's father, who is here now. Yesterday a transport of ± 30 people arrived here. Some are very old and are definitely not suited to this work. Well, I suppose they considered that.

Bep and I are finished. I ended it because I felt nothing could come of it after all. I am very wishy-washy with things like that. The mailman is here, so I'll stop this letter and will start another one tonight.

Ma, do your best to make Pa come. It is possible, so it must be done.

I end again with a big kiss

from *Flip.*

Ma and Pa,
Keep your courage up *!!*

The Germans were so intent on eradicating Jews and Jewish culture from Dutch society that they even Aryanized Jewish street names. In the photograph above, Lazarus Lane is being renamed Leprozen (Leprosy) Lane. And the street named after the universally loved Spinoza became Andriesz Street.

Well-trained teams of art historians, literary experts, musicologists, and other specialists followed closely behind the German front-line. They evaluated what was worth stealing from homes, libraries and museums. A great many works of art were removed and sent to the Reich. Most of the major works have been returned, but not the minor ones. People in Germany were given domestic items with the message that they were gratefully donated by the people in the occupied territories. *Right*: Jewish homes being emptied by A. Puls, a Dutch company, who like latter-day locusts, gutted 10,000 apartments in Amsterdam. As a result of this looting, a new word was added to the Dutch language: *"pulsen"*—to steal.

1. Vrolik Street, Amsterdam, January 2005. The houses on the left look as they did in 1942.

2. Molengoot to Amersfoort was 65 miles as the crow flies. Karel sometimes cycled, but often walked from Amsterdam to Molengoot (80 miles) and many other camps. His visits gave marvellous comfort to his friends; he brought them food, money, messages, laundry, and companionship. He journeyed once or twice a week until 1943 when there were no friends left and the Germans then called up all Dutch men to work in Germany. He, however, went into hiding in Drachten on the Baron farm where he worked as a farm hand; plowing, gathering hay and milking Friesian cows (*below*).

Until he was 84, Karel played tennis twice a week, and every year walked 26 miles a day for four days in the Nijmegen Four Day March (*Vierdaagse*), earning the medal *Vierdaagsekruis* (*right*) fourteen times.

Hardenberg, 2 Aug. '42
Sunday afternoon

Dear Pa and Ma,

This morning I received your letter and now I will write a long letter back. I am glad Pa has not left yet. As long as there is hope, there's life. The people who were brought here were warned that they were not allowed to bring any smoking materials or food-stuff. Also in Zwolle they were warned that everything would be taken away. That was not true at all in Zwolle, but many people gave everything away. So Pa, don't pay too much attention to their threats. Why don't the people at the *Handelsblad* [the newspaper where Flip's father worked] hurry up? That so-called exemption is taking much too long. I have also heard that inventories are being made of many people's things, lists are made of furniture etc., etc. Ma, I don't have to write anything about this, but think about it. Take the things to a safe place, dishes, glassware etc., etc. Yes, tonight I think I will get a visit from Dick and Liel, if not tonight certainly tomorrow at work.

We are now a long way away from where we started. We have dug a canal that is longer than the whole of Vrolik Street.[1] So we don't sit still. We worked very hard at the beginning of the week, though we have spent the last few days lying on our backs. But we still made our minimum salary. This morning we gave our bedroom a thorough cleaning. We took everything outside, beds, blankets, suitcases etc., etc. and then we mopped and scrubbed. Oh, the dirt that came out! It really was badly needed. It's bad for your health if there is a lot of dust behind the places you can't reach.

Karel[2] is planning to walk from here to Amersfoort. They [Karel, Dick and Liel] are still on vacation, but that will also happen for us again, some time. We often pass time here playing whist [a card game] and other games . . . and writing of course. Do you have the address of Harry and Henny? [Harry Elzas and Henny de Lange]. I'd like to write to them if possible. Do you ever see the fam. Elzas? They are not having a good time either, but we all have to overcome that. Us and them, and many others.

Ma, you ask where is the lens of the camera, it has <u>not</u> been removed. This one is inside. There is no lens on the outside. Ma next time you send a package will you send the automatic timer and the light meter?

I am not sending my laundry back now, it is not worth it. Next week I'll send double. Can't think of much else to write besides keep your courage up and grit your teeth. Many kisses and ~~a big kiss~~

a firm paw, [a playful way to indicate a friendly handshake]
from

Flip. daag!!!

Letter from Saint Teresa Benedicta of the Cross

20 April 1933

Holy Father!

As a child of the Jewish people who, by the grace of God, for the past eleven years has also been a child of the Catholic Church, I dare to speak to the Father of Christianity about that which oppresses millions of Germans. For weeks we have seen deeds perpetrated in Germany which mock any sense of justice and humanity, not to mention love of neighbor. For years the leaders of National Socialism have been preaching hatred of the Jews. Now that they have seized the power of government and armed their followers, among them proven criminal elements, this seed of hatred has germinated. The government has only recently admitted that excesses have occurred. To what extent, we cannot tell, because public opinion is being gagged. However, judging by what I have learned from personal relations, it is in no way a matter of singular exceptional cases. Under pressure from react-ions abroad, the government has turned to "milder" methods. It has issued the watchword "no Jew shall have even one hair on his head harmed." But through boycott measures—by robbing people of their livelihood, civic honor, and fatherland—it drives many to desperation; within the last week, through private reports I was informed of five cases of suicide as a consequence of these hostilities. I am convinced that this is a general condition which will claim many more victims. One may regret that these unhappy people do not have greater inner strength to bear their misfortune. But the responsibility must fall, after all, on those who brought them to this point and it also falls on those who keep silent in the face of such happenings.

Everything that happened and continues to happen on a daily basis originates with a government that calls itself "Christian." For weeks, not only Jews, but also thousands of faithful Catholics in Germany, and, I believe, all over the world, have been waiting and hoping for the Church of Christ to raise its voice to put a stop to this abuse of Christ's name. Is this not this idolization of race and governmental power which is being pounded into the public consciousness by the radio's open heresy? Isn't the effort to destroy Jewish blood an abuse of the holiest humanity of our Savior, of the most blessed Virgin and the Apostles? Is not all this diametrically opposed to the conduct of our Lord and Savior, who, even on the cross, still prayed for his persecutors? And isn't this a black mark on the record of this Holy Year which was intended to be a year of peace and reconciliation?

We all, who are faithful children of the Church and who see the conditions in Germany with open eyes, fear the worst for the prestige of the Church if the silence continues any longer. We are convinced that this silence will not be able in the long run to purchase peace with the present German government. For the time being, the fight against Catholicism will be conducted quietly and less brutally than against Jewry, but no less systematically. It won't take long before no Catholic will be able to hold office in Germany unless he dedicates himself unconditionally to the new course of action.

At the feet of your Holiness, requesting your apostolic blessing,

(signed) Dr. Edith Stein

Instructor at the German Institute for Scientific Pedagogy,
Münster in Westphalia,
Collegium Marianum.[A]

Edith Stein, the youngest of 11 children, was born on Yom Kippur, the Day of Atonement, October 12, 1891, in Breslau, Germany. Her father was a timber merchant who died before she was three. She earned a Ph.D. in philosophy under Husserl in 1916 with a thesis on *The Problem with Empathy* which explored the basis for understanding the inner life of another person, but she also served as a nurse in WWI. She converted to Catholicism in 1922. In 1933, shortly after Hitler came to power, she requested an audience with the Pope that was declined, so she presented her case in writing (*left*). She joined the Carmelite convent in Cologne (her investiture was in 1934), but after *Kristallnacht* (1938), she moved to the Carmelite convent in Echt in the southern tip of the Netherlands. She was offered a transfer to Switzerland, which she declined as they did not have space for her sister Rosa, who had also converted and had joined her at Echt. Edith and her sister were arrested in the chapel on August 2, 1942, and taken to Amersfoort, then to Westerbork, where according to Jacob Presser in 1965, she was an "example to all, helping and consoling wherever she could."[B] Edith commented: "I never knew that people could be like this, neither did I know that my brothers and sisters would have to suffer like this. I pray for them every hour." At her canonization in 1998, Pope John Paul II, said: "Because she was Jewish, Edith Stein was taken with her sister Rosa and many other Catholic Jews from the Netherlands to the concentration camp in Auschwitz, where she died with them in the gas chambers." At her beatification the Pope said, "We bow down, before . . . an outstanding daughter of Israel."[C]

This letter (*above*) was not included in any of Edith Stein's published correspondence. It lay hidden in the Vatican until February 15, 2003. However, on March 14, 1937, the Pope, Pius XI, issued an Encyclical *With Burning Sorrow* that criticized the "war of extermination" and the notion of a master race: "As God's sun shines on every human face so His law knows neither privilege nor exception." The Pope added: "Nothing but ignorance and pride could blind one to the treasures hoarded in the Old Testament." On April 13, 1986, Pope John Paul II became the first Pope in nearly 2,000 years to enter a synagogue. He attended service at the Great Synagogue of Rome, addressing the congregation as "dearly beloved brothers."

1. Barend Schaap was born in 1894, married Hendrika Gerritdina Eshuis, who was born in 1916. She died in 2001. Barend died in 1959.

2. Hendrika's sister, Bernarda Eshuis, was born in 1924, thus she was 18 years old in 1942.

3. Friedrich Salomonson "Call-Me-Uncle" and his wife Esther Philips had a son Lion, age 12, and a daughter Hanni, age 10.

4. Aunt Juul was Juliette Anna Salomonson-Schaap, the second wife of Koopman Schaap, Barend's brother. She complained to Flip that she suffered more than her sisters, Seline (Flip's mother) and Johanna Samas, (the mother of Philip Samas). Philip had been arrested in the February 1941 raid in Amsterdam and sent to Mauthausen. Before long the suffering of the three sisters and their husbands would be equalized.

5. Jane Fresco has kindly informed us that the Gallery was located near Frederiksplein, one mile northwest of Vrolik street. In the Gallery were houses, shops, and a little hall. Number 16 was used by the Committee to help Jewish refugees. In 1941, it became part of the Jewish Council. A group of resistance workers were quartered in house number 24. They offered temporary shelter, gave out clothes, and helped people obtain passes, sometimes by making them themselves.

Hardenberg, 3 Aug. 1942 [Monday]

Dear Pa and Ma,

Yesterday ~~evening~~ I had some great visits. First Barend's wife[1] came in the afternoon with her children, her sister,[2] and a friend of her sister's. When I saw her I didn't recognize her, but I felt immediately it had to be Hendrika. She again brought a wonderful package with the same contents as last time and also 3 jars with broad beans and a piece of meat loaf. I really had a good time with her for a few hours, and also with her sister who is almost 18. Then Friedrich with his wife and two children came to visit me,[3] and de Bruin's wife also came. And last night ~~Karel and~~ Dick and Liel came to visit. I received the envelope from Dick. Now I can get by for a while. This morning they came to where I work and stayed about half an hour.

Hendrika told me Aunt Juul[4] is not well. She goes half crazy when you tell her money is not the biggest problem. She says all the time that it is not as bad for Aunt Jo and Selien [sic] as it is for her. Well, now I ask you. She should really calm down. When I hear these things I think this will go the wrong way for her. I will write her another letter soon. Half an hour ago there were Germans here who made a quick inspection. They didn't say anything and left quickly.

This morning the new men went to work. Pa and Ma, it broke my heart to see these oldsters plodding along. Some of them have heart trouble and varicose veins. There is no light work on the moor, and they get no time to catch their breath. We have already decided that tomorrow we will dig a ditch for them.

I am now sitting in the woods behind the camp and writing while waiting for Dick and Liel.

Tomorrow I will probably get your letter. Today I had no mail at all. It is often delayed. Have you heard anything yet, Pa? I am very anxious. Has Ma been to the Gallery[5] yet? Remember, there is room in this camp. Both yesterday and today, a few people ran away again. I often say until something goes very wrong why on earth do they run away? It is better here than in the city. If they get caught, they are in even worse trouble.

Pa and Ma, I don't know much more now and end again

with a big kiss from

Young and old inmates at Molengoot

Hardenberg 4 Aug. 1942 [Tuesday]

Dear Pa and Ma,

Yesterday evening I received your letter from Karel[1] and am now writing back. I certainly understand how happy Ma is that you have not gone yet, Pa. Every day you are home is a day gained.

I am not at all depressed anymore, but yes, I did have quite a bad week because of the business with Bep. But I am holding my head high! As long as I know you are all right. But that's how it should be. Ma, will you send my light meter and my automatic timer and the tripod? And also possibly rolls of film.

I heard again that inventories are being taken of jewish homes. So if at all possible get rid of everything. Pa, please send me the address of Brilman [Brilleman] again. I lost the number. The boys paid me for the photos. Thanks a lot. I hope that later I will be able to pay back, and then some, with love, for everything and more that you are doing for me now.

No, I will never be able to be mad at Bep. She is much too fine a girl, but you know I am only just 18 and constantly searching and changing, and being here changes you a lot, too.

The head boss was here today. There is one old man who has heart trouble and varicose veins; he scrubbed the floors and then the boss said he must work whether he can or not. He has no choice. It is pathetic to watch, but that is how it goes now. I am glad that Pa is in much better shape than many of the people here. You are better off here if you are fit rather than an invalid. Yes, Pa, how in God's name do they expect to make construction workers out of them! This too is an accusation against them.

Today Dick and Liel went to Sellingen. They are not badly off there, but you know what Pa says: here you lose something, there you find something. They don't have to work hard, but there are 50 people to a room, and they have hardly any washing facilities.

Dear Pa and Ma, I end again with
a big kiss and
a speedy *tot ziens* again
from

1. Karel van der Schaaf and Wiebe van der Pol, a farm laborer, on the Baron farm in Friesland where Karel was hiding in 1943. Karel's mother rescued Bora Prijs's eight-year-old brother, Sally, by collecting him from his home on 150 Vrolik Street and taking him to the Baron farm. Mrs. Prijs thought that this separation from the family would be easier for her son because Karel was on the same farm. The Barons changed Sally's name to Wim and raised him with their own children. His two siblings, Bora and Samuel, and his mother, Sientje Blog-Prijs did not survive. Wim's father survived Auschwitz.

The Baron farm in Drachten

The Baron children and Wim Prijs.
Top to bottom: Jan; Wybren; Wim; and Tjeerd.

Waiting

by

Tootje Loonstijn Renger

Cato (Tootje) Loonstijn (Simon Loonstijn's sister). Tootje was 15 when she received a summons to report to "work in Germany." She refused to go. The Vrijlink family helped Tootje find her first hiding place. Tootje's great capacity for empathy, her intelligence, and her skill in blending with her environment, plus luck, enabled her to survive, and she was able to give some help to the resistance movement. *Waiting* is taken from Tootje's privately published reminiscences of the war.

Tootje has strong memories of her mother who had a deformed foot, about which she was occasionally teased at school. The foot did not inhibit her mother who was very active. She liking walking and swimming and swam during "ladies hour" at the local pool and afterwards had coffee with the other ladies, most of whom were Christian, although they never mixed at any other times. "We had a very large family so there were few outside friends, and none of them were Christian. My mother was unusual for her time in that she smoked pink, green, and blue "Mont Blanc" ladies cigarettes. When she wore the fashionable bobbed hair, my father would not talk to her for three days."

The family were keen readers, especially in winter when they read and played Monopoly, chess, and checkers. Tootje used to go to the cinema with friends. She loved Deanna Durbin and Shirley Temple movies, which inspired her to take up tap-dancing. Her mother always wore black shoes and fashionable clothes, but she dressed somberly after her father was arrested.

Somewhere a door slammed, and my father shook me gently. "Tootje, wake up. The security police are here, we have to leave." The night was chilly and I shivered in the darkness. My clothes lay ready on the chair next to my bed. I thought obstinately, "I'm not going. I want to stay in the Netherlands."

My mother came running in at that moment and saw my face. She whispered to my father, "Not the child." Calmly she said, "Stay there, Tootje, don't let them see you." Mother closed the door behind her and I waited, shivering. When she returned, alone, she had somehow managed to save my life. She told me only that Father had gone. We stayed up that night without talking, sitting together as in mourning.

As dawn rose over the city, I pushed back the curtains and put my forehead against the cold window. Amsterdam was staring at me with bleary eyes, as if loathe to awaken completely. I shivered and said to Mother, "I had better go and tell the family about Papa." I put on my coat and stepped outside. For a moment the city embraced me, and then seemed weary again.

As I began to walk, I pleaded with my city. "Don't let us go, we belong here. What would you do without us? Without her Jews, Amsterdam cannot have much charm. Four centuries ago, you gave us shelter and you never regretted it . . . let us stay!" How my young heart wanted to believe in the power of my city and its allegiance to generations of my family who had loved it. Yet why did I sense for the first time that my city might be willing to see us go? Was it because the horror had finally struck home? Or did I foresee the net closing in on me?

The night before had begun rather well. Before curfew, I had gone to Uncle Sam's house, as usual. He had connections with the Jewish Council; if they were on duty, it would mean the Gestapo or SS would be raiding and picking up Jewish citizens. If not, we could hope for a good night's sleep.

At my uncle's house, I had found him very busy teaching Nonnie, his young son, how to conduct an orchestra. The sturdy nine-year-old stood on a chair waving his father's baton rather skillfully to a recording of Beethoven's Fifth Symphony. This tender scene of father and son, the beautiful music, and the warmth and intimacy of their home almost made me forget the reason for my visit. It seemed like the old days, so long ago. The news was reassuring; the Jewish Council had an evening off. The Germans had given no standby orders to work that night. Happily, I ran home to tell my parents.

That night, in the middle of our deep sleep, the bell had sounded and my father had gone upstairs (our bedrooms were on the lower level) to open the door. Three men in civilian clothes stepped inside and announced they were Security Police. They ordered that all the inhabitants of the house get dressed and prepare to leave immediately.

Obediently Father went downstairs to tell Mother, and then he came to waken me. But Mother had stormed into my room and asked, "Is she on the list too?" Father shook his head, "They didn't show me a list. They just said to wake everyone in the house."

"Then the child does not go!" said Mother. And turning to me, "Hide yourself somewhere and don't make a sound."

She ran upstairs and confronted the men, "Your papers, please." But they had the right credentials. She went on, "What do you want from us?"

They replied that the whole house had to be emptied, everyone had to go with them. Mother said firmly, "That is impossible. We have elderly people living with us, and some are invalids who need help getting dressed. You must wait until morning when the maids arrive."

The Security Police said, "Well then, we will have to take you and your husband. We'll come back later for the others." Only then did my father protest, "Not my wife, she has to stay. I will go!"

They accepted that. I don't know why, but they were satisfied to take only my father away. When I heard my parents come downstairs again, I crawled out of my armoire. It had been hot behind my dresses. But heeding Mother's command, I stayed in my room. I could hear by the movements that my father was getting dressed.

There was a long silence, like a kiss, broken only by a sharp moan. Then I heard my father's footsteps approaching my room and I looked eagerly toward the door, waiting for him to enter. But the steps passed by.

I ran to the door and whispered, "Papa, Papa." He didn't stop, although I thought I heard him pause. But he continued upstairs, they all went out, and the door fell heavy in its lock.

Finally the darkness turned gray, and Amsterdam was slowly awakening. Now I had to go tell the family. Stepping out into the chilly dawn, I looked up to the streaking sky and questioned God. My first stop was Father's younger brother, the bachelor, whose job with the Jewish Council had seemed to us a beacon of protection and a source of help. How my worldly uncle's universe seemed to crumble around him at the news! Leaving him to look about at the ruins, I went to my brother's hiding place, climbed the stairs with wobbly knees, and found I had no words. In pitiful mimicry of our uncle, I stared at my brother. But he could read me. "Oh God, my father," he said, and suddenly I opened my mouth, and began to scream and scream.

"Tootje," my mother had said, "help me pack your father's rucksack. Imagine! All his life he did without a rucksack. He never carried one before, and now at his age my husband needs a rucksack."

She smiled, but her eyes looked sad. Who had told us we ought to have a rucksack ready, I cannot say, maybe the Jewish Council. But at some time we started to buy and arrange things: heavy woolen clothing, leather boots, a Red Cross box, DDT. We had laughed to think of our chubby aunts and uncles, in an outfit for North Pole expeditions. Did we really need those clothes? They looked ridiculous on us. Yet it seemed better to have them, just in case. Some people even had bad teeth removed, so they wouldn't have to worry about toothache. Girls had their hair cut short, it was easier to keep clean.

"Here is the first aid kit, check if there is any flea powder. You know, in such a work camp, vermin are common." My mother put in as much food as she could, because we all feared that food would be scarce in a camp. We hardly expected that the Germans were going to feed us well. So we had not gone to all this trouble of rucksack, boots, woolen socks, and windbreakers for nothing. I thought suddenly—what is Beertje[1] doing now, without a rucksack and warm clothes? Beertje, Little Bear, who moved so slowly and loved honey—the impoverished old woman my mother had taken in to live with us, and who screamed and carried on so when they came to take her away. My father, strangely calm and unprotesting, helped her pack and went with her to the door. I held my hands over my ears—Beertje cried out to him, "Don't let them take me away, Meneer [mister], I'm a helpless old woman, Meneer!"

I still hear your voice, Beertje. No one fought for you, no one wept for you. They willingly let you be dragged out of the house.

In the end, it didn't help us very much.[4]

Sara Biet-Loonstijn (Tootje's mother), with Tootje on her lap. She was born September 6, 1894. She went into hiding, but was discovered and arrested together with a number of family members. She was placed on a transport for Auschwitz on June 31, 1943.

Mozes Loonstijn (Simon and Tootje's father) was born March 26, 1892. A family man who loved music, especially opera, he used to sing arias as a wake-up call in the morning, and sang duets with his wife. He and his wife took care of several elderly people, all of whom were deported and killed. He had told his family that when they were summoned to go to Poland they should comply; however, he threw a note from the train between Westerbork and Cosel, telling them not to go when summoned.

1. Beertje was Vrouwtje de Beer, born June 12, 1875; died at Auschwitz on September 14, 1942.

1. Eduard Philips (*above and below*), born in Harderwijk, September 8, 1892, married Flip's father's sister, Grietje Slier, who was born on Waterlooplein in Amsterdam, March 12, 1893. Grietje and Eduard ran a laundry at 92 Vrolik Street.

CAMP ERICA IN OMMEN

2. Before the war, a camp close to the town of Ommen had been used by followers of the Indian spiritual leader Krishnamurti for their annual meetings. As it was located sufficiently off the beaten track to be neither seen nor heard, the Germans converted it to a concentration camp in June 1941. The first camp commandant, a Dutch collaborator, Karel Lodewijk Diepgrond, named it Camp Erica (Erica is an obscure but unpleasant person in Norse mythology). All reports and orders were given in German. The first inmates were black-marketeers and men who had dodged their call for forced labor camp. The 48 guards, called Kontrol Kommandos (KK), beat the prisoners unmercifully for the slightest infringement. The prisoners were housed 60 to a barrack and given little food or clothing. They slept in hammocks. As Flip reports in his letter of August 16, Camp Erica was used to teach Dutch guards from other camps "how to treat Jews."

From 1942 onwards, Jews, resistance fighters, and anyone who broke one of the many German laws were sent there.

Right: Eduard Philips outside 133 ? Street.on his laundry delivery tricycle

Hardenberg 5 Aug. 1942 [Wednesday]

Dear Pa and Ma,

This evening I received your letter from yesterday; now I am writing a short letter because Dick and Liel are coming soon. Yes, thousands are leaving; it is very sad. Will it ever end? And still we have to keep up our courage and not give up. Although that article from the newspaper does not give us much hope! Perhaps it will soon be over, and then we can just begin again with whatever strength and energy we still have.

Uncle Eduard's[1] outlook is not too rosy; we hear about all those things here. The camp in Ommen[2] is a punishment camp. They have to work hard and the pits they dig they have to fill up again with their hands. (Der Neue Orde) [The New Order]. We may perhaps also get some of that here. Just wait. In any case I will eat heartily so that I am strong and healthy and stand a greater chance to overcome these difficulties and get through. They do clean here, but not very well. So we have redone it ourselves. Harry [Elzas] and Henny [de Lange] have surely gone. I already heard that they are not allowed to write any more.

I never play for a lot of money, Pa! The only amount I ever lost was *f*0.30, so that is not so much. If it is a lot, we agree to halve our losses. So you can see we play for 50% profit.

I will keep the addresses carefully.

I close again with some big kisses and
speedy *tot ziens* in a
free *Mokum,*

Hardenberg, 6 Aug. '42 [Thursday]

Dear Pa and Ma,

From this evening's letter I again learned that luckily Pa has still not gone. You have to figure every day is a gain! Yes, in our camp it is still better than in many other camps. But . . . for how long? Dick and Liel went to [Camp] Dalfsen and saw Max van Kleef[1] and he told them that changes are coming soon. For example exercising before and after work. Anyway, we'll soon see. I can stand a bit. Tonight there was good news, right? About the coming invasion and then people will have to stay indoors. Will it be over before winter? ~~Leed~~ Let us hope so.

Indeed Pa, this is no work for middle-aged people.[2] Nothing can happen to us young people. We get stronger from it, but for men over 50 this is not the right work.

Today we worked hard again. It is the only distraction here where you can find satisfaction and not have such awful thoughts all the time.

This week I again earned ƒ9.66. So fortunately again something to live off.

I salted about 1 pound of butter for when it gets scarce.

Yes, the visit on Sunday was great. A real distraction for me again. I will also send a letter to Aunt Juul and Uncle Karel.

Dear Pa and Ma, I end again now with a big kiss and a handshake from

Flip !

Maybe we will again soon be in A *!* [Amsterdam]

1. Max van Kleef was a salesman. He was born February 2, 1912, and lived in Amsterdam with his widowed mother, Mietje Haringman van Kleef, who was born May 8, 1877, and died January 26, 1943 at Auschwitz.

2. A photograph taken by Flip of some of the "middle-aged" men in the camp. About this time, Flip comments on the unsympathetic attitude of the boss or head-supervisor of the Moor Corporation towards "these oldsters plodding along." The boss said to one old man with heart trouble that "he must work whether he can or not." It is hard to understand why a Dutch company should treat fellow Dutch citizens so brutally, or why they gave them less pay and less food and less leave than they gave non-Jews. Elma Verhey has written that after renewed protest from a few survivors of the camps, who thought that they had, at least, the rights to the wages they did not receive, the Moor Corporation (who today call themselves Arcadia) donated 150,000 guilders to so-called "good causes." It is questionable, she added, whether a judge with Flip's letters in hand would acquit the company.[4]

A typewritten list of suggested things to pack when being deported to Poland, possibly issued by the Jewish Council.

For Men	For Women	For Children
2 pajamas	2 woolen undershirts	1 woolen undershirt
2 extra pairs socks	2 undershirts	2 undershirts
1 pair slippers	2 woolen underpants	2 woolen underpants
handkerchiefs	2 cotton underpants	2 cotton underpants
1 pair work shoes	1 brassiere	2 pajamas
1 wool hat	2 pairs pajamas	2 pairs long socks or
1 extra pair pants	2 pairs socks	stockings
1 winter coat	4 pairs stockings	4 pairs socks
1 rain coat	1 woolen vest	1 pair rain boots or
2 towels	1 dress	shoes
1 scarf	1 blouse with skirt	1 pair slippers
shaving kit	1 winter coat	1 pair "wellingtons" or
	1 rain coat	clogs
	1 scarf	
	1 wool hat	
	1 head scarf	
	2 long-sleeved aprons	
	1 pair work shoes	
	1 pair slippers	
	1 pair overshoes	
	1 training suit	
	1 pair woolen gloves	
	handkerchiefs	
	a suit to wear	

General

2 towels	earmuffs	linen for foot bandages
1 watch (not silver)	hairpins	shoe cleaning kit
sewing kit	shoelaces	prayer book
identity papers	1 cake of soap	favorite book
insect powder	toothpaste	
goggles	1 toothbrush	
hot water bottle	twine	

The star must be sewn on all clothes and dresses. These are available at 9 Plantage Park Lane. "General" means that these articles are necessary for men, women, and children.

If possible, blankets can be sewn together to make sleeping bags. Paint the name on the inside as well as the outside of the suitcases and backpacks. Luggage for each person must be packed separately.

Loading baggage belonging to people who have been arrested and sent to Westerbork. They were told that they could reclaim their baggage at Westerbork; however, this did not always happen. When it did, they were allowed to take no more than 15 kilograms.

Have teeth checked.

Bring inoculation records.

Perhaps make sleeping bags from sheets or blankets.

[Religious books and things.] Rituals (small tfillis, arbang-kanfosh, tefillin, a small edition of tenach and Chumash) If you only have a large edition, trade for a smaller one.

For children have shoes one size larger than needed, for growth.

Insect powder, 50 grams of talcum powder in a box, 25 grams Vaseline, iodine, 20 aspirin tablets, 1 bottle vitamin D, 50 Noril tablets, bandages, cotton, 20 Tannalbin tablets (for diarrhea) for children under three, band-aids.

[illegible]---- and transport
Families with children under age 10 will ride in streetcars. More information about this can be obtained from the information bureaus.

Luggage can be delivered during the day of departure between 2 and 5 in the afternoon to the warehouse at 38 St. Nicholas Street between Nieuwendijk and N.S. Voorburgwal. Luggage can be picked up in the evening after 10 o'clock.

It is not yet known whether children's carriages can be taken along.

Doctors and nurses will be along on the journey from Westerbork to Germany and will also [illegible]--------
Jewish Council officials will accompany transports to the final destination.

Care of people and items left behind.
The Jewish Council will try to ensure that those left behind without care will be looked after.

A representative has to be named. The correct forms necessary for the appointment of this person are available at the information bureaus.

Cancellation of rent has to be considered.

You must give a list of family and friends to your representative so that announcements received by your representative can be passed on.

Forms are available at the post office (forms for temporary absence) for instructions to whom incoming mail should be sent.

The mailing address of the camp will be given by the representative or family or Jewish Council. If this is not possible the representative will take care of it.

The German authorities have determined that all Jews, Dutch as well as German, in the occupied territories will be sent to Germany to work. These Jews will have to undergo a registration process. Subsequently, those who are called up will go to Westerbork for initial training before their work in Germany.

Westerbork is therefore only a temporary stay. It is the intention to have men as well as women leave together, family bonds will be maintained. Only a small group of Jews will remain in the Netherlands. Who will be selected for that, as regards to age and other details, is not yet known. Work placements will continue in camps in Germany (not in Poland). The upper age limit is probably 40 years, the lower age is not yet known for sure. This includes men and women. Families [will go together] only if both the man and woman are in the age group. Children within the limits will go in any case, even if the parents are above the age limit and therefore will not leave.

Call-ups will happen from place to place. The call-ups will be by the German authorities, not by the Jewish Council.

Exchange of letters between camps will be possible.

1. Eduard Philips with wife (Grietje) and their two sons, Philipp Philips (another Flip) (*left*), born 1922, and standing in the middle is Abraham Philips (Arthur), born 1920.

2. Aunts Duif (Duifje) and Bora (Debora), Flip's father's sisters

Hardenberg, 7 Aug 1942
Friday evening

Dear Parents,

This morning I again received your letter at work. Yes, Pa, I see you are still home with Ma. That's lucky. This morning a boy got the news that his 49-year-old mother, who was the only person left at home, has to go to Germany. And also that there were raids again yesterday. The mood went all the way down. That you can understand. There is hardly a family that has not been affected by the situation. Pa, when you send a package, will you add a few packets of Esbit with the films? I make great use of it here because I often fry an egg for extra food. I think that maybe Uncle Eduard[1] might not find his experience as bad as he expects. In the beginning the work is never easy. But Uncle Eduard is strong enough to stand it.

Pa, once again, see that you come here. Ma should have seen to that a long time ago. You have to go. Pa, if you don't get an exemption, you must come here to me, then I can help you with everything. Many farmers know me here.

The mood in the camp? Oh, it's not too bad, only when bad news comes does it go down. But that is also easy to understand. This evening Dick and Liel will be with me for the last time. I arranged with them that after roll call I will go with them for an evening walk. I am already looking forward to it.

The broad beans tasted very good. There was a lot of fat with them.

Pa and Ma, I end again and see you soon in free Amsterdam.

A big kiss from

Give my greetings to everyone.
Also Grandma, Aunts Duif, and Bora.[2]

Arthur (Abraham) Philips was in the Dutch army in 1940 when the Germans invaded. He was wounded during the five days of fierce fighting and spent a year in an army rehabilitation hospital. While there, Johanna Vink, one of the nurses, warned him that a German raid was going to take place, and she found a hiding place for him, for his fiancée, Willy (Wilhelmina) van Geldere, and for Willy's brother, whom she later married. Johanna died in 2002.

Hardenberg, 9 Aug '42
Sunday afternoon

Dear Pa and Ma,

This morning I received your express letter, again in good shape. Friday night I came home with a headache because my glasses broke on Thursday night. So yesterday at eleven o'clock I went to the village to buy a new frame and bought one for ƒ6. Very simple, but a nice frame. I also had to have my watch checked. That done, we did several errands and then went to the de Bruins where we were given a delicious cup of coffee and a few sandwiches. (I was there with a camp friend). From there we went to the Salomonsons and had a delicious meal. Altogether I was gone from 11 a.m. until 7.30 in the evening. I made a fine afternoon of it. The de Bruin and Salomonson families send their regards. Neither have heard anything yet. Yes, I also hope I can stay in this camp until after the war. But still, I think that the rules here will get much stricter.

Yesterday morning we beat the free laborers at work. This is because on Friday we stood at 17 ct, and in three hours we had to catch up enough for the whole week to make an average of 20 ct. The boss was astonished. We worked like mad. But we proved that we jews can also work like horses if necessary. It is so often said that jews only eat, without taking into consideration the circumstances in which we live, but in three hours we completed work that usually takes a whole day, so we have proven ourselves. Otherwise we would have been paid hardly anything, while now we still earned almost ƒ10.- I received the bread coupons as well as the ƒ1.- from Uncle Bram. I will write him a thank you note. Now, I won't write about the conditions here. We don't tell each other any news. Anyway, I know everything.

Ma also wrote a long letter this time. Yes, I know it is great that Pa hasn't gone yet, but we must consider that he will have to go. Yes, Ma, I am still young and can easily stand it, and that is a big consolation for you too, isn't it? I will survive, just like so many of us. There will be an end to this some time.

I am still writing to Bep. Certainly you know that I am not cross with her? Friday night I took an evening walk on the moor with Dick and Liel from 10 p.m. to 12.30. It was really great to walk and sit so peacefully, just the three of us. At night you really feel peace come over you, and you can enjoy nature.

Dear Pa and Ma, I end again with a big kiss
and greetings ~~the~~ from

Flip

P.S. I have sent my laundry. It is

2 towels
2 pairs of underwear
2 shirts
2 pairs of socks.

Bep de Vries; Karel van der Schaaf; and Lena van Bienen

Flip's paternal grandparents, Philip Slier and Betje Benjamins-Slier in 1934, celebrating their 50th wedding anniversary.

Hardenberg, 10 Aug 1942 [Monday]

Dear Pa and Ma,

Today I didn't get a letter from you; maybe tomorrow there will be two. But it doesn't worry me. This evening we had a meeting in the canteen. Mr. Duisend of the J.C. [Jewish Council] attended. The same as last time, and he said the following: our camp will be just like Ommen, i.e. mornings up at five-thirty. Communal meal in the canteen. Morning and evening roll call. Orders will be given in <u>German</u>. To the faucets with bare torsos; at night wash the whole body. <u>Probably</u> we will not be allowed to receive any more packages with food. 9 o'clock to bed.

For the present that is all. Oh, no. There is also a <u>chance</u> that incoming letters will be censored. <u>Not</u> outgoing ones.

Pa and Ma, now I want to ask if this week you can still send me a package with food and <u>esbit</u>. I urgently need esbit. But first durable stuff. Like i.e. canned milk etc., etc.

The suitcases and all personal belongings are still completely free. Also laundry can be sent as usual.

We just have to accept these regulations. It probably won't be as bad as it sounds. I will also write to Barend. In any case send the package before Saturday because that is when the cook returns; at the moment he is in training.

I am not down at all, you understand. On the contrary, I don't worry about anything yet. Come what comes. We will all one day be free again.

I have moved to Room **16** with my work mates. All young people. Much more fun than with the oldsters of room 7. So in the future, <u>room 16</u>.

Dear Pa and Ma, once again, don't worry. Send <u>only</u> what you <u>can</u> spare as soon as possible.

I end again with a big kiss and
a speedy *tot ziens*
from

Flip.

Have you still not heard from Handelsblad?
Also nothing from the Gallery?

Ma, if you can, send oatmeal, sugar, a can of milk etc. Remember [only] <u>what you can spare</u>.

Opposite page:
The bridges across the canals in Amsterdam were sometimes raised during raids.

MAP OF AMSTERDAM

The 1939 tourist map of Amsterdam *(below)* shows many of the canals. There are bridges, like the one opposite, over almost all the canals. The following landmarks are indicated:

1. Central Train Station
2. Nieuwmarkt (New Market)
3. Dam Square
4. Waterlooplein
5. The Walter Suskind Bridge
6. Hollandsche Schouwburg
7. Amstel hotel
8. Frederiksplein
9. Oosterpark Street
10. Vrolik Street
11. Asscher Diamond Factory
12. Koco Ice Cream Parlor
13. Anne Frank's home until 1942

There were First, Second, and Third Oosterpark Streets between Oosterpark (9) and Vrolik Street (10). Only the first is shown.

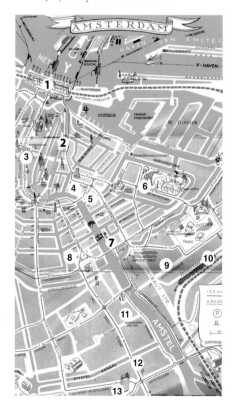

Hardenberg, 11 Aug '42 [Tuesday]

Dear Pa and Ma,

This morning at ± 12 o'clock I received your letter from Sunday night in the best of health. I also heard that there have been raids again. It seems that they never stop.

Yes Pa, it would be great if you came here. Why doesn't Ma push that now? Perhaps she can arrange it at the Gallery. Don't let my letter from yesterday bother you. I think a loophole can always be found.

Pa, if you can, will you send a box of vitamins? Not junk, but good stuff, if you can get it. You never know when it will be useful.

Yes Pa, you would be great company, and I could take care of many things for you. You get a lot of visitors now, right Pa? You will also get a visit from an old school friend of mine, who went to Amsterdam today.

How is Mrs. Bleekveld? Any better yet? Give her my regards and wish her all the best.

I would like it if I got some tea, it is really nice to have a cup in the evening.

Pa, I no longer believe that there will be an invasion this year. They are leaving us badly in the lurch. But yes, when the time comes; the greater the feeling of liberation and relief. And it has to happen sooner or later.

This week none of us feel like working. Nothing much has been done yet, but the work is very hard now. The ground is stone hard and the planks are long.

Yes, Ma, Dick and Liel are right. I look like the "Dutch Picture of Health."[1] But I buy whatever I can get to eat to make myself strong and robust to be able to stand eventual difficulties.

I don't know much more. I wrote most of my news last night.

Will you try to get the Esbit?

I end now with a big kiss and *tot ziens* in Free *Mokum*.

daaag!!

Ma, stay strong.
Don't give in and stay strong.

1. Flip looking like the "Dutch Picture of Health"

[Handwritten letter in Dutch, shown at left]

Amsterdam, 11, 8/42 [August 11, 1942]

Dear Family Feurink, [Veurink]

As you can see, I am writing to you at once. This Bible is in gratitude for what you have done for me and the boys. I hope very much that you will be able to use it in good health for a long time.

Fortunately I had a safe trip. I first walked to Lutte [Lutten is shown on the map on page 57]. From there I took the bus to Zwolle, and then from Zwolle to Amsterdam. I had no trouble whatsoever. My wife is very happy that I am back home with her. And I am too, of course.

The mood here, however, is nervous. And of course there is little to eat. But all that does not matter. The most important thing is that we are back together again. My father also had to go to G[ermany] last night.

I was fortunate to be able to say goodbye to him. If you ever have an extra ration coupon for one thing or another, could you send it to me? I will be more than happy to pay you for it.

Well, dear Feurink family, I want to thank you very much once more for all the good things you have done for us. God will reward you for it. I wish you all the best and I hope that you will be spared all sorrow. Bye, best regards and best wishes from

Jules Scharis
Vrolik Street 90 III [3rd Floor]
Amsterdam

A thank-you letter to a local farm family, the Veurinks (misspelled above), from Jules Scharis, one of the inmates who escaped from Molengoot. Along with the letter, Jules sent the Veurink family a 1940 reprint of the 1619 edition of the Bible. His fate is unknown, but his wife, Fanny Colmans Scharis, who lived at 90 Vrolik Street, died at Auschwitz October 8, 1942, when she was 21 years old. The Digital Monument lists a David Scharis (perhaps his father) of 94 Tugelaweg who was a 47-year-old tailor who died 21 days after Jules's letter (*above*). Both of Fanny's parents, Helena and Louis Colmans, and her siblings, Alida (age 23), Adolf (age 27), and Marcus (age 31), died in Auschwitz.

Deep gratitude to a local farmer, perhaps the Veurinks, was expressed by Ab van der Linden, who was evacuated from Molengoot in the mass round-up in October but then escaped from Westerbork. He was interviewed by Roel Gritter in 1995:

> At that point, acquaintances or family members who were not Jewish and who threw food to us over the fences from time to time stopped doing this out of fear. I remember that I would steal away to visit a farmer who lived nearby and who would give us food and mail letters. He was a giant in my eyes! How memorable it would be to meet this hero once more! I will never forget his courageous acts, thank you so much. You were a human being such as God must have intended![4]

Hendrik Jan Veurink marries Aaltje Seinen in 1920

Arrival at Hollandsche Schouwburg

Registration at Hollandsche Schouwburg

Interminable waiting at Hollandsche Schouwburg for transport to Westerbork

THE HOLLANDSCHE SCHOUWBURG

Between 1892 and 1941, the Hollandsche Schouwburg was one of the leading theaters in Amsterdam. The theater was stripped by the Germans and from August 1942 until November 1943 it was used as a collection point for people being sent to Westerbork. The facilities were inadequate for the large numbers of men, women, and children who were often forced to spend many days there. There was little food, insufficient seating, inadequate sanitation, and little privacy, and sleeping arrangements were virtually nonexistent. Transfer to Westerbork was carried out at night, out of sight of Amsterdam's gentile population. During 1942 and 1943, thousands of men, women, and children passed through the theater.

The operation was overseen by SS Hauptsturmführer Ferdinand Hugo aus der Fünten (Captain Fünten), but daily affairs were run by the Jewish Council, who appointed a German refugee to supervise the registration of everyone entering and leaving. He had the necessary background; he spoke German, knew the culture, and was a skillful diplomat. His name was Walter Suskind. He was a 39-year-old German-born company director.

RESCUE FROM THE SCHOUWBURG

The Hollandsche Schouwburg is remembered as a holding pen from which many thousands of Dutch Jews were transported to Westerbork and from there to the concentration camps or death camps. But the Hollandsche Schouwburg is also remembered as the place where Walter Suskind[1] found a way to save some of the children passing through the theater.

To reduce the noise and chaos in the theater, permission was granted for infants and children under the age of 12 to spend the daytime at the kindergarten across the street. Parents were secretly asked if they were willing to allow their children to be taken into hiding, and if they agreed, Suskind was able to "lose" the records of some of the children. Occasionally, as a cover, he would supply alcohol or prostitutes to the guards. Suskind exploited his common background with Aus der Fünten to fraternize and thereby earn some freedom of movement, but he also earned the animus of those who did not know the motive behind his behavior

Once a child's registration card was lost, Suskind informed Henriëtte Pimentel,[2] the kindergarten director. Working with an underground organization called "Naamloze Vennootschap" (Unnamed Public Limited Company), students at Amsterdam and Utrecht Universities rescued as many as 600 children.[4] Almost all were passed over the kindergarten wall or "disappeared" while out for a walk, but a few tiny ones were smuggled out in knapsacks, baskets, and even empty milk urns. Early in her work as a rescuer, Marion van Binsbergen, who was then a university student, was asked to collect a "package" from behind the crèche. She did so and delivered the baby to a family in the north of the Netherlands.

Dr. Bert de Vries Robles, Felix Halverstad, Waffen-SS Sergeant Alfons Zündler, and many others assisted in the rescues. The scale of Suskind's rescues, their daring, and their flamboyance were remarkable, but himself he could not save. When Suskind learned that his daughter, Yvonne, and wife, Johanna, born January 1, 1906, were on the next transport, he chose to join them. They were sent to Theresienstadt and then to Auschwitz where they died. A plaque on the Walter Suskind bridge over Niewe Heren canal near Waterloo Plain states: "With great danger for his own life, he saved many Jewish citizens from deportation during the German occupation." Henriëtte Pimentel died in Auschwitz on her 67th birthday. When Zündler's role was discovered in 1943, he was court-martialed and sentenced to death. The sentence was commuted to 10 years in Dachau. He survived, as did Halverstad.

1. Walter Suskind

2. Henriëtte Pimentel

Hilde Jacobsthal, Margot Hertz, and Margot Stern (*below*), three child-care workers from the kindergarten

The plaque (*below*) is on the Walter Suskind bridge over the Nieuwe Herengracht (New Heren canal) in Amsterdam (page 107).

Children in the kindergarten

WALTER SUSKIND

* LÜDENSCHEID 29 OCTOBER 1906
† NA EVACUATIE AUSCHWITZ
JANUARI - FEBRUARI 1945

HIJ ONTTROK TIJDENS DE DUITSE BEZETTING.
MET GROOT GEVAAR VOOR EIGEN LEVEN.
VELE JOODSE MEDEBURGERS AAN DEPORTATIE

> *Schouwburg 20–3 [March 20]*
>
> Dear Neighbor van Elst,
>
> Would you be so kind as to ask Kunstlinger to send us one or two things from the apartment? For my wife, some underwear, her good summer shoes are in Rudi's room. Sewing and darning things. Also her raincoat. For the children, anything left which is still useable. Especially for Willy, diapers and so on. There are vitamin pills in the sideboard. For myself, shaving soap. There are two wrapped sticks in the top of the linen cupboard. In the little bookcase there is my new shaving brush. Mrs. van Elst, you can well believe that saying goodbye was very painful for us. I would not wish to go through that a second time. We did not sleep at all last night; neither did the children. We are all exhausted. At 11:30 this morning we were in the Schouwburg, and there it is even more wretched; it is packed full.
>
> The following is for Kunstlinger and his wife. Of course you understand that it is painful for us to leave you. We got on so well with each other, and let this be our comfort to continue thinking of each other as good friends. Further, we thank you all, both neighbor and friend, for your open-hearted help. Let us hope that we will meet again,   Z. de Wolf and wife
>
> and lots of kisses from the children.

The letter above was written on toilet paper by Zadok de Wolf to a neighbor named van Elst, while the de Wolf family was held in the Hollandsche Schouwburg on 20 March 1943. What Mr. de Wolf was asking his neighbor to do was illegal.

Zadok de Wolf, of 6 Benkoelen Street, was born June 29, 1905. He was married to Frieda Schlockoff, born February 2, 1912, at Zabrze, about 45 miles northwest of Auschwitz. They had five children: Betsy, age 10; Ella Lina, age 8; Emanuel, age 6; Rudolf, age 3; and Willy, age 1. All were killed at Sobibor on April 2, 1943.

After families were arrested, their homes were sealed, all their goods and chattels were taken away (*right*) and the Germans declared it illegal for anyone to re-enter.

Hardenberg, 12 Aug. '42 [Wednesday]

Dear Pa and Ma,

This morning at work I got your letter. Fortunately, everything is still OK.

Yes, Pa, it would certainly be good if I had a spare pair of glasses, but I don't think they can be had any longer. The glasses lying in the drawer are no use. They are no good anymore. Pa, can you send the package before Saturday? On Sunday some changes may go into effect. That is when the cook comes back from his "training."

If anything happens, I can leave my stuff with a reliable farmer. I am sure someone will help me here.

Pa, see if you can get some Esbit for me. I have asked before, it is extremely useful, and I use it for everything.[1]

Ma and Pa, I am enclosing a few photos with some negatives. One is of our dinner when we ate the chicken, and one is with our farmer. Don't we look close?[2] But don't worry, it is just a little joke.

Don't I look well?

I put a number on each negative to show how many prints I want. If Ma has time she can take them to be printed. Is this OK?

I would like to have a box of "Davitamon."[3] It is made by the Zwanenberg laboratory in Os [Oss] and costs ƒ2.88. It is not available around here.

This evening we are going to visit our farmer again. So I close again with a big kiss and *tot ziens* from

Will you send the photos back?

1. When Flip said he uses Esbit for everything, he meant for all types of cooking. It is unlikely that he knew that it can be used as a urinary antiseptic. When eaten, it is well absorbed and excreted in an acid urine as formaldehyde, which kills all micro-organisms.

2. *Below left*: Flip and his farmer friends

3. Davitamon is a multivitamin tablet that was and still is made by the Zwanenberg company that started in 1923 when Dr. Saal van Zwanenberg and Professor Ernst Laqueur began to manufacture insulin under license from Banting and Best, the discoverers. As the owners were Jews, the Germans appointed a German administrator during World War II. Zwanenberg fled to London; Laqueur remained in Oss and survived, thanks to the help of friends and the Wehrmacht Field Marshall Wilhelm Keitel, who in 1945 signed Germany's surrender in Berlin.

Today the Zwanenberg Company is an international pharmaceutical company, still based in Oss, with a Cambridge, Massachusetts research laboratory.

Prewar advertisement for Davitamon

From left: Sina Vrijlink; Flip; Seine Vrijlink; and local farmers, Jan and Geert Klein

1. Flip was not alone in thinking this. Even some of the more reflective Germans would have agreed. For example, in occupied Warsaw, a Wehrmacht Captain, Wilm Hosenfeld, was thinking along the same lines and observed the following in his diary:

> Warsaw, 23 July 1942. The love of freedom is native to every human being and every nation, and cannot be suppressed in the long term. History teaches us that tyranny has never endured.[A]

According to Moore (1997, p.195), the Dutch bureaucracy had an accommodating attitude to the Germans that could not be attributed to those NSB members in senior posts. This was consistent with Rauter's boast to Himmler (page 69):"The hundred new units of the Dutch police are doing good work on the Jewish question, arresting hundreds of Jews by day and by night." However, Gerrit Renger[B] pointed out that the administration was Nazi controlled and most people feared the dire consequences of non-compliance. Hosenfeld once tried to save a Polish child who was about to be shot for stealing an armful of hay, but was prevented by the Gestapo who said; "If you don't get out at once, we will kill you too."[A]

Hardenberg, 13 Aug 1942 [Thursday]

Dear Pa and Ma,

When I came home this evening the letter and package were already here. Now that is again a surprise. There was so much in it. I now have a suitcase full of foodstuff and I hope I will be able use it for a long time and that they will keep their hands off everything. But we must wait and see. I have already arranged with a good, honest farmer (where Liel and Dick stayed) that I can leave my belongings with him. Everything you listed was in the package.

I have already written before. I hope that I will be able to repay you when we all live again in freedom and health. When will that time come again? It is taking so long.[1] But we mustn't lose our courage. Dick and Lily [Liel] bought me 2 packages of Esbit, with 50 pieces in each. Great, huh? I can make good use of them. Will you send some soon? Preferably insured! Then they won't disappear. Pa, when those rules are in place they [the farmers] will bring things to me in the camp, i.e. bread, milk, etc.

Again, today we did not do very much. This week I again got ƒ9.75. But now I think I won't get anything, for this reason. The boss had the list ready on Friday when we stood at 17 ct. Then we worked so hard that we achieved an average of 20 ct. So for that reason he had to do the lists all over again and he was really p[issed]. Now we have been given very hard work, namely ground as hard as rock and a long strip of land, and now he finds fault with everything, but we don't let it bother us.

I stop again here because I want to do a lot more writing and end with a very big kiss and again *tot ziens*

from

Pa, see to it (that is when you have to go) you come to me, you hear!

As people learned the true meaning of "work in Germany" or "resettlement in Poland," fewer and fewer people responded to their call-up summons. Those who could, went into hiding. The rest waited at home to be picked up. Street searches became more frequent, as did police raids in which the Dutch police arrested whomever they could on the street or in their homes.

Hardenberg, 15 Aug '42
Saturday afternoon

Dear Pa and Ma,

This is the last letter I can write that won't be censored.[1] This afternoon we were called into the canteen. The cook spoke. There are now 1,001 rules. I will mention them one by one. The cook must not talk to the jews. He is not allowed to grant favors or give any privileges. The camp will be split into 3 or 4 parts. Everything will be numbered. Several jews will become Kapos[2] i.e. commanders. 5.30 get up. 5.35 line up in front of the room. 5.45 make beds and wash. 6.10 roll call and eating. Talking while eating is forbidden. Then we go marching. Speaking is forbidden then also.

We must not be late for work. Buying food is strictly forbidden. We are not allowed to smoke at work. Evening, marching again. 6:15 roll call. Laziness will be punished. After eating, wash feet. Then in the mornings wash upper body. 18.45 [6:45 p.m.] roll call and at 21 hours (9 o'clock) to bed. Then everything must be quiet.

We may only receive clean underwear. Everything has to be eaten before Wednesday!!

And now comes the most important:

I and also you may only write a maximum 2 x per week and everything will be censored.

In the morning each man gets dry bread and no more jam or sugar, and also no butter.

There, that is all behind us. I can only receive money, and I ask you, Pa, to still send me money by reg. mail. The mail is free until Tuesday. If this rotten business gets to be too much, I'll beat it. Money orders are still allowed. Picture postcards and postcards will be burned. Except for the fact that there are no beatings, it is a complete concentration camp.[3] Maybe that will come too.

If we don't follow the regulations, we will be sent to Ommen [Camp Erica]. That is the camp where the cook had his training. He said it is terrible there. Th When you leave there, you don't walk anymore, you ride or you are driven. Your coffin is ready, according to our good cook.

But, dear Pa and Ma, don't be upset. I won't let myself starve. A p[ox] on them. Remember, don't be upset; keep your head up, and it will all work out someday. I will send some things back tomorrow.

Pa, decide carefully what to do if you get a summons. Maybe it won't be so bad. In any case today and tomorrow I will stuff myself.

Dear Parents, I stop again. Tell everybody they must not write.

Remember, stay strong, I do too, and don't let your courage sag.

Keep your chin up; *tot ziens*

and a big kiss
from
Flip

Send money on Monday, express and insured.

CENSORSHIP

1. The censorship at Molengoot was described by Flip. The censorship at Westerbork was described by Mechanicus and by Flip's aunt, Grietje Slier Philips (*below*). Mechanicus met a Catholic man who was being deported because he wrote a private letter supporting the Jews that was intercepted by the censor.[A] Aunt Grietje was only allowed to write 12 lines on a postcard (p. 119) once every two weeks, provided she made no mention of the transports or internal Westerbork affairs.

Grietje Slier Philips when she was 27 years old with her son Arthur

2. Kapo is an acronym of **Ka**mp **Po**lice. At Westerbork, kapos were known as the OD.

3. If concentration camps are defined as on page 152, then the work camps were not concentration camps since there were no beatings or killing. Ab van der Linden, a Molengoot survivor, said that the staff there had a ditty: *In Molengoot is geen Jood dood* (In Molengoot no Jew dies). However, a civil servant quoted by Louis de Jong inspected the work camps and he reported that they were concentration camps run by the State Employment-Creation Office.[B]

Flip's parents. This is the only available photo of his father, Leendert (Eliazar) Slier, born March 26, 1890. He worked as a typesetter for the newspaper, *Algemeen Handelsblad*. Postcards of Flip *(below)*, as a toddler on his first birthday in 1924, and at five years of age *(bottom)*. These photos were sent to his uncle, Jack Slier in South Africa, with the message, "Ask Andries to tell you what a nice boy he is."

This letter to Flip is the only one from his parents that was found with his other letters.

A'dam, 16 August 1942 *Sunday evening*

Dear Flip,

We received your letter Sunday night and we ~~are~~ very concerned by it. Even though you have been in camp, until now everything has gone well. But what will happen now? [Referring to the introduction of censorship and other restrictions]. We don't know how to respond to your letter because we heard the same about other camps, and you certainly know that too. But I do know for sure, that Uncle Jonas and Andries still regularly write letters from camp Kremboong in Hoogeveen which are not censored and they also receive uncensored letters. Also, at first they were not allowed to receive anything to smoke, but now that can also be sent. They can also still buy some things in the canteen. So Flip, wait and see what will happen. How strictly all these regulations are enforced depends a great deal on the leader of the camp. We enclose ƒ 50 (fifty guilders) in this letter. Flip, you still have that money we gave you? Write and tell us clearly and exactly what you really want. You must consider the fact that ~~you are not alone in the camp~~. If you need more money, write to us immediately, and we will send it gradually in money orders. Don't let yourself be influenced by others.

Hardenberg 16 Aug '42 [Sunday]

Dear Pa and Ma,

We have just one more day to write uncensored letters. We are allowed to write once a week, on Sunday. We have to give our unsealed letters to the cook, who since yesterday, does not talk to us any more. He is totally upset by what he saw there [Camp in Erica in Ommen Ommen]. He said, The coffins stand ready. It is not going to get pretty here. Pa, if it gets too crazy, should I leave? In any case send a money postal order or registered letter by express. We are not allowed to have any foodstuff in our possession after Wednesday and also no Esbit. I don't know yet what to do, send the food home or keep it here. There is a good chance it will all be taken away if I keep it in my suitcase. But Ma and Pa, don't let your courage sag. Maybe we will be home again before the winter. So whatever happens, chin up!

On Tuesday, the daughter of our farmer is coming to our home.[1] Ma, she is a good-looking unmarried woman. In the few weeks that we have known her, she has taken good care of us (namely, me and Simon Loonstijn) who I am with now and am with all the time.[2] I hope you will receive her warmly, and let Pa discuss with her if I can eventually go and stay with her if it all gets too crazy here. She is very trustworthy. See what you want to do, Pa.

Now I want to arrange something as far as the censor is concerned. You may write to me 2 x per week. Of course, we do not know how strict the censor will be. In any case when I write about the cook, I will say Simon. If I am discussing food I will say "weather." I just stopped to arrange several things. On Monday or Tuesday you will receive two packages. No foodstuff, however. It is here and hidden in the lion's den. A boy from our room has now been appointed cook, and he gets along very well with our former Christian cook.

We now do everything together. The cans of milk and the tins of stew, etc. are probably all safe. If they find them, well in God's name, then it had to be, and we did our best. When I send clothes, check the pajama pants thoroughly, inside the hole the tape goes through. There may be a letter in there. But maybe all this won't be too bad and will be strictly enforced for the first few weeks and then become more lax. Right now, he [the cook] is brutal to the people; he swears and curses up a storm.

We also have drills. But at least we don't have German guards yet, and if we want to, it would still be easy to take off. For the time being it's not necessary, and I won't do it. The Esbit and the laundry are safely in my possession. I have hidden the Esbit between my clothes.

Dear Pa and Ma, till next week. Don't worry; I will get through.

For the time being we have food, and I end again with a big kiss and

speedy *tot ziens*.

from

[signature]

[signature]

1. The Vrijlink sisters; Gerridina; Johanna: Gees, and Sina

2. Simon Loonstijn (*above*) wearing clogs. He was born on August 9, 1922; he planned to study law but was unable to do so because the Germans would not allow Jews to attend university. He worked as an office clerk before being sent to Molengoot sometime around the beginning of July 1942. He was a avid reader and a keen sportsman; he played ice-hockey in the AJC and Maccabi teams.

Yes, we are the Red Falcons, we are the labor youth;
Flags and singing show our struggle and our truth.
We remain faithfully together, each knows his duty to fight;
One day we'll carry the flags, high in freedom's golden light.

The AJC had songs (*above and page 147*), uniforms (*below and pages 10 and 60*), a pledge (*page 32*), and members (*below and elsewhere*) whose compassion and camaraderie is plain. Of those in the photo below, only three survived the war: Karel, Little Bep, and Sally Vogel. After the war Sally unexpectedly turned up at Karel's home saying that he had been in hiding in France and had changed his name to Charlie Bird. *Vogel* is Dutch for "bird."

1. Henny's sister, Debora de Lange is in the back row, second from the left.
Back, left to right: Big Bep (Elisabeth) de Vries; Debora de Lange; Bora Prijs; and Chelly (Rachel) Borzykowski.
Middle, left to right: Little Bep (Elisabeth) de Vries and Reina Kroonenberg.
Front, left to right: Benny Haringman; David Blits; Sally (Salomon) Vogel; Karel van der Schaaf; and Sally (Salomon) Waas.

2. Flip failed to sign his name to his letters on July 31, August 11 and August 17 (*above*). Each time, he was writing at night with not enough light to see.. However, if he had light enough to write the letter, why balk at the signature? Unlike most signatures, Flip's were not routine marks that could be written automatically without looking; his signatures were more like variable artistic expressions that reflected his mood (see endpaper). Perhaps he needed light so that he could inspect the work in progress.

Hardenberg, 17 Aug. [1942] ~~Tues~~
Monday evening

Dear Pa and Ma,

It is nine o'clock and we are already in bed. The first day is over. We decided to look on the bright side and just laugh about it. It's ridiculous how crazy we have to act. Real military discipline. The cook is out of his mind. It's crazy how a person can change so quickly. He swears and rants and still can't pull it off. The comedy is so obvious. Our suitcase is gone, no longer in the camp. Eating will now become difficult, but we will have to adjust. We also have to stand at attention, etc. Pa knows how that goes.

This letter has obviously been sent secretly. I hope to be able to send many this way. This evening the mail wasn't opened. I received a letter from Henny's sister.[1] If you had sent me a registered letter by express mail, nobody would have read it. Isn't that what I asked for?

Tomorrow other things can happen. I don't worry and just let everything pass over me. It is getting dark so I can't write much longer.[2]

Ma, don't worry. I can stand a lot. Maybe on Wednesday I will write a longer, more detailed letter.

Dear Pa and Ma, I end again with greetings to everyone.
A big kiss and a speedy
tot ziens.
I can't see any more.

Also look thoroughly in my washing,
there might be a letter inside,

Hardenberg, 18 Aug '42 [Tuesday]

Dear Pa and Ma,

This evening I received two letters from you with the ƒ5.- enclosed. One letter, namely the registered one, I had to open in the presence of the cook.[1] The other one had not been opened. In fact, I am only allowed to write once a week, but there is nothing I can do about that. About all the other stuff, it may not be so bad. We have to march and mustn't greet anybody. That's not too bad; only it is a real pity that we cannot buy extra food, but we will figure out a loophole for that one.

Yes, Pa, I still have all the money you sent me. But, who says that we will be staying here? Any moment we might have to leave, and then I have to be able to take care of myself for a while. Ma, I am happy that Karel and his father[2] are coming again, but I will have to wait and see if I can be with them for any length of time. Send the vitamins with them Pa. Here I will be able to make very good use of them!! Just buy things, ~~neither~~ perhaps money may not be worth anything soon. Ma, I still have money. I still have ƒ32,5.0 altogether, you understand? So I can take care of myself for a few months. If Uncle Bram wants to send me a loaf of bread, I can make good use of it.[3] So now I can start the second letter. You can write to me a few times a week without fear. But, Pa, don't enclose anything, you hear, ~~annthil~~ and watch your words. Write everything very carefully; even though the censor is not too bad, it is still bearable. Today you had a visitor right? Was it very nice? Isn't she a really nice girl?

It has now begun to get much more difficult for us. Roll call ten times a day, standing at attention etc. etc. But still, we don't let it bother us. Dear Pa and Ma, I end again; a speedy *tot ziens*, and stay strong, from *Flip*

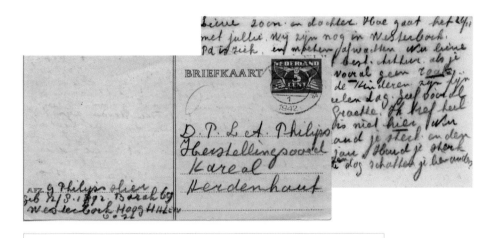

Dear son and daughter, How is it going? We are still in Westerbork. Pa is sick, and we must wait. Now dear children, we make the best of it. If you send anything, no tobacco because that's not allowed. The children are fine and play the whole day. Special regards to Mr. Harmsen. I meet the whole of Amsterdam here. Bard is not <u>here</u>. Now my dear boy, be strong and we think about you very much. We may write 12 lines every 14 days. 'Bye darlings, your loving parents.

[2nd side]   date stamped 5 December 1942
G Philips Slier
Born 12/3/1892 Barrack 69
Westerbork, HOOGHALEN 6026

1. Flip had to open his letters in the presence of the cook. His aunt at Westerbork, Grietje Slier-Philips, who sent the postcard *(below left)* to her son, Arthur, and his wife, Willy, was allowed to write exactly 12 lines and so left the second side blank. In her *Shoah* interview, Willy said that she would rather have died than go to Westerbork.[A]

2. The van der Schaaf family *(left to right)*: Dirk (father); Hanna Cecilia Meyvogel (mother); Dick; Liel (Lily) van der Berg (friend); and Karel.

3. Uncle Bram [Samas], was married to Flip's mother's sister, Johanna. He was a baker who lived on Professor Tulp Street, Amsterdam.

A letter from the Mayor of Vriezenveen *(above)* states that Uncle Bram's son Salomo Samas, a typesetter from 25 [Professor] Tulp Street, Amsterdam, was put on a train and sent [back] to Amsterdam on March 4, 1941. Two weeks earlier, on February 22, 1941, Salomo's brother, Philip, had been arrested and sent to Mauthausen.

The first page of the three-page summons for transport to the east, detailing instructions.

Walking to an assembly point

1

Central Office for jewish
Emigration Amsterdam   No. 19446

Adama v. Scheltema Square 1
     Telephone 97001

SUMMONS!

To   Ida E. van Raalte-Simons   **L.** 31 **No.** 13
          Franken Street 3.
          Scheveningen

You must present yourself for possible participation, under police supervision, in a work creation program in Germany, and must report for a personal and medical inspection at the Westerbork transit camp, station of Hooghalen.

Therefore, you must on **19 AUG. 1942** at 1.00 P.M.

be at the assembly place   THE HAGUE RAILWAY STATION
                                        see appendix

As luggage you may bring:
          1 suitcase or backpack
          1 pair of work boots
          2 pairs of socks
          2 pairs of underwear
          2 shirts
          1 set of overalls
          2 woolen blankets
          2 sets of bedding (cover and sheets)
          1 bowl
          1 mug
          1 spoon
          1 sweater
          towel and toiletries
also food for three days and all your ration coupons.
The baggage must be packed in two parts:

a.   **Necessary travel items:**
         the 2 blankets, 2 sheets, food for 3 days, toiletries, a plate,
         cutlery and mug

b.   **Large baggage:**
         All other items must be packed in a strong suitcase or backpack,
         clearly marked with first name, family name, birth date, and the
         word "Holland."
         Family baggage is not allowed.
         The above must be adhered to precisely, because the large baggage
         will be loaded separately at your place of departure.
         The various identification and personal papers, as well as the
         ration cards, must <u>not</u> be packed with your baggage, but
         carried with you so that you can show them immediately.
         You must leave your residence orderly and locked behind you; the
         keys must be taken along.
         Things that may not be taken: household pets

K 372

2

Illness is no excuse for failing to report to this summons. Those who are sick on the day of departure and considered by their doctor to be unable to travel will be examined by a German police doctor.[1] In such cases, the first doctor will assume full responsibility, and will need to send the various papers, together with a written declaration, to the Central Office, by return post.

If you are a veteran of the war of 1914-1918, or in possession of war decorations, then, at the appointed time, you must come forward with proof of this. Postponement of deportation or dismissal from the Westerbork transit camp can only occur if you have all necessary personal papers with you. If you do not report for this summons, you will be given no special treatment, and will be punished in accordance with Security Police measures.

At the bottom of this summons, you will find a travel permit and a transportation ticket, which will allow you to travel free by train. You can use the travel permit on the tram or bus, but you will need to pay for these trips. The travel permit and transportation ticket must be voluntarily presented to the conductor, and, upon your arrival at the Hooghalen station, he will tear them off.

This summons,[2] along with your personal identification and all other family papers and ration cards, including your ration stamp card, must be brought with you.

On your arrival at Westerbork, you must have **COMPLETE AND ACCURATE INFORMATION** about the following (relevant documents must be brought along and presented):

I.   a. bank transfer account balance (both postal and city)
       b. bank account balance
       c. saving account balance and
       d. information about other financial institutions

II.   a. securities (stocks, third-party claims), domestic and foreign
       b. policies (life insurance, study insurance, annuities, such as
                 national insurance, burial funds, etc.)

III.   claims, both domestic and foreign

IV.   safety deposit boxes (bring along the keys, as many as you
       have in your possession)

V.   a. inheritances
       b. temporary possession of property
       c. patent rights

VI.   a. art objects
       b. collections
       c. jewelry
       d. precious stones
       e. gold or silver objects
       f. other valuable items

VII.   a. gifts
       b. transfers
       c. compensations

The second page of the summons

1. Being examined by a German police doctor was not likely to be helpful: "At Amersfoort, Ellecom and Vught the doctors spurned Jews suffering from injuries, fevers, or diseases, telling them they could rot or die, for all they cared. 'Die, you Jew!'"[4]

WESTERBORK - AUSCHWITZ
AUSCHWITZ - WESTERBORK
<u>DO NOT UNCOUPLE WAGON</u>
RETURN TO WESTERBORK.

2. The final destination was not stated on the summons but it could be seen on the trains. "We had read the name of Auschwitz on the label on the trucks, the trucks of the wagons, but nobody of us knew what Auschwitz meant."[B] —Primo Levi

The third page of the summons

People waiting to be deported on Polder Way, about a half-mile from Vrolik Street.

No. 19446

VIII.   exact enumeration and description of debts

IX.   shares in businesses and companies (full description with address, purpose, and legal status)

X.   a. real estate holdings
         b. co-rights to real estate holdings
         c. claims on landed property (a, b, and c all refer to domestic and foreign property)
            You are required to note the following:

Province	Place Name
City	Street Name
Plot number	House Number
Section	Book Value
Number	Mortgage

XI.   Mortgages (see X).

XII.   Building plot (see X).

All this information must be provided, even if the objects concerned have already been delivered to
° Lippmann, Rosenthal and Co., Sarpharti Street 47-55, Amsterdam

° "The Economic Audit Authority," The Hague

° "Dutch Land Plot Administration," The Hague.

By order of
W.H. Wörlein
SS Captain

Central Office for jewish
Emigration Amsterdam   No. 19446   L......... No.......

Adama v. Scheltema Square 1
   Telephone 97001

TRAVEL PERMIT AND TRANSPORTATION TICKET!

The holder of this travel permit and transportation ticket, of the same number as the summons, may travel on the prescribed train from the station   *Scheveningen*

to the Hooghalen station on ...**19 AUG 1942**.........free of charge.

The travel permit and transportation ticket must be shown unrequested to train personnel and may only be torn off by the conductor upon arrival at the Hooghalen station.

By order of
W.H. Wörlein
....   ⚡ Captain

When this card is shown, upon payment, the holder may use a trolley or bus on the date listed above.

Hardenberg, 22 Aug '42 [Saturday]

Dear Pa and Ma,

I received your letter from Thursday morning ~~evening~~ in good health. It is now Saturday afternoon; this morning we didn't work but still had to get up at half past five, just like the others. It is now real military discipline. Orders and commands during drills[1] are now mostly in German. But that's not really so bad, if we only had enough to eat, but we get very little and the worst quality. Most people were hungry this week, because we are not allowed to buy anything extra and there is no opportunity for that. Things for Simon and me are still all right. They [the farmers] put it under the wheelbarrow at work for us.[2] For example, yesterday we had 8 eggs, 1 kilo of tomatoes and some little carrots. When you have this, it is still manageable, but otherwise it's almost unbearable. Friday at lunch break I took off and went to our farmer and ate wonderfully. Yes Pa, I received the $f50$, but because I am sending off black letters,[3] I wrote 5.

It's a pity that the girl didn't come to you on Tuesday, isn't it? She is not here yet so I don't know why she didn't come. When I have the opportunity, I will ask her.

I thought you had gone back to work long ago, Pa, but yes, stay home for the time being; that's always a good idea. You now have a lot of visitors, right? Yes, Pa was always liked.

Now I go to bed earlier than you; at quarter to nine. We have to go to our room and get undressed. But we also have to get up at exactly 5.30. We then get dressed quickly (in the dark room) and then at 5.35 must stand outside the room. (Everything done exactly by the whistle.) Then we go and wash and have to stand ready, exactly in time for the "Mealtime'"!!!, which consists of coffee or "porridge!!" that resemble ditch water and starch. Before I never ate it . . . but now it has to do.

Pa and Ma, you can certainly send me a few letters a week. But be careful; don't enclose anything special because all letters are opened. Also, the laundry is examined. If you want to send something, put it in the lining of a pair of pants or a jacket. They are not that thorough. Ma will you send me my sweater and long pants? Then I can wear those for a change.

Remember we were not supposed to earn any money this week? Well we had achieved 11 cents and now are supposed to make 20 cents. On Wednesday the boss brought the money to the camp. (I was on duty), and there were $f9.73$ in the envelope. Then he said to me, "Slier, hear, see and . . . be silent!" So at least I got that much.

The suitcases have not been checked at all, so I could have safely kept everything here. But it doesn't matter now. It is pretty safe. Dear Pa and Ma, I hope I won't keep you waiting for letters as long as I had to wait this week. And now I end with a big kiss and speedy

tot ziens, from ~Flip.~

Give everybody my greetings
and a kiss from me.

~Daaag!~

Keep in mind that I am allowed to write only once a week.

1. Drill and roll call became the order of the day at Molengoot. Above, members of the Westerbork camp police, the Ordedienst (ODs or Kapos), most of whom were German Jews and were detested.

2. Two local farmers' daughters in 1946: Miena (Hermina) Vrijlink (*right*) and her friend Riek Veurink (*left*) who put food under the wheelbarrows every day for the boys at Molengoot.

3. Following the introduction of censorship, Flip advised his parents that he would camouflage references to sensitive subjects. On Sunday, August 16, Flip's parents sent him $f50$. On Tuesday, August 18, Flip wrote that he received "the $f5$, making $f32.5.0$ altogether, you understand?" But they didn't, so he explained that he had divided by ten and henceforth avoided using coded messages.

THE BATTLE OF STALINGRAD [A]

STALINGRAD
Myth and Reality

These photographs are from a 32-page booklet dropped by the RAF on Germany in early February 1943, in order to tell the German people that the costly German advance into the USSR was stopped at Stalingrad.

1. Horse racing slang for £500 to £1.

The city of Stalingrad stretched for 25 miles along the west bank of the Volga river, 1,600 miles from Molengoot, yet the battle infiltrated into everyone's consciousness. The victories in the Egyptian desert at El Alamein on November 4, 1942, and on the frozen streets of Stalingrad on February 2, 1943, were the turning points of World War II.

On August 23, 1942, the German army launched a massive, five-day, round-the-clock bombing offensive with over 2,000 planes against the city of Stalingrad. Hitler, who had appointed himself Commander-in-Chief of the Combined forces, had predicted that the city would fall on the 23rd and ordered that it be taken no later than August 25. His direction of the battle continually conflicted with that of the generals in the field. One of them, General Halder, the Army Chief of Staff, wrote in his diary that Hitler "pathologically overestimated his own strength and criminally underestimated the enemy's." The German ambassador to Italy, Ulrich von Hassel, deplored "the irresponsible leadership of this wanton and megalomaniac corporal." General Beck, Field Marshall Witzleben, and Admiral Canaris wanted Hitler arrested and tried publicly for his crimes against the state and violation of international law. General Halder, Colonel Hans Oster, and Dr. Hans von Dohnanyi thought it preferable that Hitler be declared insane and committed to an asylum. By 1944, Field Marshal Rommel favored assassination: "The pathological liar had gone completely mad."

Under Hitler's command the battle became a nightmare. On September 30, he boasted that the Germans would never leave Stalingrad. Since the Germans had artillery and air superiority, the Russians fought them at close quarters, effectively hindering their use of either one. Consequently, the fighting was house-by-house, street-by-street. The central train station changed hands 15 times—four times within a single day! Vasily Grossman, a special correspondent for the Red Army newspaper, reported from the front lines: "Sometimes the trenches dug by the battalion are twenty meters from the enemy. . . . I was shooting point-blank, at a range of five meters . . . We wandered into an empty house and decided to stay there for the night. Then some soldiers appeared . . . They turned out to be Romanians . . ."[B] When in October, Halder asked Hitler for support for the flanks, Hitler promptly replaced him with General Kurt Zeitzler. On November 19, the Soviets attacked the north flank; a day later they attacked the southeastern flank and two days later they linked up, trapping 250,000 German troops. Finally, on February 2, 1943, having lost 850,000 men, Field Marshal von Paulus surrendered. The total battle casualties were between 1.7 and 2 million. The Soviets took as prisoners of war: one field marshal, 23 generals, 2,500 officers, and 91,000 men, of whom only 6,000 survived the war. By most reckonings, Germany suffered a historic defeat.

When Germany invaded Russia on June 22, 1942, all the experts predicted that Russia would fall as rapidly as France and Poland had done. Winston Churchill was host to the American Ambassador and British cabinet ministers, Anthony Eden and Stafford Cripps, who said Russia would not last six weeks. Churchill disagreed: "I will bet you a Monkey to a Mousetrap[1] that the Russians are still fighting, and fighting victoriously, two years from now."[C] In his BBC broadcast that evening, Churchill said,

> At four o'clock this morning Hitler attacked and invaded Russia. All his usual formalities of perfidy were observed with scrupulous technique. We are resolved to destroy . . . this bloodthirsty guttersnipe . . . No one has been a more consistent opponent of Communism than I have for the last 25 years. I will unsay no word that I have spoken about it. But all this fades away . . . Any man or state who fights on against Nazidom will have our aid . . . We shall fight him by land, we shall fight him by sea, we shall fight him in the air, until with God's help we have rid the earth of his shadow . . . The Russian danger is therefore our danger and the danger of the United States, just as the cause of any Russian fighting for his hearth and home is the cause of free men and free peoples in every quarter of the globe. It follows that we shall give whatever help we can to Russia.[D]

Hardenberg, 23 August '42 [Sunday]

Dear Pa and Ma,

Today I'm allowed to write a letter to you again and therefore begin by asking how you are doing. For me it is still OK, as you probably know. Everything is still the same as I wrote last week. Only the food is so terribly little for us young people, but Pa and Ma, we have to keep up our courage. Maybe by winter I will be safely with you again. I do hope so because I am very fed up with this. How are Karel and his father? I have not heard anything from them. I spoke to Rosette de Bruin. She left Aunt Jenny (and is back in Hardenberg). She told me Aunt Jenny is pregnant again.[1]

Ma, I enclose a soap coupon and a soap powder coupon. I would like to receive them soon.

Will you send me my long pants and my sweater? You can also safely send vitamins. Only no foodstuff or smoking stuff.

Ma, did you get last week's packages? I sent two. One with laundry and one with the Primus stove. Write and tell me.

Isn't it a long time since we saw each other? It is already 18 weeks since I left. Do you remember on the platform that Saturday morning? And when will we see each other again? We don't know that! But still, I am optimistic, some day there will be an end to this war, and possibly soon.

Have Gees[2] and Stien been?[3] I think so because they have also been at Simon's. But I will hear about that, right? Cannot think of much more to write so I end with a big kiss from

Filip.

Encl. 2 soap coupons

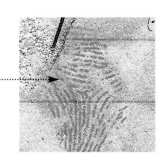

Two *zeep* (soap) coupons

1. Aunt Jenny gave birth to a boy, Philip, on February 22, 1943; he died at Auschwitz two weeks later. Aunt Jenny (Jeanie Muriel Gestetner-Salomonson) was married to Flip's mother's younger brother, Alfred Salomonson, who is listed as a metal dealer, a polite description for a scrap iron merchant.

2. Gees went to Amsterdam with her father Jan Vrijlink (*above*), to explore ways in which they might help Flip and Simon.

3. There was a local resident called Stien, but it is not known whether she accompanied the Vrijlinks.

On Flip's original letter (*left*) he stuck a soap coupon with a serrated edge to the right of his signature. A remnant of the serration is visible, and just below it is a finger print (enlarged below) that Flip probably made as he stuck down the coupon.

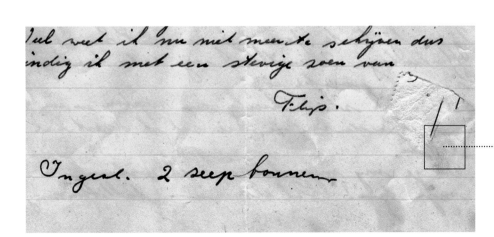

Hardenberg, 24 Aug. 1942 [Monday]

1. Ap (Abraham) Waterman, age 26, of 34 Hofmeyer Street, Amsterdam, was a mechanic who died in Auschwitz on February 28, 1943. His sister, Alida Bromet-Waterman, age 24, and their mother, Schoontje Waterman-Waterman, age 51, died in Auschwitz on September 30, and October 15, 1942.

2. On August 19, 1942, the Allies, using mostly Canadian troops, raided the French town of Dieppe, chosen because the Allies thought it was lightly guarded. Lord Louis Mountbatten, Chief of Combined Operations, informed Churchill that the raid was a success, despite the loss of about 100 aircraft and the raid's failure to achieve its objectives. Of the 6,000 Allied troops, 1,000 were killed and 2,000 were taken prisoner.[A]

Below: One page of the leaflet dropped by the Germans on southern England "to inform the people in Britain that you also invaded France but your raid on Dieppe has been a disaster."

Dear Parents,

This letter is brought to you by a very good roommate of mine from room 7 and who has always been with me in my work group. The reason he is in Amsterdam is that he is getting married today. So congratulate him heartily, and, Ma, will you give him a nice cup of coffee? He was a great comrade, and if he hadn't left, I would have stayed in my old room, but I have again found a good friend. I think Ap[1] will tell you a lot about camp life.

(I had to interrupt [this letter] because we had drill for an hour.)

Pa, in your previous letter you wrote that you had received my letter of the 18th. I would prefer you didn't do that, Pa, because I am only allowed to write once a week. Ma, will you send my laundry? I accidentally used up all my regular towels, and now I have to dry myself with a tea towel. Pa, if you send a package, you can safely put something between the clothes, not openly, in such a way that it could fall out. Pa, you must absolutely not let anyone read my letters in which I write about the extra food I buy; you never know what harm it can do.

Until now we have muddled through; when this is no longer possible, I will let you know. Even though now I must be satisfied with less than during the past week. Yesterday there was a German in the camp. He raised hell, yelled as though he was having a fit. A real Kraut, though at the end he wasn't too bad.

Will you have the shoes I sent repaired, Ma? And if possible, I would like to have them back as soon as possible.

How come Karel and his father did not come? They were planning it, right? I was really looking forward to it.

This evening we (Siem [Simon Loonstijn] and I) made a big pudding; it's not yet finished. It looks great.

Rosette de Bruin [Ru de Bruin's eldest daughter] was here on Sunday and brought me some little pears and tomatoes.

~~She~~ This morning I heard that their two sons [Emanual and Lion Emanual] have been sent to Germany. Yes, they are just taking everybody away.

I am glad that I have not sent anything home; now at least I have something, and it is also great that sometimes we get help.

I guess you haven't heard anything yet from the people who are gone, right? That is one of the worst things they have done to us, and they will not escape their proper punishment. What did you think of the occupation of Dieppe?[2] Will they wait a long time for the invasion? I hope for me and for everybody else that the whole rotten business will soon be over.

Pa and Ma shall I write down again what I need? Here goes: a few towels, my long pants and blue jacket, my shoes, <u>vitamins</u> and some candy (I enjoy that too) and a tin of shoe polish, and those whalebones with the little chain.

If you want to send something, hide it well in the laundry, so it can't be seen. They just feel the laundry. It's too dark to write any more. Soon I will go and get the potatoes that are waiting outside the camp. I end with a big kiss and a speedy *tot ziens* from

until in *Mokum*

Hardenberg, 25 Aug. 1942 [Tuesday]

Dear Pa and Ma,

This evening I got your letter and learned from it that things are still all right. I must say, in contrat to many others, I haven't yet been hungry. That is lucky, but also, I am as brazen as can be. So I will tell you what happened to me and somebody else last night. In the evening, before dinner, one of the boys from our room took a large mess tin and put it in the woods across the road. We had arranged with a farmer that he would put potatoes and eggs in it. On the way back the boy was caught and had to dig a hole as punishment. So last night I went to get it and was already standing in the woods when [one was] from the cook I heard voices. But . . . . they didn't catch me. I went back, took a roundabout way, and came back from the w.c. [toilet]. They stopped me and asked me where I had been. I acted as if I didn't recognize them and asked, "What do you want?" When they reprimanded me, I said I had not seen it was them. When they asked me again, "Where are you coming from?" I said "from the toilet," and they could not prove anything, and a quarter of an hour later I went yet again. So you see we live just like prisoners, but we still are always helped.

This afternoon during break I went to our farmer and again ate wonderfully. I don't suffer from hunger. Again, under the wheelbarrow there was a lot. This evening de Bruin came and gave me a loaf of bread, a little bit of butter and some apples and plums. You see, so far I manage to get through. But Pa and Ma, let only trusted people who don't talk read these letters; otherwise, they will ruin it for us. Yes, the money is safe, and I still have it all.

No, Pa, we don't get ice cream any more. It is now really a prison camp but I don't need that for nourishment.

Dear Ma and Pa, I end this letter again with a big kiss from *Flip* good night and sleep well. Until tomorrow night.

(I get German lessons from a camp friend). Give Grandma[1] a kiss from me.

It is now already Wednesday night and I am writing again.

Today I was at our farmer and talked to Gees.[2] She was full of praise for you and had a good time. I now eat there all the time in spite of all the risk. She also said that you said I should only leave here if it becomes unbearable. Well, you can trust me in this. This evening I got the package with the clothes, there was nothing in there, right? I am not writing much now and end with a very big kiss from *Flip*

See you soon, O.K. Keep your courage up!
Luckily you don't have to worry about me.

P.S. Pa, if you are called up, either for a camp or Germany, I can only advise Don't go because you will suffer hunger.
Only if you can come to me, then you won't have to be hungry.

Flip

1. *Back, from left to right*: Grietje Slier-Philips, holding her son Elie; name?; Eduard Philips; Debora Slier. *Front:* Flip's cousin, Philipp Philips; and grandparents, Philip Slier and Betje Benjamins-Slier.

This signature (*above*) was taken from a card that Aunt Bora sent to her brother Jack in South Africa (page 58). Betje Benjamins-Slier added a note and signed herself *Moeder* (mother). [On a final proof read we noticed that the signature above is written in the same hand as the rest of the card, so we wonder whether perhaps the greetings had been dictated not written.]

Flip addressed his parents as Pa and Moe, Moe being an abbreviation of *moeder* that has been translated as Ma.

2. Gees Vrijlink was the eldest of six siblings. Following the death of their mother in 1937, she became the bedrock of the family.

Hardenberg, 30 Aug. '42 [Sunday]

Dear Pa and Ma,

On Friday I received your letter in the best of health and I hope it's the same for you. I also received the package with the jacket and the shoes. Now I am also sending a package back. The underwear is really dirty, Ma. But this is because it is so warm. It is possible to get my shoes repaired in the village, but then I have to wait such a long time for them.

Ap [Abraham] Waterman is now back in the camp. He thought it was better not to stay in Amsterdam. A pity, huh? that he had no time at all there.

Yes Ma, I believe you would give anything to speak and to see each other. But yes, we have to wait. Who knows how soon the war will be over and then we will all be together again forever.

Also for Simon things are going fairly well again. He is getting better.[1]

I had thought that Karel[2] might have come today. It is nice, isn't it, when you have a lot of visitors, then you always have good company.

I look very well. My back is dark brown so you can understand how I look.

I end again with a few big kisses and a handshake from

P.S. I enclosed a roll of film in my package. If Ma has the time, can she take it to be developed? But then you must also ask for a new roll of film. Can you also send me a few more flashlights and a few batteries? The batteries should be the same size as the enclosed ones.

Again, my warmest greetings, speedy *tot ziens*.

1. Simon and a friend doing gymnastics

2. Karel van der Schaaf's ID issued in 1941 when he lived at Oosterpark Street, no. 103 [III]

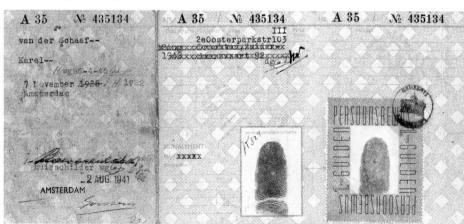

Hardenberg, 1 Sept. 1942 [Tuesday]

Dearest Parents

So, now I am again going to write a letter while I wait for yours. We have been warned again by the kapos, these are our jewish leaders, that it is absolutely forbidden to eat with farmers or get food from them. How far this will go we don't know yet. We will wait and see. The cook put in a request for more bread, but of course, it was refused; I could have predicted that.

This week I received a loaf of bread from de Bruin, but yesterday Rosette [Rosetta de Bruin] was here and told me you had sent the coupons. Now, that was great! Until now we have not been hungry. Pa, if you have anything to send to me, you can confidently send it to the Vr[ijlinks]?[1]

Someone just came in and said the German civilian(s) saw us collecting food so for the time being, that is finished. Only . . . no food, no work.

It is becoming more and more difficult for us; and it may become much worse, but don't worry, the porridge is never eaten as hot as it is served.[2] I'll get through.

Pa, I enclose a negative. Could you a have few prints of it made? About 5. You never know what they can be used for, maybe they could be traded for bread.

This week I got a whole loaf of bread from Klein[3] for 50 cents. Cheap, huh?
I stop again with a big kiss and see you very, very soon from

Flip.

Chin up and
keep your courage up.

daag

1. Members of the Vrijlink family, *left to right;* *back:* Gerridina, Gerrit, Sina, Gees *front:* Hermina and Seine

2. A Dutch idiom

3. It is likely that Flip was referring to Salomon Klein, born November 13, 1923.

4. This is the only letter with a number. Flip may have written the number on the envelopes of subsequent letters which Manus de Groot preserved but have since disappeared.

Letter No **1**[4]

Hardenberg, 2 Sept 1942 [Wednesday]

Dear Pa and Ma,

Today I came home from work because I did not feel well. So now I have 1½ days off, so will take a nice rest. You need that here. The food situation is still the same; we are not allowed to eat at the farmers at all and may not accept anything from them. For many that means it's hunger again. Simon and I take precautions and again get eggs, fruit, etc. every other day.

Tonight four of us went to collect the suitcase of foodstuff and the cans of vegetables and milk.

Tomorrow new people arrive again, ± 30 of them. Now, fortunately, we can't eat in the canteen anymore and will be eating again in the rooms. That is a great relief for us because eating in the canteen is really awful.

Pa you can safely send an extra letter now and then. It doesn't matter at all. But don't enclose coupons. If you want to send something, send to Vrijlink and I will get it from there. Have you heard anything yet from the Gallery or from the *Handelsblad*? They are making you wait a long time, but as long as you are still together it's fine and also very reassuring for me.

Hasn't the weather changed suddenly? Yesterday we sat in the shed for several hours again.

Now I am lying comfortably on my bed, writing and getting a good rest.

[Flip did not end this letter, and he started the following letter on the same page.]

Johan and Jan Kemink, two Vrijlink nephews, beside a haystack on the Vrijlink farm

3 Sept. 1942 [Thursday]

Today I am still off. This afternoon I am going to the village[1] to see if I can get a lens for my glasses. Only it's a pity I have to have a guard with me. Then I'm not nearly as free.

Pa, I don't know if you receive all my letters because I always give them to others. So now I am going to number my letters and then you can always write back and tell me which number you received. I also got your letter from Tuesday morning. Yes, we are gradually going into winter again. I think we will have to get through this winter, though I hope not. Because once again there will be many victims.

One pair of shoes is enough for here in the camp. I very often wear my slippers. Yes, my underwear is always very dirty, isn't it? But I still always get it back clean. Maybe Lou[2] is coming to the camp here. This afternoon I'll see.

I got all the vitamins and immediately locked them in a tin. Yes, the cook doesn't carry on as much as he did, but we still have to be extremely careful. Even the jewish kapos give us a hard time. The one is even more scared than the other. I am so glad that I am still free and don't have to worry about a family or anything like that. For those people it is much, much worse. How can their wives live on the few pennies they earn? Ma, I am allowed to receive fruit in my package. So see if you can get any. But don't take it out of your mouths. I am not short here because Siem and I get some regularly. Is the butter gone? Yes, you can't get it all the time. I now also manage on my ration.

Dear Pa and Ma, I stop now with a big kiss and a speedy *tot ziens*

from

I bought a watch for ƒ5 it is not in good condition, but if I have it fixed, I will have a good thing.

Stay strong! We made it through last winter. And we can do it again

1. Heemserveen is the village where the Vrijlinks lived at number 10, and the Veurinks at the adjacent farm. But the village where Flip went for a haircut and glasses was Hardenberg which is now a thriving town of 58,000 people with a fine Coat of Arms, *below*.

2. Louis Slier's photograph (above), was glued on the back of his street market trader's card, dated 1935, (*above*). It allowed him a stall on the Nieuwmarkt (New Market), which was midway between the Amstel Hotel and the Central Railway Station. It provided a valued source of employment. Louis was Flip's cousin, the son of Jonas Slier and Anna Plas-Slier. He married Elisabeth Aluin. They had one son Johnny (Jonas Philip, page 158).

Hardenberg 6 Sept '42 [Sunday]

Dear Parents

This morning, very much on the sly, Karel and I had been talking to each other for half an hour when the whistle blew for roll call, so I had to rush back. After that the cook arranged for guards to see to it that we would not be in contact with other people. He said that if it happens, he would phone "Erica!!" immediately and have the people involved arrested. Now I absolutely dare not take that risk. I did, however, receive the package with laundry because Karel left the packages with V[rijlinks]. It was nice and clean again, Ma. I also got the two and a half guilders.

Tonight K[arel] will probably tell you all about everything and I'll write a letter.

Hardenberg, 6 Sept. '42 [Sunday]

Dear Pa and Ma,

I could not talk to Karel alone again. It is one rotten mess here. Today a roommate of mine, [van Beets]⁴ whose parents live on Vrolik Street, got the news that his father, 71 years old, and his mother have been sent to Westerbork. He ~~brought~~ packed his suitcase and left an hour after he got the news. Right after, the cook got a phone call, and another boy got the same news. You can imagine the dismay. I couldn't even shake hands with Karel. The cook sympathizes with us, but he is unbelievably scared.

Pa and Ma, now something very important. Ma still has a photo of me. She <u>must</u> give it to Karel. If we also get in serious trouble soon, that may be my only salvation *!!!*

So do it. Don't think about if this or that may happen . . . In these times you must not hesitate! Then there is something else to which I would like an answer very soon. Have you considered the fact that you may have to leave today or tomorrow? What are your plans about that, Pa? What should I do if you have to leave. These are all very important things which I really should have known much sooner. Write about them to me quickly. You don't know a damned thing today what tomorrow will bring.

Have many people that we know from our street been taken away?

I received my package of laundry with the rolls of film and the batteries. I still have to collect the other.

I read your letter that Karel brought very quickly, and it is now also at the farmer.

Pa and Ma, you cannot imagine what nice people the Vrijlinks are. The day before yesterday they literally took care of everything for us. Butter for 60 cents per half pound, cookies, fruit and even more.

Tonight Mr. Duisend from the J.C. [the Jewish Council] is coming again. He will probably have something "nice" to tell us. I count on the worst. I will immediately write tonight to tell you what he said, so now I'll stop.

Oh, before I forget it! Pa, can you now get me a good pair of gloves? Probably I will soon need them.

This evening we had a drill. Fortunately Duisend did not come, so I worried about that for nothing. Dear Pa and Ma, I end again. Give Karel the passport photo.

<u>I have decided that if and when you are arrested, I will come to you immediatly!</u>

Give everyone my greetings, especially Grandma, Aunt Duif, and Bora.¹

Consider yourselves kissed and *tot ziens* in free Amsterdam.

Flip.

Ma, stay tough, and, Pa, you too must
keep well, you hear!

Daäág

Another big kiss from

Flip

1. Aunt Bora (Debora Slier, *above*), Flip's father's sister, worked as a seamstress for the Hollandia-Kattenburg clothing factory in Amsterdam, which made raincoats for the German army during the occupation. There were many Jews among the 740 employees, all of whom had deportation exemptions. Debora had worked at the factory since February 1935 and was an active member of the Garment Workers' Union. On October 17, 1942, the Germans arrested Sally Dormits, a Jewish leader of the *Nederlandse Volksmilitie*, a resistance group with communist sympathies. Sally committed suicide in his cell, to avoid betraying anyone, but the police searched his home and found a list of people who were then arrested. Under SS interrogation, one of them, Martha Korthagen, dreamed up a large group of saboteurs at the Hollandia factory. At 4:30 p.m. on Wednesday, November 11, 1942, Willy Lages directed the SS to raid the factory. The Jewish staff members were taken away to the Scheveningen penitentiary and photographed. Some of them were charged with distributing the illegal underground publication *De Waarheid,* or with planning to sabotage the production of raincoats by working slowly or deactivating the conveyor belt. In January 1943, a Nazi court in Utrecht tried five of the "saboteurs." Two were executed, and three were taken to Westerbork and from there deported to Auschwitz. Debora Slier was one of the three deported.*B*

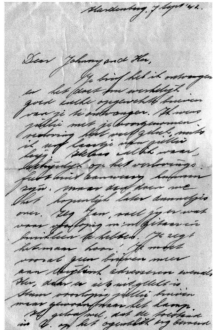

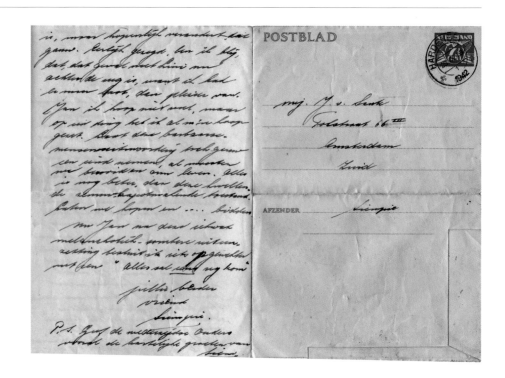

This letter dated Sept. 7 (*above and translated right*) was not sent. However, a similar letter (*opposite*) to the same friends was sent Sept. 9. On Sept. 28, Simon mailed the first letter. Why would he send two similar letters to the same people three weeks apart? It is likely that initially he held off "because something has leaked out here." Two days later, the leak was resolved ("You can send your letters to J. Vrijlink"), so he wrote the second letter. It is probable that Simon sent the Sept. 7 letter on Sept. 28 because Johnny and Her did not live together, and thus he sent one to each address.

Above: Simon Loonstijn and unknown inmate, in Molengoot camp

This letter is from Simon Loonstijn to Janny van Santen and Herman Weisberg in Amsterdam.

Hardenberg, 7 Sept '42 [Sunday]

Dear Johnny and Her[man],

I received your letter, and it really does me good to get such cheerful letters from you. I wish you both a great deal of happiness in your planned engagement, as long as I get a card from you. Alas, I probably will not be able to come to your engagement party, but I hope we can manage a small repeat [party] later. By the way, Jan, would you like to take care of my guitar, for now, as a loan? It's up to you, let me know. Above all, don't send any more letters addressed to Vrijlink; that goes for Her[man] too because something has leaked out there. For now, just send them to the camp. I can well believe that the situation is really bad in A[msterdam] at the moment, but hopefully things will soon change. Frankly, I'm happy that the business with Lini is behind us now because it gave me more trouble than pleasure. Jan, I don't hope for much, but there's one thing I've set all my hopes on. Let the barbaric slaughter of people come to a quick end, even if our lives have to be destitute and poor. Anything would be better than this nerve-wracking state of things. Let's hope and . . . pray.

So, Jan, after those somewhat melancholy, somber words, I'll close a little more cheerfully with an "everything will __again__ be fine."

Your friend, both of you,
Siempie
P.S. Give my very best wishes, especially, to your parents on both sides.

Siem. [Simon]

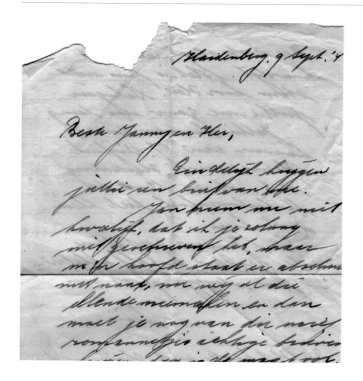

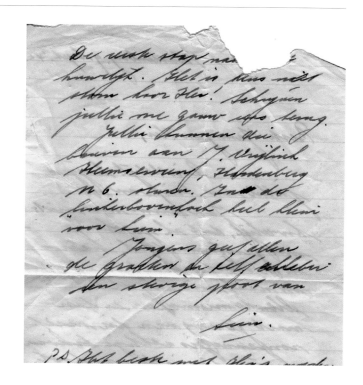

Hardenberg, 9 Sept. '42 [Wednesday]

Dear Janny and Her[man],

At last you receive a letter from me.

Jan, please forgive me for not writing to you in so long, but I really haven't been in the mood for it now we are going through all this misery, and then one is supposed to come up with these happy letters like naive novellas, then it's just too much.

Congratulations for your planned engagement.

The first step towards your wedding. And Her, no it isn't stupid!

Please write back soon.

You can send your letters to J. Vrijlink, Heemserveen, Hardenberg nr. 6. In the top left hand corner, very small, [write] "For Siem."

Guys, give our best wishes to everyone and a warm handshake to you both from

Siem.

P.S. All the best for Her's work.

Simon Loonstijn's letter from Molengoot to friends in Amsterdam. In this letter, Simon addresses Johnny as Janny. In the photograph below, she is the first on the left in the middle row.

Left to right, back row: Ben Prins; Wim Tak; name?; Piet name?; Mautje Vischjager; Charles name?; Simon Loonstijn. Middle row: Janny van Santen; name?; Betty name?; name? Front row: Tootje Loonstijn; Hanna Vischjager; Hilda name?

Mautje (Maurice) Vischjager, age 23, his sisters Hanna (17) and Alida (12), his father, David, and his mother, Maria Vischjager-Blits, all died in Sobibor on June 4, 1943.

1. Just 15 miles north of Molengoot, between Hoogeveen and Emmen, is the village of Nieuwlande, where during the war everyone was trustworthy and where almost every family was inspired by the Reverend Frits Slomp to hide Jews. Almost everyone took in at least one *onderduiker.* In all, 300 were hidden.

Johannes Post (*below*), municipal politician and farmer, led the way, along with his brother Marinus, Arnold Douwes, and Max Nico Leons. Post was a brilliant resistance leader who was elected head of the resistance combat units. He was betrayed and executed on May 15, 1944.

Virtually every Nieuwlande villager received a Yad Vashem medal, and in 1985, the village itself was awarded the medal for being a community that in its entirety welcomed strangers into their homes.

Johannes Post

Hardenberg, 9 Sept '42 [Wednesday]

Dear Parents,

When I got to the Vrijlinks this morning, my letter was already lying on the table. Because I had been worried, I was doubly pleased. I will begin by answering the letter. Pa, it seems best to me that you prepare everything for your departure and have it ready. Don't forget vitamins and first aid material also.

I also don't know what is best, Pa. Maybe it would not be a bad idea for you to go to the Gallery yourself. Try to request our camp. There is space! Even in our room!

I would not advise going into hiding[1] unless you can absolutely trust the people. But in any case, if you have to leave, I am coming too! If it should be the other way around, I will beat it.

I would like you to send my black shoes, Pa. They are solid walking shoes that ~~every~~ can take a beating.

Do you think it is a good idea for me to have my winter clothes sent here, or shall I wait a little while? Then if you are taken away, let's hope not!! I would at least have everything I need here.

Pa, the reason that Karel took the letter with him was because I had to leave in a great hurry for roll call.

Pa, I advise you to buy anything you think you might need. Money has no value to us any more. Buy yourself a pair of good work shoes and work clothing.

Ma, see if you can get me a few or at least one pair of warm overalls. I would also like a warm wool scarf and a pair of <u>good</u> <u>fur</u> <u>gloves.</u> Don't worry about the cost! I'll stop with this part of the letter, and now I am going to write about something else.

In spite of everything we still eat well every afternoon. They [the Vrijlinks] are really lovely to us. For example, this afternoon they again gave us tomatoes and so we nearly always have something. I haven't yet been hungry. Against all odds, I have grown taller and stronger here.

The boss has also helped us and put us right near the area of V[rijlinks]! Nice, huh? Tomorrow I will probably go to the village for arch supports; I have ordered them.

Since I still have a few things to write to the boys and girls, I end this with the hope that we will all be together again soon and everything will shortly be behind us.

A big kiss and greetings by

your

Get everything ready, you hear*!*
and keep your courage up*!*

The graves of the Post brothers

Postcard of the Nieuwlande Dutch Reformed Church and school

Hardenberg, 10 Sept 1942 [Thursday]

Dear Parents,

First, I want to begin by wishing you strength and energy for the coming difficult time in the New Year [the Jewish new year], and have it behind you and to live in health and freedom. Let us hope it will be soon!

Pa and Ma, today I heard the following: when parents are sent to Westerbork and the son or daughter chooses to go willingly with them, they are <u>still</u> separated and the boys and girls are sent away separately. I can trust this news item. It comes indirectly from the J.C. [Jewish Council].[1]

Dear Pa and Ma, if this is really true, and it seems so to me, of course there's no use in me coming to you in Westerbork to be separated <u>over there</u>. Write back to me about this in great detail, Pa! You must understand that if we could be together, I would not hesitate for one moment. On the contrary it would do me good (and also the other way round) to be able to support you. On the other hand, I don't know how long (short) I may still stay here in the camp, but I can always take care of myself !! Until the end of the war! Dear parents, I end this letter expressing hope that soon, very soon, we can be together in freedom and health and [I] end with warmest greetings and a big kiss from

Be strong
and *tot ziens !*

```
JOODSCHE RAAD VOOR AMSTERDAM
Nieuwe Keizersgracht 58          Amsterdam, 8 April 1943
A M S T E R D A M/C

I Voorz.
C/dL/vdL/HE                      Aan de Medewerkers van den Joodschen Raad
                                 voor Amsterdam.

Mijne Heeren,

        Nu U Uw woonplaats gaat verlaten,,en daardoor ook Uw
functie als vertegenwoordiger van den Joodschen Raad moet opgeven,
voelen wij het als een plicht U van ganscher harte dank te zeggen
voor al wat U in deze functie hebt volbracht.

        Wij weten, dat Uw werk niet alleen met groote toewij-
ding is geschied, maar dat U zich ook vele belangrijke opofferingen
daarvoor heeft getroost,-

        Wij wenschen U van ganscher harte het beste in Uw nieu-
```

JEWISH COUNCIL FOR AMSTERDAM
Nieuwe Keizersgracht 58   Amsterdam, April 8, 1943
AMSTERDAM/C

I Voorz
C/dL/vdL/HE   To: Staff members of the Jewish Council
of Amsterdam

Dear Sirs,

Now that you will be leaving your place of residence, and therefore will also be obliged to give up your position as representative of the Jewish Council, we feel that it is our duty to convey our heartfelt gratitude for all that you have accomplished while holding that position.

We are aware, not only that you have carried out your work with great dedication, but also that it has demanded great sacrifices on your part.

Please accept our sincere best wishes for the future in your new place of residence. We wish to assure you that your efforts will not be forgotten.

1191   We remain yours faithfully
Jewish Council for Amsterdam
A. Asscher   Prof. Dr. D. Cohen
Chairmen

1. It is strange that Flip should have trusted news because "It comes indirectly from the Jewish Council." Mechanicus wrote that at Westerbork, the Council was not well regarded and when the directors, Asscher and Cohen arrived, people expressed hostility towards them to which they seemed somewhat oblivious. They were also oblivious of German intentions. For a year or so after May 10, 1941, Asscher said the German's evil intent was not at all clear. By April 1943, Asscher and Cohen's letter (*below left*) offered employees, "our sincere best wishes for the future in your new place of residence." Cohen said that when running the Jewish Council, they never knew that the 100,000 people under their care had been killed.

Cohen and Asscher might have seen through German deception had they kept in mind the history of Asscher's diamond company. The world's largest diamond, weighing 1.3 lb, was found in South Africa in 1905. It was sent to Asscher's company in Amsterdam via London. A stone was shipped from Cape Town to London, accompanied by guards and photographers. The real diamond, however, was mailed anonymously to London at the same time, by parcel post, for three shillings without insurance.

After the war, most people judged Asscher and Cohen harshly. However in some situations they behaved courageously. Cohen refused an offer of a visa to Switzerland and Asscher once hit a German soldier. He told Lages (head of the German security police) that Hitler was an arch-criminal, and when Goering visited his diamond factory, he refused to let him sign the distinguished visitors book. In 1946, Asscher and Cohen were tried by a Jewish court and found guilty on five counts, five aspects of their collaboration with the Germans. Asscher responded by distancing himself from Judaism, Cohen by writing his memoirs explaining that he would never have assisted the Germans had he had any inkling of what deportation meant. When Jo Spier went to visit Cohen on Cornelis Schuyt street in Amsterdam in 1967, six months before he died, Cohen greeted him: "Have you come to look up the little mass murderer?"

Left: A card from Asscher and Cohen to the Jewish Council workers with sincere best wishes for the future in "your new place of residence."

Philip Bromet and his son Alfred, and other members of Hardenberg's Jewish community

Dear Pa and Ma,

Last evening I got your letter from Thursday, again in the best of health.

I read that Pa has already prepared several things, but that Ma does not feel like doing so. Well, that's stupid. You must get everything ready, you know they can come and get you any time. Ma, if you still have anything <u>valuable</u> that you must get rid of, send them to me. I know what to do with it. Also, I would like my winter clothes sent here. Ear muffs, warm woolen clothes etc. etc. Especially gloves. The mother of a boy in my room has been taken away. His father is in Apeldoorn. He wanted to go immediately to Westerbork and went to the cook-boss. But he told him that he should not make difficulties for himself because he had heard from the cook at Westerbork that he ~~wanted~~ would absolutely not be able to be with his mother. It is so difficult, Pa and Ma, to make a decision. If I knew for sure that I could at least be with one of you, I would not hesitate, but now . . . ?

Well, I will hear about that from you later.

Yes, Pa and Ma, there is a chance I will come on leave, but if that happens I will hear. I am not letting myself be happy over a dead sparrow. [This Dutch idiom is the equivalent of: Don't count your chickens before they are hatched.]*A*

Ma, I don't know if that brown coat still fits me. Send it in any case. I would also like you to tell Dick about everything as far as clothes are concerned etc. etc. You never know how it might be useful. Dear parents, I end this letter again with a big kiss and a speedy *tot ziens*,

Stay strong*!!!*

Write everything to me as usual

Marcus Bromet (*above*) was the brother of Philip Bromet, whose arrest is described in the Hardenberg police records (*right*). They were distant relatives of Flip's mother. Philip Bromet had an uncle Philip (*above top*) and two more brothers called Philip, who died in infancy. After his attempted suicide, and capture, Philip (57) was sent to Sobibor on April 27, on the same transport as David André Slier. Philip's three brothers, Marcus (68), Asser (70), and Meijer (79) were sent to Sobibor on May 11, 1943.

Below: A Report from the Hardenberg police records from 1943.*B*

April 8, 1943 [Thursday]

"After the departure of the jewish family Bromet, living at Hardenberg, there was a rumor that there was still a member of the family in their home. We, Gerrit Jan van der Berg and Arie Johannes of Prince Court, policemen of the Royal Police at Hardenberg, by order of our group commander, searched the house of the jew Bromet, which had been entirely emptied and had been sealed. In a wall cupboard that had been fastened from the inside we found Philip Bromet, a Dutchman, was living at Hardenberg, Station Street no. B/83, born there on February 14, 1884. When Bromet was discovered, he took the opportunity to cut his wrists with a razor but he was not successful. Bleeding heavily, Bromet was brought to the hospital at Hardenberg. There his wounds were not stitched but were bandaged to stop the bleeding and by order of the SS in Enschede, he was sent to Zwolle and locked up. It is likely that Bromet will attempt suicide again."

Hardenberg, 13 Sept 1942 [Sunday]

Dear Pa and Ma,

There is shul [synagogue] service, but I did not feel like going and I started to write. Yesterday I did go, but it seemed such nonsense to me to look for strength that way, so today I did not go. What good does it do? Lately I see more clearly than ever that this situation has nothing to do with religion.[1] I cannot help it, but that is how I feel. What is a person? What is all of life? Nothing. And still we don't want to lose it, and that is why we have to be strong and have faith. Someday we will be liberated !!! I am sure of that.

Pa, will you send me several things? e.g. among others, my winter clothes, as I have already written several times, also my fountain pen, and if there is anything else of value, you can send those also or have them brought here. But in the first place take care of yourselves. I would also like some soap and a small piece of shaving soap. Will you get me some gloves soon? Preferably fur. It is already quite cold here in the morning, while the afternoons are still very warm. I have not had any news from you.

Pa, again, send me a short letter every day; then I don't have to worry each time. Just send them as usual to the camp, and if there is something special, you can send it to the Vrijlinks. They take very good care of us, and if anything should happen, then I am sure I can count on them!

Dear Parents, it is once again a short letter, but now I will again write every day.

My best greetings and a
very big kiss from Flip

daaaaag!!

The Hardenberg synagogue (*post war photo, below*) was built in 1903, and razed in 1980. A better photo and an elevation of the synagogue can be found in Roel Gritter, 2005, which gives a first-rate glimpse of Hardenberg's erstwhile Jewish community.[A]

1. Flip was correct. Hitler's hatred of Jews was racial not religious. He hated secular Jews no less than religious Jews; the reverse of his opposition to Christians. Hosenfeld wrote that National Socialism forbids people to practice their religion.[B] Hitler did not mind Christians provided they did not practice Christianity. Bormann, Hitler's secretary, said that "National Socialism and Christianity are irreconcilable."[C] In 1938 Pastor Martin Niemöller told his Lutheran Church on the outskirts of Berlin, "We must obey God rather than man." That cost him seven years in Sachsenhausen and Dachau concentration camps.[D] Jehovah's Witnesses fell foul of the National Socialists because they placed their primary allegiance in God and they opposed war and moreover, they disdained the Nazi salute, but they were pardoned if they renounced their religion.

". . . The task of the priest is to keep the Poles quiet, stupid, and dull-witted."[E] —*Hitler*

The Nazis began replacing all Christian religions with the National Reich Church that held 30 Articles of Faith, for example:

Article 5: The National Reich Church is determined to exterminate irrevocably . . . the Christian faiths imported into Germany in the ill-omened year 800.

Article 7: The National Church has no scribes, pastors, chaplains or priests, but National Reich orators are to speak in them.

Article 13: The National Church demands the immediate cessation of the printing, publishing as well as the dissemination of the Bible . . .

Article 14: The National Church decrees that the most important document of all time is our Führer's *Mein Kampf*. This book embodies the purest and truest ethics.

Article 18: The National Church will remove from the altars of all churches the Bible, all crucifixes and religious objects.

Article 19: In their place will be set our most saintly book, *Mein Kampf*; and to the left of the altar, a sword.

Article 30: The Christian Cross shall be removed from all churches, cathedrals and chapels inside the Reich and will be replaced by the swastika.[F]

Heemserveen 13 September 1942

Dear Loonstijn Family,

We received your letter yesterday (Saturday). Siem was very happy about it since he was a little worried because he had not heard from you for a few days.

And now I want to thank you for the splendid brooch that you sent me. I am truly very grateful for it, although it was really not necessary! We absolutely cannot stand by and see someone else go hungry. As long as it is at all possible for us, we will help the boys to go on.

We have heard that things are bad in Amsterdam, so you all have enough problems to worry about. You must therefore no longer worry about Siem because I promise you that as long as Siem is here, we will take good care of him. We will do as much as we can for him. If everything continues this way, he will be fine, and he is looking very well too. They often come to us in the evening and then we have a very nice time sitting around talking, playing games, etc.

We'll just have to hope that we will see each other again and also hope for better times. Thank you again so very much for the brooch, which will always remind me of all of you.

Very best wishes to all of you from Gees and the rest of the family.

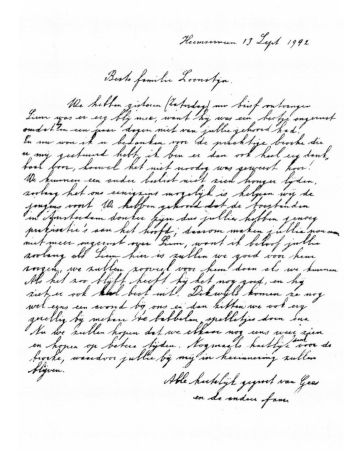

From left to right: Vrijlinks, Seine, Gerridina, Sina, Johanna and Gees; and Simon Loonstijn.

Gees Vrijlink (*below*) wrote the letter (*above*) to Mrs. Loonstijn, Simon's mother. Gees died May 26, 1987 at the age of 72.

Hardenberg, 14 Sept '42 [Monday]

Dear Parents,

This evening I received your Saturday morning letter. I am glad that now I know what you also think about it. Yes, it is terrible if it happens sometime, but we do have to face it. I will then be all on my own, with nobody who cares about me except for my friends. Don't think it is cowardly of me if I don't go with you. I have thought it all ~~over~~ through thoroughly and then asked the cook for information. He strongly discouraged all of us, said there is no way we would be together.

Send several of my things of any value here, Pa.[1] Also I would like to know where and with whom you have our stuff. You do understand me well, Pa! So that in case it might become necessary I can take possession of it. Yes, how much I would like to see you again, but there is a small chance we will get leave. By now we have earned some right to that, huh? Well, wait and see, maybe luck is with us.

Today I got work in another place. I now have to walk almost an hour in the morning and then cut sods of turf. Dirty rotten work. It is getting to me more and more, and I am very indifferent to it. I am now terribly tired, and have absolutely no idea why. I think for once, tomorrow I will go to the doctor.

Door Vr. worden we nog steeds met alles geholpen. Ze is gewoon een moeder voor ons zo aardig en lief. We kunnen Gees nooit dankbaar genoeg zijn, terwijl haar vader en zusters ons ook zo graag mogen.

The Vr[ijlinks] still help us with everything. She is really like a mother to us, so kind and loving. We can never be grateful enough to Gees. Her father and sisters also like us a lot.

Tonight I will go to them again to eat something or collect something good. I don't know much more now and end this letter with a big kiss and wishes
for strength from

Be strong and in any case get everything ready,

Dáááááy !!!!

Many kisses and a strong embrace.

Tot ziens.

THIS IS FLIP'S LAST LETTER

1. Aside from the very long farewell "byeeeeee," the tone and the content of this letter suggests that Flip was expecting to be around for a while: "Send my things here and tomorrow I will see the doctor." Clearly something unexpected happened that evening at dinner with the Vrijlinks. Maybe he was warned by one of the 13 friends or relatives who had been transported in the past two weeks. Perhaps the Vrijlinks heard that all the camps were to be emptied, or perhaps he felt free to leave as they gave him a letter that contained the false ID that he had been expecting. A week before, Flip had asked his parents to give Karel his passport photo so that he could get a false ID. He wanted one like Bep Wijler's (*below, top*), that had a new name, and no "j". It enabled Bep Wijler to survive the war. She married Jozef Vomberg.

FLIP'S ESCAPE

Flip's September 14 letter was his last before he escaped. At least 20 members of Flip's family or people he knew died in Auschwitz during September 1942, including Bep's brother and Ru de Bruin's brother. It is possible that he had heard about the fate of one or two, either from his parents or from the Vrijlinks. He had no illusions as to what transport to the east might mean.

Flip returned safely to Amsterdam where he was offered a hiding place by Karel van der Schaaf's brother, Jo, who lived on the corner of Derde Oosterpark Street that was only two streets north of Vrolik Street. Truus Tokkie Sant who lived on the same street, saw him from time to time and she recalls that he looked pretty much as usual. He was near enough to see his parents comfortably and Karel remembers going with Flip, who had dyed hair and false papers, to visit their friends Hella[1] (Seliena) and Stella[4] (Esther) Aluin, on Derde Oosterpark Street, Amsterdam. While they were there, the Germans arrived. The Germans ordered Flip and Karel to leave. Karel thinks that the Aluins were then arrested, since they were not seen again. Stella, Hella, their sister Hendrika[1], their mother Roosje, and their father Abraham, all died in Auschwitz.

It is not known why Flip moved his hiding place from Oosterpark Street to Professor Tulp Street just behind the Amstel hotel, but it was usual for onderduikers to move frequently and Professor Tulp Street was only about half a mile away. His Uncle Bram Samas and Aunt Johanna, lived on the same street, and perhaps they had found him a job washing dishes in the basement of a restaurant, although it was a dangerous area because the Amstel Hotel[2] was the Gestapo's preferred watering hole. Karel visited Flip there once but was not able to do more than wave to him through the basement window of the restaurant[3] (the hotel is the building on the left). In May 1943, Karel and Dick were themselves summoned for work in Germany. They ignored the summons and went into hiding on the Baron farm in Drachten in Friesland.

1. *From left to right*: Appie Reis, Bep de Vries, Hella Aluin, Dick van der Schaaf, Henny (Hendrika) Aluin, and Maupie (Maurits) Vogel

2. A pre-war photograph of the Amstel Hotel

3. Karel believes that these basement windows on Professor Tulp Street is where he last saw Flip.

4. *Back, left to right*: Stella Aluin, Liel (Lily) van der Berg, Big Bep de Vries, Little Bep de Vries. *Front*: Lena (Lea) van Bienen

This photo of a German raid on De Lairessestraat was taken in 1944. It was how the streets looked to Flip when he was in hiding.

Ab van der Linden, who escaped from Westerbork, later gave Roel Gritter the following account of the day the men were sent from the work camps to Westerbork:

In October 1942, I think it was the 14th [sic], the SS came to get us at Molengoot. Under guard by these SSers, we walked to the station in Hardenberg in order to be transported by train to Zwolle. I remember that residents of Hardenberg watched us go and wished us courage . . . or looked the other way and acted like they did not see anything. There were also people who made a sign silently. The people of Hardenberg did not give me the impression of enmity or of friendship. It was really fear that held everyone in its grip.

Westerbork was the portal to the gas chambers. It was there also that I saw my wife being brought in one day. We were both able to escape as a result of a ruse and simple good luck. We were helped by a German tailor who had to make clothing for the camp managers. He was a Jew as well. Back in Amsterdam after a lot of wandering around, we remained underground until the liberation. We got our little daughter back who had been cared for lovingly by a sister-in-law all those years. I also found my brother again, the only family member who had survived. My wife and I finally calculated that, between the two of us, we had lost 170 family members.[A]

THE DIARY OF A BAGGAGE HANDLER

On October 2 and 3, all the men in the Dutch work camps were transported to Westerbork. At the same time their wives and children were rounded up and also sent there.

October 3: I shall always remember this day . . . As women and children were crammed into the barracks, all hell broke loose. No one could find anything or anybody; men, women, children, and rucksacks were all one inextricable confusion . . . None of them had had anything to eat. People stood about outside and asked, "Has my husband got here yet?" "Where are the women from Amsterdam?". . . The whole situation was quite hopeless. No one could be found. Absolutely hopeless. We went on with the farce of sorting out the baggage, but in fact, anyone could just pick up anything he fancied; there were not nearly enough of us to keep an eye on the things.

October 4: Today it was even worse than last night . . . Altogether some 13,000 new arrivals, on top of the 2,000 already in the camp. Lorries and trains poured in from all directions and spat out their human cargoes—what the SS would call a splendid operation. Yet for us it was nothing but confusion . . . the people felt completely helpless and deserted . . . many deportees—we do not know precisely how many, but I think at least half—will have to leave without their luggage. Not only men and women, remember, but babies in need of clean diapers.

12October 5: A day of real horror. I can't imagine a worse one . . . this very morning, some 200 to 300 women had come with their children to join their husbands. Their luggage had been left in Hooghalen and was expected later. The women were waiting in a side-lane near the camp entrance, guarded by gendarmes. When Dischner, the German Camp Commandant, heard that the trains were not full—that is, the standing room was not crammed to capacity—he gave orders for all the women to be registered and then hustled off to the station. The unsuspecting victims, waiting anxiously to be reunited with their husbands, gladly gave their names. But when, instead of being let into the camp, they were shepherded to the station, the awful truth began to dawn upon them. They all began to scream and some offered resistance. Dischner hurried to the scene and made liberal use of his riding whip. Some of the gendarmes, too, kicked and pushed the women. A few succeeded in escaping into the camp; the others, particularly those with children, were shoved remorselessly into the train. The whole thing was horrible enough to behold, but worse still were the frightened screams of the bruised women and children, whose only wish was to catch just one more glimpse of the husbands and fathers from whom they had been separated for so many months. There were women from every rank of society and of all ages, though most were working-class wives between 20 and 40. Some were warmly dressed for the journey; others, who had clearly not been given enough time by the police, were in the filthiest of dresses and slippers . . . Their screams attracted a gang of men, who were busy road-building near by, and some of whom suddenly recognized their wives. They raced to the spot, broke through the police cordon and, unable to bring their wives back to the camp, tried to board the train themselves. To make room for them, some of the luggage had to be thrown out. When the train left, the whole platform was strewn with suitcases, backpacks, baby carriages, and other articles . . . In the afternoon, I had to sort out the women's luggage, with the aid of a list. Men, anxious to discover whether their wives were among the deportees, crowded around me. Some gave horrible groans when they saw their wives' and children's rucksacks in the heap and thus realized that their families were on the way to Poland . . . Some decided to volunteer for the next transport; other begged me to send the luggage on the next train . . . I stood there in the darkness and rain, guarding their pitiful belongings . . . countless rain-soaked parcels . . . that had been lovingly packed and still bore such messages as: "To father, with love" or "Bon appetit, my darling."[B]

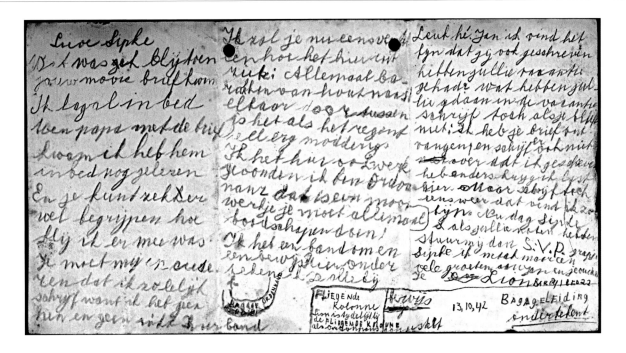

Dear Sipke,

I was so glad when your beautiful letter came. I was in bed when father came with the letter and I read it while still in bed. You can imagine how glad I was with it. You have to excuse the fact that my writing is so sloppy because I do not have pen and ink here. I will now tell you what it looks like here. There are lots of wooden barracks, all attached to each other.

In between them it is very muddy when it rains. I have found a job here, too. I am an orderly; it is a good job, you have to run lots of errands. I wear an armband and I have a card. I will draw it all below. Isn't it nice? Jan, I am happy that you have written as well. Did you all have a vacation? What did you do during the

vacation? Please do not write "I did not receive your letter" and do not mention that I have written, or I will be in trouble here. But please write again; it means so much to me. Bye now, Sipke. If you all have nuts, please send some. I am going to end now. Many greetings to Jan and Sjoukje

Lion Bar 89185022

LUGGAGE ORDNANCE
armband

FLYing
Column
Lion is temporarily
in the THE FLYING
COLUMN as as an orderly.

Identification
LUGGAGE MANAGER
13, 10, 42   signed [by]

This letter (*above*) was written by Friedrich Salomonson's son Lion, age 12, from Westerbork camp on October 13, 1942, to his friend Sipke. The photograph shows Lion (*right*) with Sipke and Jan Sipkema.

CAMP VUGHT

Vught was a concentration camp that held 18,000 people. It was near 's-Hertogenbosch, 50 miles south of Amsterdam. The camp was established in January 1943, primarily for Jews, but also for political and resistance prisoners. It was run by the SS and controlled from Berlin. The first commandant, Karl Chmielewski, had been commander of Gusen, a sub-camp of Mauthausen. There were strict instructions from Berlin to refrain from mistreating the prisoners. Selma Wijnberg from Zwolle had been in hiding but was betrayed and imprisoned in Amsterdam, and then from January until March 31, 1943, in Vught. She observed that men were starved and treated more harshly than women.[B] R. P. Cleveringa reported, "The Jews were driven like cattle and had to stand for hours wearing hardly any clothing. Many of them were sick and infirm. I saw some of them pull up tufts of grass, only to have it snatched out of their hands. They were treated like dirt."[C] Philip Mechanicus described the state of the S-prisoners, like Flip, on arrival at Westerbork from Vught: "In the night, 316 Jews arrived from Vught . . . Not a single one of them had a winter coat—they had been taken away from them. Several of them had literally no underclothing, no shirt, no trousers, no socks. 120 S-detainees from the concentration camp. The people were starving."[D]

Vught had a gallows and crematorium. Several hundred people were murdered there, including over 300 members of the resistance who were executed in the woods close to the camp. The prisoners were poorly fed and often starved, and some were tortured. Most prisoners worked inside the camp. The Philips Electronics company of Eindhoven, ten miles south of Vught, employed 1,200 prisoners.[E] The company insisted that all its workers have a hot meal every day, and be exempt from deportation. But like all exemptions, they eventually proved to be worthless, and the Jews were deported to Poland. Vught's 3,017 children were treated no better than the adults. They were forced to drill, sometimes standing at attention for almost two hours, and in June 1943, children, babies, toddlers and teens, the sick and the healthy, were loaded into cattle trucks and sent to "work" at Sobibor. In September 1944, as the Allies approached, Vught was evacuated; the women were sent to Ravensbrück, and the men to Sachsenhausen.

After the war, Chmielewski was tried in Germany and sentenced to life imprisonment for crimes against prisoners, in particular for killing prisoners by freezing them to death.

FLIP IS ARRESTED

Karel van der Schaaf recalls that shortly before he himself went into hiding, sometime around February 1943, Flip's parents asked Karel to go to an address in Bussum or Hilversum, he cannot remember which, to contact someone who had undertaken to arrange Flip's escape to Switzerland. Karel went to the given address but formed the impression that the person that he was supposed to meet did not want to meet him, leaving Karel with the impression that he or she was untrustworthy.

On March 3, 1943, Flip was arrested at Amsterdam Central Station and taken to Vught concentration camp, where most men were treated very harshly. "Things surely can't be as bad in Poland as they are at Vught. It's hell, sheer hell!"[A] The file card (*below*), gives the reason for his arrest as "*Ohne Stern*" [without a star]. The answer to question 7a (next page) suggests that he did not go quietly. On March 31, 1943, Flip was sent from Vught to S-Hut 67, the punishment barrack at Westerbork.

A	B	C	D	E	F	G	H	I	J	K	L	M	N	O	P	Q	R		T	U	V	W	X	Y	Z

Name	First name	Religion	Number	Block		Source:
Slier	Philip	J.	5540	2	⬛	AZC
Address	**Birthplace**	Day	Month	Year		
Amsterdam Vrolik Street 128III		4	Dec	1923		AZC
Notes		Day	Month	Year		
Arrival Date typographer Criminal Offense: No Star		3	March	1943		AZC JDL 00057 31(=924)

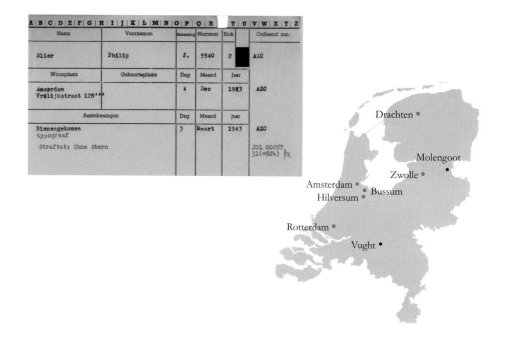

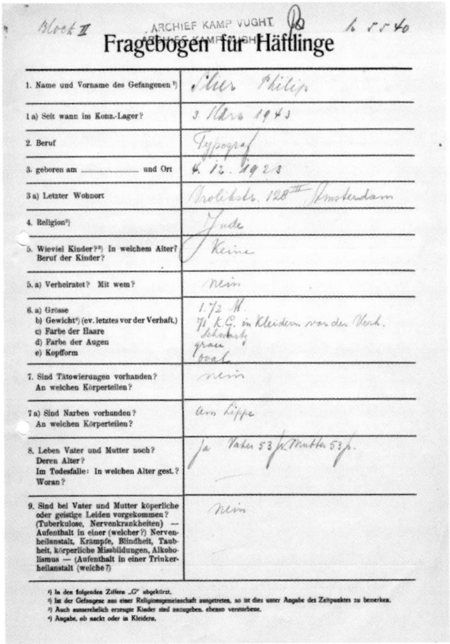

Fragebogen für Häftlinge

(German original form with handwritten entries)

Questionnaire for Prisoners

1. Name and first name of prisoner?	Slier Philip
1a). Since when in Concentr camp?	3 Mar 1943
2. Occupation	typographer
3. Birth date	3 Mar 1923
3a). Home address	Vrolik Street 128III Amsterdam
4. Religion	Jew
5. How many children? Occupation of children?	None
5a) Married? To whom?	No
6. a) Height b) Weight (e.g. before arrest) c) Color of hair d) Color of eyes e) Shape of head	5ft 7¾ in. 156 lbs. clothed dark brown gray oval
7. Are there any tattoos? Which part of the body?	No
7a) Are there any scars? Which part of the body?	On lip
8. Are father and mother alive? Their ages? If dead: at what age? Cause of death?	Yes Father 53 Mother 51
9. Did father or mother have physical or mental disease? (tuberculosis, nervous illness) Admission (which) mental hospital? convulsions, blind, deaf, deformity, alcoholism- addiction clinic (Which?)	No

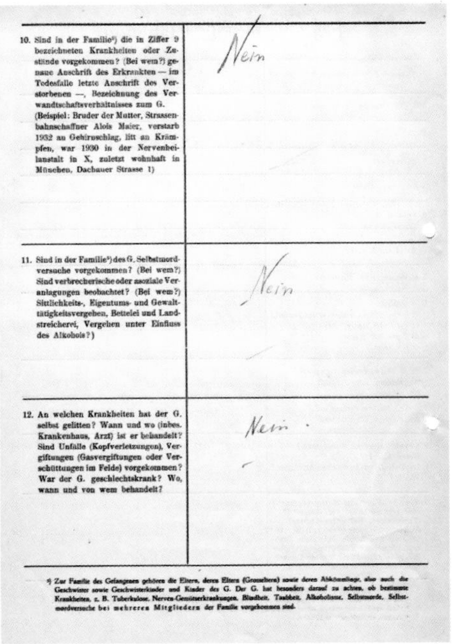

1) Note "p" is abbreviation for prisoner
2) When the prisoner has a religious community, it should be noted and time given.
3) Also illegitimate and deceased children should be noted.
4) State whether naked or dressed

10. Did any of the disorders mentioned under 9 occur in the family? 5 (Who was affected?) Supply exact address of the affected — in case of death give last address of the deceased Detail the relationship to P. (For example: Brother of the mother, a street car conductor, Alois Maier, died in 1932 from a stroke, suffered from cramps, was hospitalized in 1930 in a mental institution in X, last address in Munich, Dachauer Street, 1.)	No
11. Where there any suicide attempts in the family of P. (Who). Did anyone note any types of criminal or antisocial behavior? Did any of the disorders mentioned in 9 occur in the family? also sexual misconduct, stealing or abuse, begging, vagrancy, sexual aberrations, abuse under the influence of alcohol?	No
12. What diseases does the P. suffer from? When and where (especially hospital stays, or treatment by physicians)? Did the P. suffer a head injury, gas poisoning, or other trauma during the war. Did the P. suffer from STD? Where, when and who delivered the care.	No

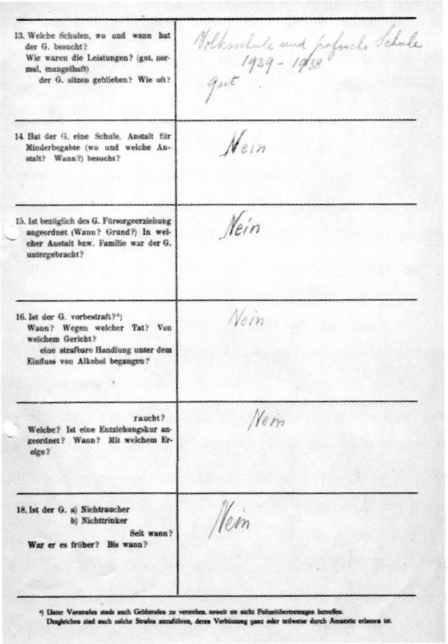

Family members of the prisoner are the parents and their parents (grandparents) and descendants, siblings and their siblings, also children of the prisoner. The prisoner needs to write very accurately name illnesses of family members, e.g. tuberculosis nervous illnesses, blindness, deafness, alcoholism, suicide, attempted suicide.

13. Which schools, where, and when did P. attend? What were the grades? (good, normal unsatisfactory) Did P. repeat classes, how often.	elementary and technical school 1929-1938 Good
14 Has P. attended a school or institution for the retarded (Where and which school, institution? When?)	No
15. Is it indicated that P. received special education? (When, reason,) In which institution or family?	No
16. Does P. have a police record?[1] When? What was the offense? From which court? Did he commit offenses under the influence of alcohol?	No
17. Smoked? What? Was rehabilitation indicated? When? What were the results?	No
18. Is the P. a) non smoker b) A teetotaler Since when? Did he abstain previously? Until when?	No

1. This includes previous convictions and also fines as far as they do not concern police violations. In the same way such punishments are to be stated, whether completed or amnestied or otherwise.

TRANSPORTS LEAVE WESTERBORK

Cato Slier

1. Philip Mechanicus was born in Amsterdam on April 17, 1889. He travelled to the Dutch East Indies, where he worked as a reporter and an newspaper editor. On return to Amsterdam, he wrote several books, edited for *Algemeen Handelsblad* and when the Germans banned Jews from newspapers, he worked on under a pseudonym. When seen on a tram without a star, he was reported, arrested, imprisoned in Amstelveenseweg and sent to Amersfoort camp, where he was tortured and beaten so badly that at Westerbork he was in hospital for nine months from November 7, 1942. Even though he was well liked, and well respected, he was deported to Bergen-Belsen on March 8, 1944, and transferred to Auschwitz on October 9, where he was shot on October 12, 1944.

On Wednesday, March 31, after three weeks in Vught, Flip was sent to Barrack 67, the punishment hut at Westerbork. Two young women were in Vught with Flip, on the same train to Westerbork and they were on the same train to Sobibor. The women were Selma Wijnberg, and Ursula Stern. On Tuesday, April 6, all of them were loaded into cattle trucks, along with Joseph and Cato Slier, Flip's uncle and aunt, their children Henri and Elisabeth Anna, and AJC friends Bora and Samuel Prijs. There were 364 S-prisoners out of a total of 2,020. Selma remembers all her Vught friends being loaded with her into the same wagon. They arrived at Sobibor on April 9, 1943.

On May 24, 1943, Flip's parents were arrested and sent to Westerbork to Barrack 63—not a punishment barrack—indicating that they had not been in hiding. On Tuesday June 1, they, their sister-in-law Anna Plas-Slier, Chelly Borzykowski-Schelvis, her family and her husband, Jules Schelvis, and 3,000 others were loaded into cattle trucks. The loading of this very transport was witnessed and recorded by Philip Mechanicus[1] in his diary.

"**Tuesday June 1.** The transports are as loathsome as ever. The wagons used were originally intended for carrying horses. The deportees no longer lie on straw, but on the bare floor in the midst of their food supplies and small baggage, and this applies even to the invalids who only last week got a mattress. They are assembled at the hut exits at about seven o'clock by OD men, the Camp Security Police, and are taken to the train in lines of three, to the Boulevard des Miseres in the middle of the camp. The train is like a long mangy snake, dividing the camp in two and made up of filthy old wagons. The Boulevard is a desolate spot, barred by OD men to keep away interested members of the public. The exiles have a bag of bread which is tied to their shoulder with a tape and dangles over their hips, and a rolled up blanket fastened to the other shoulder with string and hanging down their backs. Shabby emigrants who own nothing more than what they have on and what is hanging from them. Quiet men with tense faces and women bursting into frequent sobs. Elderly folk, hobbling along, stumbling over the poor road surface under their load and sometimes going through pools of muddy water. Invalids on stretchers carried by OD men. On the platform the Commandant with his retinue, the 'Green Police,' Dr. Spanier, the Medical Superintendent, in a plain grey civilian suit, bareheaded and very dark, with his retinue, Kurt Schlesinger, the head of the Registration Department, in riding breeches and jackboots, a nasty face and straw-colored hair with a flat cap on it. Alongside the train doctors holding themselves in readiness in case the invalids need assistance. The deportees approaching the train in batches are surrounded by OD men standing there in readiness (now NB men also, i.e. men from the Emergency Squad), to prevent any escapes. They are counted off a list brought from the hut and go straight into the train. Any who dawdle or hesitate are assisted. They are driven into the train, or pushed, or struck, or pummeled, or persuaded with a boot, and kicked on board, both by the 'Green Police' who are escorting the train and by OD men. Noise and nervous outbursts are not allowed, but they do occur. Short work is made of such behavior—a few clips suffice . . . [The OD man] base their uncouth behavior on that of their German colleagues who are lavish in the use of their fists and inflict quick, hard punishment with their boots. The Jews in the camp refer to them as the Jewish SS. They are hated like the plague and people would gladly flay many of them alive if they dared. Men and women, old and young, sick and healthy, together with children and babies, are all packed together into the same wagon. Healthy men and women are put in amongst others who suffer from the complaints associated with old age and are in need of constant care, men and women who have lost control over certain primary physical functions, cripples, the old, the blind, folk with stomach disorders, imbeciles, lunatics. They all go on the bare floor, in amongst the baggage and on it, crammed tightly together. There is a barrel, just one barrel for all these people, in the corner of the wagon where they can relieve themselves publicly. One small barrel not large enough for so many people. With a bag of sand next to it, from which each person can pick up a handful to cover the excrement. In another corner there is a can of water with a tap for those who want to quench their thirst

"When the wagons are full and the prescribed quota of deportees has been delivered, they are closed up. The Commandant gives the signal for departure—with a wave of his hand. The whistle shrills, usually at about eleven o'clock, and the sound goes right through everyone in the camp, to the very core of their being. So the mangy-looking snake crawls away with its full load. Schlesinger and his retinue jump up on the footboard and ride along for a little bit for the sake of convenience, otherwise they would have to walk back. That would wear out their soles. The Commandant saunters contentedly away. Dr. Spanier, his hands behind his back and his head bent forward in worried concentration, walks back to his consulting room."[4]

Three eye-witnesses, Selma Wijnberg,[1] Ursula Stern,[2] and Jules Schelvis,[3] described the train journey.[B] Ursula's summary: "The journey to Poland was dreadful." Jules gave the most detail: "We kept wondering all the time and arguing why we had to go to Poland to work and what would happen there to the sick and the old . . . Herman, our Benjamin [*below*, Herman Borzykowski, Jules' 15-year-old brother-in-law], just wept. He could not be comforted. It was hard to fathom his thinking, this dear young boy who had learned at the AJC, the song, "Man is good."" ["Man is good", is the refrain from the song, "Hang out the Flag"][C]

1. Selma Wijnberg-Engel's 1945 passport photograph

Hang our flag up high.
It is as red as sparkling blood
Proclaiming what our heart longs for,
Man is good! Man is good!

Herman Borzykowski

2. Ursula Stern (Ula), who after the war went to Israel, where she married and became Ilana Safran.

Selma found the train stops intimidating: "Every time the train stopped, the guards started shooting, and the dogs began barking, it was very scary."

Nonetheless both Selma and Jules recall contact with passers-by. One of the workers asked Jules out of curiosity who they were and where they were going. Selma saw some who seemed to know. She said: "They pulled their fingers across their throats; we thought they were just anti-Semitic—didn't like us—we had no idea they were telling us that we were going to our deaths." After three days' lack of sleep, and for some, lack of water and food, crying children, arguments about the right to spend a few minutes at the ventilator—a 1 x 2 foot head height hole— Jules reported that ". . . the door was opened by an SS man with a gun who snarled: 'In a few minutes you will come into the camp, there you will have to hand over everything of value, so to speed it up, it will help if you give everything to me now.'"

When they arrived, Selma had no idea where they were: "We thought we were in Russia, the people looked so poor, and then we saw a big sign, SOBIBOR, everything looked very nice, little windows and flowers and the houses were painted green and red."

The train had stopped on a rail spur on the southeastern edge of the 143 acre camp with only 540 yards to walk from the train to the gas chambers.

3. Jules Schelvis and Chelly Borzykowski-Schelvis in 1942

AUSCHWITZ[A]

Oswięcim was a small, relatively unknown town in southwest Poland that lies in flat damp scrubland 50 miles west of Krakow. In the spring of 1940, the Germans built a concentration camp in the city's suburb, calling it Auschwitz, a name which will be remembered as the place where more people were killed than ever before in human history. The first prisoners were Poles who arrived on June 14, 1940. Auschwitz "was never conceived as a camp to kill Jews, it was never solely concerned with the 'Final Solution'—although that came to dominate the place."[B] In the fall of 1941, gassing was tried as a method to kill people with a minimum of noise or mess. It proved to be quick, efficient, and stress-free (for the Germans). It kept the dying out of sight and muffled the screams. By the summer of 1942, gassing was well established and by the fall of 1943 over 4,000 people could be killed every day. Prisoners younger than 15 or older than 40, the unfit, and women with young children were gassed on arrival. The death rate was only slightly lower than at Sobibor, but at Auschwitz there were 30,000 SS guards because half the prisoners were exploited in various ways before they were killed. Some were used as human guinea pigs:

> The transport of 150 women arrived in good condition. However, we were unable to obtain conclusive results because they died during the experiments. We would kindly request that you send us another group of women, the same number and at the same price.[C]

Those 150 women were sold to Bayer (for $68 apiece at the 1940 exchange rate). Auschwitz expanded because many industries, power plants, and factories were attracted by the slave labor: IG Farben bought Simon Loonstijn, Primo Levi and 30,000 others. The slaves worked in the power plants, mined coal, and made gravel, cement, armaments, and chemicals. Primo Levi was 25 years old when he arrived in Auschwitz in 1944; he was first assigned to the general labor force before IG Farben acquired him as a chemist:

> It was my good fortune to be deported to Auschwitz only in 1944, that is after the German Government had decided, owing to the growing scarcity of labor, to lengthen the average life span of the prisoners destined for elimination; it coincided with noticeable improvements in the camp routine and temporarily suspended killing at the whim of individuals.[D]

Whereas Sobibor was a secret, Auschwitz was not. For example, a courageous and compassionate Wehrmacht officer, Captain Wilm Hosenfeld, who saved the life of the pianist Wladyslaw Szpilman and five others, wrote in his diary on April 17, 1942, from Warsaw:

> Auschwitz, the deeply feared concentration camp in the east. Auschwitz, the deeply feared concentration camp in the east. The G. Sta. Po. [Gestapo] torture people to death there. They drive the unfortunates into a cell and make short work of them by gassing them. People are savagely beaten during interrogation. And there are special torture cells; for instance, one where the victim's hands and arms are tied to a column which is then pulled up, and the victim hangs there until he becomes unconscious. Or he is put in a crate where he can only crouch, and left there until he loses consciousness. What other diabolical things have they devised? How many totally innocent people are held in their prisons?[E]

The answer is given by Laurence Rees: "Of the 1,300,000 people sent to Auschwitz, 1,100,000 were killed, of whom 1,000,000 were Jews; 70,000 were Poles; 10,000 were Russian POWs, 20,000 were Gypsies, and a few hundred were Jehovah's Witnesses."[F] Of the 73,000 Dutch who were sent to Auschwitz, only 1.75 percent (1,277) survived. At the liberation on January 28, 1945, "a prisoner watched empty baby carriages being wheeled out of Auschwitz, five abreast. It took one hour for them to pass by."[G]

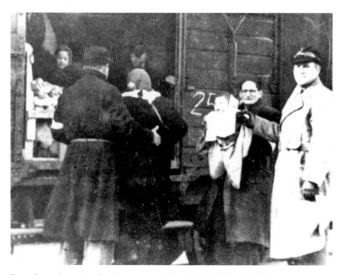

Boarding the train for the east at Westerbork (above left).

At Auschwitz.[H] (above), most women and children were gassed on arrival.

Opposite page: Families awaiting transport to Westerbork

SOBIBOR[A]

On Friday April 9, Flip, Uncle Max (it was his birthday), Aunt Cato, cousins Henri and Elisabeth, AJC friends Bora and Samuel Prijs, and fellow prisoners Selma Wijnberg and Ursula Stern arrived at Sobibor. During SS Kurt Bolenger's trial in Germany in 1962, SS Sergeant-major Erich Bauer, who had been in charge of the gassing, explained what happened to Flip and everyone else on arrival. "At the moment of the transport's arrival, all the work in the camp stopped and continued only after the extermination of the Jews. In time, the whole procedure went like clockwork and all of us were in the exact place at the right time."[B] All 16-20 SS camp guards together with a score of camp workers met each train. They whipped people readily to induce fear, confusion, and compliance. "Some of the mothers had small children sleeping in their arms, clearly they had no idea that they were going to their death." "They heard screamed orders, walk fast, throw down your bags, hurry! When one woman threw away her backpack, her child was snatched from her. She cried, 'Oh, God! my child! my child!' An SS guard hit her. Blood streamed down her face, but she screamed, 'My child!' and he hit her again and she screamed, 'my child.' He said, 'we will look after your child.'"[C] In 1965 Esther Terner-Raab testified that she saw SS Frenzel through the window of the officers' quarters, banging the head of a tiny infant against a cattle car.[I] From the assembled batches of 500 people, the Germans selected workers to supplement the Sobibor work force of 200 to 600 who built new buildings, ran a farm, cared for the animals, chopped wood and "processed" the new prisoners. Selma and Ursula were two of 28 women who with 30 men were selected to work.[D] Henri and Elisabeth were too young to be selected (both were 13), and Max (58) and Cato (45) were too old. Flip would have been a good candidate if he had recovered from Vught.

After walking two hundred yards from the train, they were given a welcoming speech in German by SS Sergeant-major Michel who apologized for the inconvenience, and politely explained that for sanitary reasons they must undress, put their clothing in neat piles, leave their purses and possessions, and take a shower before relaxing in the comfortable living quarters that had been prepared for them. He said that postcards were available so that everyone could send a message home to let their families know that they had arrived safely.[E] The people applauded. They were then forced to walk about 160 yards along a narrow passageway leading to the gas chambers in camp III. Sobibor was divided into four subcamps, named Camp I-IV. Luka, an 18-year-old with short brown hair from Hamburg was rebuked for smoking by Sasha Pechersky, a fellow worker. She explained that it was due to nerves, she said that he didn't know how hard it was for her, looking after 100 Angora rabbits in Camp IV, close to the passageway:

> I can see the naked men and women and even the children march to Camp III. I watch them and begin to shake as if I had typhus. But I can't turn my face away. I can't close my eyes. Sometimes they call out, 'Where are they taking us?' as if they sensed that I was there listening. I tremble when they call out to me. But I just peer at them through the crack.[F]

Half way along the passageway, the women were diverted into a hut where their heads were shaved. Chaim Engel, a worker in the camp for about a year during which he was assigned many jobs, told Selma that: "Of all the terrible things the Germans made me do, the one that upset me the most was shaving the women's hair." Most people were compliant but some objected and some bolted, but the corridor was fenced on both sides with barbed wire and at either end there were well-armed guards. Several survivors recall hearing people cry out as they were entering the gas chambers: "Eli, Eli, lama sabathani." That is to say, "My God, my God, why hast thou forsaken me."[G] Camp III was sealed from the rest of the camp, but a worker in Camp III bribed one of the 100 Ukrainian guards to smuggle a letter to Schlomo:

> In that place, they loaded hundreds at the same time. After it is packed tight, the door is hermetically locked and then they turn on a big diesel engine whose exhaust is introduced into a hole in the wall, in order to throw the exhaust into the interior until everyone has suffocated. At the same time, big trenches are dug. After the mass extermination, we, the "saved" from the same transport as you, start to pull out the bodies and throw them into the trenches. Sometimes, THE DIRT MOVES OVER THAT MASS OF BURIED BODIES; THEN, THE BANDITS COME AND FINISH LIQUIDATING THEM WITH BULLETS. I tell you this because, if some day you manage to escape, you could tell the world everything that happens here, as there is no hope that you will see me again. Those who come to Camp III will never leave. Your friend, Abrao.[H]

Schlomo was selected to work in camp II as a goldsmith, Abrao was selected to remove the bodies from the gas chambers, search them, extract teeth, then bury or burn them. Soon after Flip arrived, a kapo reported to SS Frenzel that the Dutch were planning an escape. In reprisal, the Germans shot 72 prisoners, nearly all the Dutch men in the camp with the exception of the artist Max van Dam and his two assistants and one or two others. In Camp I and II, the conditions were less disgusting, but there were many barbarities and many killings. Samuel Lerer still has scars from the 50 lashes he received from Frenzel. He saw SS Bauer kill a young lad because he refused his order to eat dog poop. However, another guard, SS Johann Klier, often smuggled some extra bread to the workers. When Esther Raab asked him for a pair of shoes, he asked her to sit down, helped her, made her feel like a customer and offered her a second pair.[I] He soon asked for a transfer.

The Sobibor workers did not look like prisoners for their clothes and hair were normal, they were not thin for they stole food from each transport. They played clubbiash, sang, danced, fell in love, and some held religious services daily and on holy days. On Friday, October 9, the eve of Yom Kippur, at the Kol Nidrei service, the question: "Who will live and who will die?" held added significance for those who knew that a revolt was planned within a few days. Of the 34,000 Jews from Holland who entered Sobibor, there was only one Dutch survivor.[J]

REVOLT IN SOBIBOR[A]

Alexander Pechersky (Sasha), a tall, 34-year-old Soviet army officer, along with a few hundred other Soviet POWs, was transported from Minsk on September 18, 1943. After four days without food or water, he arrived at Sobibor. Even though he had endured two years in German captivity, months of illness from typhus, an escape and capture, and ten days in a Minsk prison for Jews, he said that he couldn't believe his eyes—the screams of victims, the foul smell, the smoke from the burning bodies, and the guards' brutality. He and 80 POWs were selected to work in the north camp. He soon demonstrated defiance,[B] and resolved to escape. Leon Feldhendler, a well-respected old hand who also had escape strategies, told him of the behavior of the SS, of the anatomy of the mine fields, the double row of barbed wire fences, the number of guards, and the arms of the Ukrainians.[C] He told of ten to one reprisals following an escape in June 1943 (two survived), and in July 1943 (seven survived) and other attempted escapes. They decided that this time there would be no reprisals because everyone would escape. With Feldhendler's help, Sasha presented his plan: "My dear comrades, here is a plan that is the only one that I consider possible; we must prepare weapons—steal or make knives, axes, hand-grenades, ammunition, rifles, wire cutters and ladders, we have to kill all the German officers, one by one, in a short time period, and to do this we have no more than an hour. If we capture the armory, we can fight them, march out through the main gate and join the partisans—if not, we have no choice but to storm out."

Selma Wijnberg wrote: "At 3pm [Thursday October 14] Chaim [Engel] came to me and asked me to be at the warehouse at 3:30. I was punctual. Five minutes later Porzyczki [a Kapo] arrived and 10 minutes later he killed Wolf. After that, five men including my beloved husband [Chaim] made mince-meat of Beckmann."[A] Chaim killed SS Beckmann in his office with a pointed kitchen knife: "With every jab I gave him, I yelled: 'This is for my father, this is for my brother and all the Jews you killed.'" At 4 p.m., an hour and three quarters before sunset, acting commander SS Second Lieutenant Niemann rode up on his horse and entered the tailor shop to collect a new jacket that he was told would be waiting for him. As the tailors patted Niemann and marked the alterations, Yehuda Lerner killed him with an axe. At 4:09 in the blacksmith's shop, Simon Mazurkevitch killed a guard, and at the same time Arkadij Vajspapir and Semyon Rozenfeld killed another and then a Ukrainian. At 4:15, Boris Tsibulsky told Sasha that he had accomplished his goal to liquidate all four guards in Camp II. By 4:45 p.m. the telephone lines had been cut and the electric generators disabled, eleven of the sixteen SS had been killed including the three senoir offices, all in silence without the other SS guards or the watchtower seeing anything or noticing anything amiss.

Selma Wijnberg, baby and Chaim Engel

Most prisoners escaped through, over or under the fence. Of the approximately 300 who managed to escape, about 80 were shot or blown up by mines. The next day, search teams aided by two Luftwaffe spotter planes combed the forests to the southwest. About 100 prisoners were captured. The remaining escapees were then at the mercy of the local farmers. After five nights in the forest, Sasha crossed the heavily guarded Bug River, and he and his platoon reentered the Soviet Union, joined the partisans and eventually rejoined the Red Army.[D] Semyon Rozenfeld, from Baranowicze, 80 miles southwest of Minsk, escaped, was shot by Poles, but hid until the Red Army arrived. He volunteered for the front, was wounded, hospitalized, recovered, returned to the front, marched into Berlin, and there left his card; he graffitied the Reichstag wall: BARANOWICZE—SOBIBOR—BERLIN.[E] Feldhendler escaped but one month before the end of the war, was killed by Poles in Lublin. After Chaim Engel killed Beckmann, he grabbed Selma, they climbed the ladder, and escaped over the fence. They were hidden for nine months by Stefka Nowak and her courageous family, whom the Engels never forgot. Ursula Stern escaped and became Ilana Safran, an Israeli. Esther Terner-Raab escaped with Samuel Lerer and Avrum Kohn; they were hidden in Stefan Marcyniuk's barn in Janow. Esther called him "a kind, decent man who helped Jew and gentile alike."[F] She has never forgotten him. Schlomo Szmajzner escaped, became a rancher in Brazil and wrote an early book about Sobibor. Thomas Blatt escaped and wrote exciting accounts of the revolt. Kurt Thomas escaped, was hidden in a pigsty by kindly Poles and then rejoined the Czech army.[G] He did not forget the family who risked their lives to save his. Bora Blits-Prijs and Samuel Prijs may have escaped.[H] It would be good to report that Flip also escaped and survived, at least for a while, but it is unlikely. The Sobibor escape had no assistance and has no equal. The Germans killed all the remaining prisoners in the camp, and 43,000 in nearby camps. They then burnt the buildings, removed the fences and barbed wire, plowed the entire area, and planted trees to conceal the site of one of mankind's largest mass murders. The remaining watch tower looks down on the ashes of 0.1% of the Jews of the USSR, 1% of the Jews of France, 3% of the Jews of Poland and 30% of the Jews of the Netherlands..

Left to right: Semyon Rozenfeld, Arkadij Vajspapir and Alexander Pechersky

CONCENTRATION CAMPS

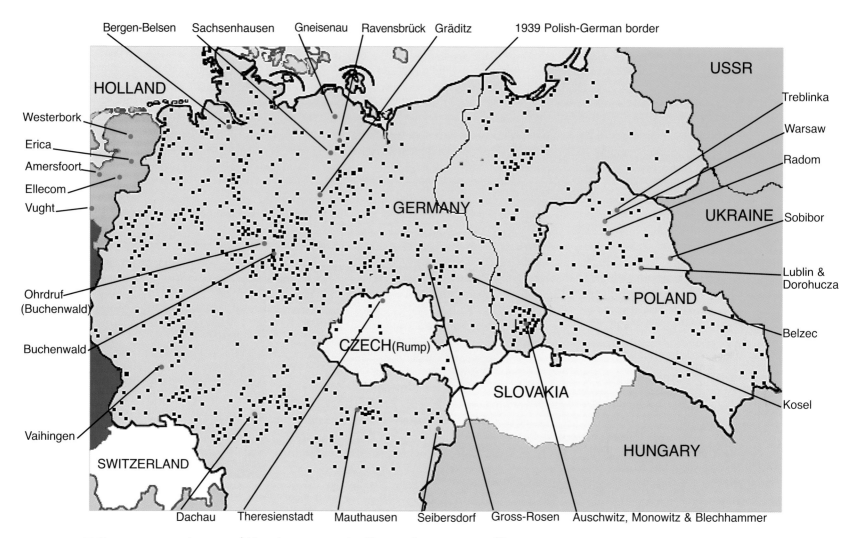

■ German concentration camps (although many are omitted because the map is too small).
● German and Dutch concentration and death camps that are named in this book.
● Death places of those who did not die in camps.

The Dutch concentration (C), work (W) and transit (T) camps are listed on the opposite page. Westerbork is included in the map above as it is the best known and biggest camp in the Netherlands and was administered by the SS, even though it allowed more freedom and had less maltreatment than Vught, Ellecom or Erica. All the camps were part of a sinister continuum, varying from Molengoot where the probability of death was 0, to Sobibor where the probability of death was close to 1.

In general, concentration camps have four characteristics. They are camps for the detention of people:

a) who have committed no crime by the accepted norms (see note 5 page 38);
b) who are detained without any rights (e.g. no trial);
c) who are deliberately given inadequate facilities;
d) who are maltreated, beaten or killed.

The work camps were not concentration camps in so far as the last element was lacking. Sobibor was not a concentration camp because the second element is lacking, prisoners were not detained, they were just killed. It was one of seven death camps.

CONCENTRATION, WORK AND TRANSIT CAMPS IN THE NETHERLANDS

Camp	Location	Type
Amersfoort	Amersfoort	C
Arriën #	Ommen	W
Balderhaar #	Bergentheim	W
Beenderribben*	Blokzijl	W
Betlem	Hardenberg	W
Beugelen#	Staphorst	W
Castle De Schaffelaar	Barneveld	T
De Bruine Enk #	Nunspeet	W
De Bruynhorst #	Ederveen	W
De Conraad *#	Rouveen	W
De Fledders *#	Norg	W
De Landweer *#	Elsloo	W
De Slikken B *	Westernieland	W
De Wittenbrink #	Hummelo	W
De Vanenburg #	Putten	W
De Vecht *#	Dalfsen	W
De Wite Pael #	St. Johannisga	W
De Zomp #	Ruurlo	W
Diever A *#	Zorgvlied	W
Diever B *#	Zorgvlied	W
Echten #	Echten	W
Erica (Erika)	Ommen	C
Geesbrug *#	Nieuweroord	W
Gijsselte#	Hoogeveen	W
Het Overbroek #	Ochten	W
Hornhuizen *	Juliana Polder	W
It Petgat #	Blesdijke	W
Kloosterhaar #	Bergentheim	W
Kremboong *#	Nieuweroord	W
Lievelde *#	Lichtenvoorde	W
Linde #	Zuidwolde	W
Mantinge #	Mantinge	W
Molengoot #	Hardenberg	W
Oranjekanaal #	Hijkersmilde	W
Orvelte #	Orvelte	W
Palestina	Ellecom	C
Ruinen #	Ruinen	W
Schaarshoek #	Heino	W
Schoorl	Groet	T
Sellingerbeetse #	Sellingen	W
Sevenum *	De Peel	W
Stuifzand #	Hoogeveen	W
'T Wijdeveld *	De Ginkel	W
't Wijde Gat' #	Den Hulst	W
Twilhaar #	Nijverdal	W
Vledder *#	Vledder	W
Vught	's-Hertogenbosch	C
Westerbork	Hooghalen	C/T
Ybeneer *#	Fochteloo	W

This provisional list (*left*) comprises four or five Dutch concentration camps (C), 42 work camps (W), and two or three transit (T) camps.

On September 11, 1942, the Germans sent the Jewish Council a list (now held by the Jewish Historical Museum) of 37 work camps (marked #) in 5 of the 12 Dutch provinces. The list gave the name, location, number of prisoners, and capacity of each camp. The average occupancy was 118; there were only 17 men at Ruinen and De Zomp but 330 at Sellingerbeetse. The total number of prisoners in all 37 camps totalled a little under 4,500. There is reason to expect that there were more than these 37 work camps. On September 24, Rauter had informed Himmler (page 69) that "There are about 7,000 Jews in these camps. By October 1, we hope to increase this number to 8,000." As only 4,500 of the 7,000 prisoners are accounted for in this German list, 1,500 of the shortfall could have been added to the existing camps as they were only 75% full, and the rest must have been held in some other work camps, perhaps in the seven provinces that are not listed. There are now (July 2007), 42 work camps that have been found, one with help from Flip who provided useful confirmation of the existence of Betlem (page 52).

* Photos of these camps are available at the Jewish Historical Museum in Amsterdam.

Palestina (Ellecom) concentration camp had only a brief existence because its prisoners arrived at Westerbork in such bad condition that the chief medical officer, Dr. Spanier, complained to Camp Commandant Gemmeker who passed on the complaint and the camp was closed (David Cohen, 1982).

Children at Westerbork camp

SIMON LOONSTIJN ESCAPES

Tootje Loonstijn-Renger recalls that on October 1, 1942, when they saw German trucks arriving at Molengoot, her brother Simon escaped with a fellow inmate, Ruud (Rudolf) Wolf who died in Auschwitz as the camp was liberated. The Vrijlinks hid them for three days under a haystack (*right*), and then Mr. Vrijlink lent Simon a suit for his journey back to Amsterdam.

One wonders what drives some people to rescue those being being hurried away to their deaths. It is true that the Vrijlinks, Veurinks and van der Schaafs were brought up with the instruction to love thy neighbor as thyself, but many receive the same instruction yet few obey and most of us choose our neighbors carefully. When a lawyer once asked the excellent question: "Who is then my neighbor?" he received the excellent answer in the form of the parable of a Good Samaritan who came across a Jew who had been set upon by thieves and was lying half dead in the street. He went to and bound up his wounds and took him to an inn, paying the inn-keeper to look after him. The Samaritans were a sect of Jews whose relationship with the mainstream was about as friendly as Protestants and Catholics in the sixteenth century. Nonetheless, that Samaritan accepted as his neighbor a half dead total stranger.

The assistance that the Vrijlinks gave Simon was the same that they had given Flip a few days earlier and was the same that Karel repeatedly gave to Flip and others and the same that Captain Hosenfeld gave to Szpilman, an enemy and a Jew. All these acts of compassion exceeded the original Good Samaritan's in two respects: they were undertaken at considerable personal risk, and they are not parables; they actually happened.

The Vrijlink's haystack. In the foreground (above, *from left to right*) are Hermina, Johanna and Seine. On the stack are Mr. (Jan) Vrijlink, Gerridina and Sina.

Gees Vrijlink beside her house

May 9, 1913, the wedding of Jan Vrijlink and Willemina Eshuis who died April 30, 1937.

LAST NEWS FROM SIMON LOONSTIJN

Simon hid in Amsterdam, first at home, and then with a friend nearby. Tootje brought him the news that their father had been arrested (page 99). He later went to hide with friends in The Hague, but while taking a walk on July 31, 1943, he was arrested and was sent to Westerbork, Barack 67. He was put on the August 24 transport to Auschwitz. This transport comprised almost entirely of S-prisoners (three of whom tried to escape). Sometime before January 28, 1944, Simon was trans-ferred to Monowitz, a sub-camp of Auschwitz, which IG Farben owned and where they had their Buna synthetic rubber factory. From there he wrote a postcard (*below*) to his friend "Her" (Herman Weisberg) cleverly suggesting a shortage of *achala*, Amsterdam-Jewish slang for food. Simon was in the hospital at Monowitz from May 27 to July 6, 1944; he recovered and was seen by a friend on January 18, 1945 during the evacuation of Monowitz, nine days before the Russians arrived.

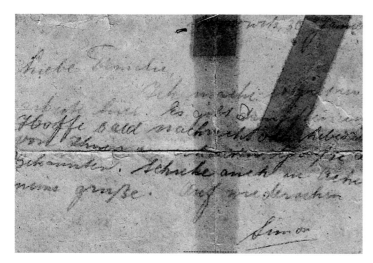

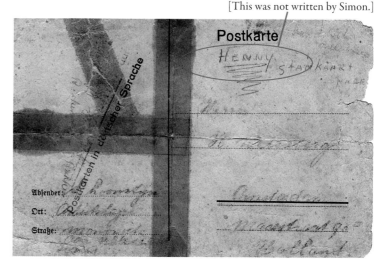

[This was not written by Simon.]

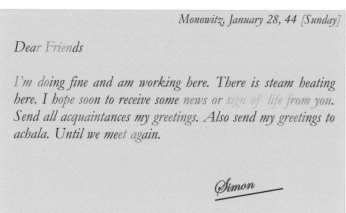

Monowitz, January 28, 44 [Sunday]

Dear Friends

I'm doing fine and am working here. There is steam heating here. I hope soon to receive some news or sign of life from you. Send all acquaintances my greetings. Also send my greetings to achala. Until we meet again.

Simon

When the Russians reached Auschwitz on January 27, 1945, they found only 2,819 prisoners, including Primo Levi, who was too sick to walk. The other 58,000 prisoners from the Auschwitz complex of camps had already been force-marched and transported to Mauthausen and other camps. Many died en route from the freezing weather and lack of food and water, and the Germans shot many more. "Anyone who dared to bend over—who stopped even for a moment—was shot."[4] Flip's cousin Philip, the son of Andries and Anna, had been at Gross-Rosen at the same time that Simon was in nearby Monowitz. It is likely that Simon and Philip died on one of these death marches.

Simon, age two   Simon as a teenager

The International Red Cross has provided humanitarian care to millions and it has also served as an important source of information about the fate of people killed or uprooted by wars or natural disasters, but it said nothing about the fate of Jews in concentration camps. Below are a few Red Cross responses to enquiries from Dick and Karel about their parents and Tootje's enquiries about the fate of her brother, Simon Loonstijn from March 1949 to November 1999, illustrating how Tootje refused to abandon hope as long as there was no confirmation of Simon's death.

```
                                    Diaconessenhuis,
                                    Hogeveensewez 38,
                                    MEPPEL.


Naar aanleiding van Uw aanvrage nopens het lot van:

     SIMON LOONSTIJN,

geboren: 9 Augustus 1922, Amsterdam

ben ik voorshands slechts in staat U mede te delen, dat gezochte

op 24 Augustus 1943 van Westerbork    uit met bestemming Auschwitz

worxxgodxxxxxxxxxxxxxxxx        xx            xxxx

Xxxxxxxxwxxdxxxxjx/xxjxxxp        xxxxxxxxxxxxxxxxxxxxxxxx


A.  Gezochte behoorde niet tot een groep van personen, van welke het
    overlijden op of omstreeks de dag van aankomst in een concentra-
    tiekamp kan worden aangenomen.

B.  Gezochte behoorde tot een groep van personen, die langere of kor-
    tere tijd in onderscheidene kampen hebben vertoefd.

C.  In de bekend gebleven resten van kampadministraties, noch in enig
    ander documentair gegeven, is het overlijden van gezochte vermeld.

D.  Het vaststellen van een datum van overlijden kan pas langs de weg
    van collectieve reconstructie te zijner tijd geschieden.


Op grond van het bovenstaande kan derhalve op dit tijdstip geen ver-
klaring van overlijden onder vermelding van plaats en datum worden
uitgereikt.
Het onderzoek wordt evenwel voortgezet; de resultaten daarvan zullen
U, zodra ik over positieve gegevens de beschikking krijg, kenbaar
worden gemaakt.
```

The letter (*below*), written May 6, 1945, and sent via the Red Cross, was from Karel van der Schaaf: "Dear parents, Dick and I are in good health. How is it with you? Hope to be home soon. Greetings, Karel and Dick."

RÉPONSE   REPLY   ANTWORT

Van het
Centrale Informatie-Bureau van het Nederlandsche Roode Kruis
Markt — Eindhoven (Nederland)

Aan het
Comité International de la Croix-Rouge
Palais du Conseil Général — GENEVE (Suisse).

DEMANDEUR — ENQUIRER — ANFRAGESTELLER

Nom - Name ____van der Schaaf____
Prénom - Christian name - Vorname ____Karel____
Rue - Street - Strasse ____Zuiderdwarsvaart 9e____
Localité - Locality - Ortschaft ____Drachten____
Département - County - Provinz ____Friesland____
Pays - Country - Land ____Nederland____

Message à transmettre — Message — Mitteilung
(25 mots au maximum, nouvelles de caractère strictement personnel et familial) — *(not over 25 words, family news of strictly personal character)* — *(nicht über 25 Worte, persönliche Familiennachrichten).*

____Lieve Ouders,____
____Dick en ik zijn goed gezond.____
____Hoe is het met Uw. Schrijf____
____gauw terug. Hopelijk zijn____
____we gauw thuis. Gegroet____
____Karel en Dick.____

```
PA/18.411/RF                  Den Haag        0 2 NOV. 1999
Informatiebureau              Doorkiesnr.  003170-4455827
LOONSTIJN, Simon              Bijlage(n)
geboren: 09-08-1922 te Amsterdam
EU 108.702


Geachte heer Renger,

Met referte aan uw schrijven d.d. 8 juli 1998, betreffende
bovengenoemde en met excuses voor de ontstane vertraging in
de behandeling, het volgende.

Omtrent de broer van uw vrouw -uw zwager- is dezerzijds de
volgende informatie voorhanden.

Uw zwager was bij de Joodse Raad geregistreerd op het adres:
Amsterdam, Amsteldijk 18.

Op 31 juli 1943 werd hij (komende uit Den Haag) ingesloten
in Lager Westerbork, barak 67.

Betrokkene werd op 24 augustus 1943 van Westerbork uit op
transport gesteld naar Auschwitz (Auschwitz was de Duitse
benaming voor het Poolse plaatsje Oswiecim).

Vanuit Auschwitz werd uw zwager voor tewerkstelling (bij de
IG-Farben AG) overgebracht naar het buitencommando Monowitz-
Buna; zijn gevangennummer was: 139795.

Hij was van 27 mei 1944 tot 6 juli 1944 (entlassen) opgenomen
in de ziekenbarak van Monowitz.

Vanaf 18 januari 1945 vonden er evacuatie-transporten plaats
van Monowitz naar Gleiwitz. De bevrijding van de gevangenen
vond plaats op 27 januari 1945.
```

```
PA/18.411                  -2-


Een overlevende * van het transport van 24 augustus 1943 naar
Auschwitz verklaarde in 1947 het volgende:

"Den heer Loonstijn was een vriend van mij maar in evacuatie
zijn wij gesplitst en niets meer vernomen."

* Ter bescherming van de privacy worden nadere gegevens
omtrent getuigen niet aan derden gemeld.

Blijkens publicatie in de Staatscourant van 29 mei 1952 werd
vanwege de Minister van Justitie aangifte gedaan van het
overlijden van betrokkene op 21 januari 1945 in Midden-Europa.
Zie bijgaande fotokopie.

Verdere gegevens omtrent uw zwager zijn niet aangetroffen.

De kosten van behandeling van uw verzoek, ad f 110,-,
brengen wij niet in rekening. Wel doen wij u bijgaand
een blanco acceptgiro toekomen waarmee u ten gunste
van het Informatiebureau een tegemoetkoming in de
kosten kunt overmaken.

Vertrouwend u voldoende te hebben geïnformeerd.

Met vriendelijke groet,



R. Fieret, Oorlogsnazorg
```

THE WAR ENDS

On September 12, 1944, Allied troops entered the south of the Netherlands. On September 13, the last transport left Westerbork. It included 50 children, 2 to 11 years old, from the Westerbork orphanage.[A]

On September 17, while the Allies were fighting to secure the bridge at Arnhem, the Dutch declared a general rail strike. The Germans retaliated by withholding food and fuel from Amsterdam and the west of the Netherlands for the remaining seven months of the war. The food and fuel shortage caused severe and widespread suffering in what became known in the Netherlands as The Hunger Winter. There was no meat, no fat, no eggs, no sugar, few vegetables and no fuel.[B] People ate tulip bulbs. On January 28, two Swedish ships offloaded food and medical supplies, but the Germans refused to allow it to be distributed. Twenty-two thousand people died of starvation.

On March 7, the resistance wounded Hanns Rauter, the chief of the SS. In retaliation, the Germans killed 263 Dutch hostages.

Hitler committed suicide on April 30, 1945. He had named Admiral Dönitz as his successor and Seyss-Inquart as foreign minister. On May 6, General Blaskowitz, head of the German forces in the Netherlands, signed the Dutch surrender documents at the Agricultural College in Wageningen, back-dated to May 5. Everyone from Amsterdam (*above right*), to Nieuwlande (*right*) and Drachten (*below right*), suddenly burst out singing. They marked the end of five years of war with joyous celebration but without vindictiveness. In front of the Royal Palace, on May 7, some Germans fired into the celebrating Amsterdam crowd killing 19 and injuring 119 people.

On May 6, Karel and Dick van der Schaaf sent a message to their parents that they were well and hoped to be home soon (page 156). They later attended the reunion of the AJC, where they and Bep de Vries were the only members of the Hortus branch. Jules Schelvis was in hospital, recovering from typhus. In 1946, Karel and Bep married and eventually had three children and seven grandchildren (page 187).

Of Flip's relatives in the Netherlands, there were almost none left: no de Bruins, no Salomonsons, no Samases, no Sliers and no Philips except two first cousins, Nol Slier and Arthur Philips, and their wives, Carrie and Willy. There were two first cousins once removed: Louis Slier's son Johnny, and Nol Slier's son Hans who now lives in Spain, although he no longer calls himself Slier. A second cousin, Stella Slier, survived two years in Auschwitz. She said that her clearest memory of Vrolik Street was Grietje and Eduard's laundry cart.

Of Flip himself, nothing remains except his letters and photos, which create an image of an optimistic, courageous young man whose affection for his parents, for Karel and the Vrijlinks, for Nico and Bep and many other friends, still leaves a warm glow.

Although Hitler's intention to establish a one thousand year Reich was a total failure, his intention to exterminate the Jews of Europe was a partial success. About 100,000 (over 70 percent) Dutch Jews were killed.[C] About 137,000 (about 1 percent) Dutch non-Jews were also killed. Hitler was more successful in the Netherlands than in Belgium, Luxembourg, France, Italy, Austria or Germany (page 174). Flip's funeral pyre was one of 170,000 at Sobibor. All those deaths at Sobibor accounted for less than three percent of the Jews, and less than one percent of non-Jews who, as civilians, were killed in a war that Adolf Hitler started on September 1, 1939.

People in front of the Royal Palace in Amsterdam celebrating the end of the German occupation on May 7, 1945.

People of Nieuwlande celebrating the end of German occupation.

Bep de Vries and Karel van der Schaaf writing home from Drachten, Friesland at the Liberation day celebration.

SURVIVORS

Flip immediate family comprised 58 relatives who were alive in the Netherlands during World War II. Only six of them are known to have survived (10 percent). Excluded from this number are the South African Sliers, such as his uncle Jack Slier, (*below right*), who emigrated from the Netherlands to South Africa in 1922. Other survivors were: Lily (Liel) van der Berg, Felix Halverstad, Kiek van Kleef, Ab van der Linden, Tootje (Cato) Loonstijn, Mrs. Peekel, Wim (Sally) Prijs and his father (from Auschwitz), Hendrika and Barend Schaap, Simon van der Sluis, Jules Schelvis (despite two death camps and three concentration camps); Truus Sant who hid three onderduikers and married one of them, Wim Tokkie; Bep de Vries, her parents, Sally (Salomon) Vogel and all the van der Schaafs.

Left: Flip's cousin, Arthur Philips, and Willy (Wilhelmina) van Geldere-Philips and their sons, Eddy born in 1946, and Jules born in 1948. Willy and Arthur were hidden during the war.

Right: At the end of the war, Nol Slier worked for the Canadian army as a translator.

Left: Carrie (Carolina) Cartoef-Slier, Nol Slier's first wife, and their son, Hans, born May 22, 1943. Carrie had false papers and passed as a Christian. Nol was hidden in their home.

Right Jack Slier; *far right;* Johnny (Jonas) Slier who was the son of Elisabeth and Louis Slier who was the oldest son of Flip's Uncle Jonas. Johnny survived in hiding. Johnny's great uncle, Jack (who survived because he lived in South Africa) wanted to adopt his orphaned great-nephew, but was informed that it would be better for Johhnny to remain in the orphanage where he had bonded with the cook.. Photo taken in 1957.

Flip's family listed by family name, then first name, with dates of birth and death

Name	Relationship to Flip	Occupation	Date of birth	Date of death	Camp
de Bruin, Alex Sallie	Ru's son	age 16	Nov 26 1927	May 28 1943	Sobibor
de Bruin, Emanuel	Ru's son	Farmer	Oct 20 1921	Sep 30 1942	Auschwitz
de Bruin, Lion Emanuel	Ru's son	Farmer	Mar 29 1918	Sep 30 1942	Auschwitz
de Bruin, Rosetta	Ru's daughter	Mother's help	Sep 5 1916	Jul 9 1943	Sobibor
de Bruin, Rudolf Emanuel	"Uncle" Ru (Seline's cousin)	Deputy mayor	May 29 1887	May 28 1943	Sobibor
de Bruin, Sallie (Samuel Emanuel)	Ru's brother	Merchant	May 3 1889	Sep 7 1942	Auschwitz
de Bruin, Rosalchen Salomonson-	Ru's wife	Housewife	Sep 1 1889	May 28 1943	Sobibor
de Bruin, Sophie Abrahamson-	Ru's brother's wife	Housewife	Aug 30 1880	Sep 7 1942	Auschwitz
Philips, Arthur (Abraham)	cousin (Eduard & Grietje)	Soldier	Aug 2 1920	Nov 7 1986	Survived in hiding
Philips, Betje	cousin (Eduard & Grietje)	Housewife	Nov 11 1928	Feb 5 1943	Auschwitz
Philips, Eduard	uncle Grietje's husband	Laundryman	Sep 8 1892	Feb 5 1943	Auschwitz
Philips, Elie	cousin (Eduard & Grietje)	age 15	Nov 11 1928	Feb 5 1943	Auschwitz
Philips, Grietje Slier-	aunt	Laundrywoman	Mar 12 1893	Feb 5 1943	Auschwitz
Philips, Philipp	cousin (Eduard & Grietje)	Clerk	Aug 23 1922	Sep 30 1942	Auschwitz
Philips, Wilhelmina van Geldere-	cousin Arthur's wife	Housewife	Sep 10 1921	Jan 3 1997	Survived in hiding
Philips, Schoontje Frinkel-	cousin Philipp Philips wife	Tailoress	Feb 13 1921	Sep 30 1942	Auschwitz
Salomonson, Alfred Sallie	Uncle Alfred, Seline's brother	Iron merchant	May 26 1895	Feb 2 1944	The Hague
Salomonson, Esther Philips-	"aunt," wife of Friedrich	Housewife	Mar 25 1895	May 21 1943	Sobibor
Salomonson, Friedrich	"uncle," Ru's brother-in-law	unknown	Dec 16 1897	May 21 1943	Sobibor
Salomonson, Hanni Bertel	Friedrich's daughter	age 11	Feb 29 1932	May 21 1943	Sobibor
Salomonson, Jeanie Muriel Gestetner-	Aunt Jenny, Alfred's wife	Cook	Jul 24 1903	Mar 6 1943	Auschwitz
Salomonson, Lion	son of Friedrich	age 13	Jul 7 1930	May 21 1943	Sobibor
Salomonson, Izaak Lion	father of Friedrich	unknown	May 27 1861	Sep 1 1942	Auschwitz
Salomonson, Martha Sophie	cousin (Alfred and Jeanie)	age 9	Oct 27 1934	Mar 6 1943	Auschwitz
Salomonson, Philip	cousin (Alfred and Jeanie)	Baby	Feb 22 1943	Mar 6 1943	Auschwitz
Salomonson, Rosalie Johanna	aunt, Seline's sister	Domestic servant	Jun 11 1887	Mar 20 1943	Sobibor
Samas, Bram (Abraham)	uncle, Johanna's husband	Baker	Nov 21 1884	Feb 12 1943	Auschwitz
Samas, Johanna Sophie Salomonson-	aunt, Seline's sister	Housewife	Oct 6 1888	Feb 12 1943	Auschwitz
Samas, Philip	cousin (Johanna & Abram)	Baker	Jun 25 1920	Oct 3 1941	Mauthausen
Samas, Salomo	cousin (Johanna & Abram)	Typographer	May 1 1918	Feb 29 1944	Gräditz
Schaap, Karel (Koopman)	Aunt Juul's husband	Butcher	Jul 26 1882	Oct 22 1942	Auschwitz
Schaap, Juliette Anna Salomonson-	Aunt Juul, Seline's sister	Housewife	Sep 21 1892	Jan 25 1943	Auschwitz
Slier, Andries	uncle	Diamond worker	Apr 25 1888	Oct 12 1942	Auschwitz
Slier, Anna Plas	aunt, Jonas' wife	Housewife	Aug 26 1891	Jun 4 1943	Sobibor
Slier, Anna van Es-	aunt, Andries' wife	Housewife	Mar 8 1894	Oct 12 1942	Auschwitz
Slier, Nol (Arnold)	cousin (Jonas & Ana)	Bicycle repairer	Mar 18 1917	Jan 19 1995	Survived in hiding
Slier, Betje Benjamins-	paternal grandmother	Housewife	Nov 15 1862	Feb 17 1943	Westerbork
Slier, Carolina Carrie Henrietta Cartoef-	cousin Arnold's wife	Housewife	May 22 1925	Dec 22 2003	Survived as Christian
Slier, Cato (Catharina) Vleeschhouwer-	aunt, Joseph's wife	Housewife	June 28 1898	Apr 9 1943	Sobibor
Slier, David André	cousin (Andries & Anna)	Clerk	Dec 31 1919	Apr 30 1943	Sobibor
Slier, David Leo	cousin (Joseph & Catharina)	Electrician	Nov 13 1926	Sep 30 1942	Auschwitz
Slier, Debora	aunt	Seamstress	Sep 18 1896	Jan 21 1943	Auschwitz
Slier, Duifje	aunt	Dressmaker	Jul 13 1891	Feb 12 1943	Auschwitz
Slier, Leendert (Eliazar)	father	Typographer	Mar 26 1890	Jun 4 1943	Sobibor
Slier, Elisabeth Aluin-	cousin Louis' wife	Housewife	Aug 30 1911	Dec 11 1942	Auschwitz
Slier, Elisabeth Anna	cousin (Joseph & Catharina)	age 13	May 6 1930	Apr 9 1943	Sobibor
Slier, Hans	2nd cousin (Nol & Carrie)	Baby	May 22 1943		Survived as Christian
Slier, Henri	cousin (Joseph & Catharina)	age 14	Jan 16 1929	Apr 9 1943	Sobibor
Slier, Jonas	uncle	Merchant	Mar 22 1886	Nov 5 1942	Auschwitz
Slier, Jonas Philip (Johnny)	2nd cousin (Louis, Elisabeth)	age 3	Sep 13 1940		Survived in hiding
Slier, Joseph	uncle	Sales rep.	Apr 9 1885	Apr 9 1943	Sobibor
Slier, Louis	cousin (Jonas & Ana)	Market seller	Dec 19 1912	Jan 31 1943	Auschwitz
Slier, Philip	cousin (Joseph & Catharina)	Clerk	Feb 14 1922	Sep 30 1942	Auschwitz
Slier, Philip	cousin (Andries & Anna)	Sales rep	Oct 29 1916	Feb 2 1945	Gross-Rosen
Slier, Flip (Philip)	**(Eliazar & Seline)**	**Typographer**	**Dec 4 1923**	**Apr 9 1943**	**Sobibor**
Slier, Seline Salomonson-	mother	Housewife	Mar 14 1890	Jun 4 1943	Sobibor
Slier, Sophie Roselaar-	cousin, Philip's wife	Housewife	Oct 7 1916	Oct 8 1942	Auschwitz

Name	Address		Date of death			Age	Place of death
Samas, Philip	25	Professor Tulp St. Amsterdam	Oct	3	1941	20	Mauthausen
Salomonson, Izaak Lion	16	Van Hogendorp St. Haarlem	Sep	1	1942	81	Auschwitz
de Bruin, Sallie (Samuel Emanuel)	A 118	Hardenberg	Sep	7	1942	53	Auschwitz
de Bruin, Sophie Abrahamson-	A 118	Hardenberg	Sep	7	1942	62	Auschwitz
de Bruin, Emanuel	A 118	Hardenberg	Sep	30	1942	20	Auschwitz
de Bruin, Lion Emanuel	A 118	Hardenberg	Sep	30	1942	24	Auschwitz
Philips, Philipp	92	Vrolik St. A'dam	Sep	30	1942	20	Auschwitz
Philips, Schoontje van Geldere-	57	Zwanenburger St. Amsterdam	Sep	30	1942	20	Auschwitz
Slier, David Leo	6	Schelde St. Amsterdam	Sep	30	1942	16	Auschwitz
Slier, Philip	6	Schelde St. Amsterdam	Sep	30	1942	20	Auschwitz
Slier, Sophie Roselaar-	44	Uithoorn St. 46 Amsterdam	Oct	8	1942	26	Auschwitz
Slier, Andries	44	Uithoorn St. Amsterdam	Oct	12	1942	53	Auschwitz
Slier, Anna van Es-	44	Uithoorn St. Amsterdam	Oct	12	1942	47	Auschwitz
Schaap, Karel (Koopman)	61	Wijk, Vriezenveen	Oct	22	1942	53	Auschwitz
Slier, Jonas	12	Oude Doelen St. Amsterdam	Nov	5	1942	55	Auschwitz
Slier, Elisabeth Aluin-	83	Tugelaweg Amsterdam	Dec	11	1942	30	Auschwitz
Slier, Debora	291	Vrolik St. Amsterdam	Jan	21	1943	47	Auschwitz
Schaap, Juliette Anna Salomonson-	61	Wijk Vriezenveen	Jan	25	1943	51	Auschwitz
Slier, Louis	83	Tugelaweg A'dam	Jan	31	1943	30	Auschwitz
Philips, Betje	92	Vrolik St. Amsterdam	Feb	5	1943	15	Auschwitz
Philips, Eduard	92	Vrolik St. Amsterdam	Feb	5	1943	51	Auschwitz
Philips, Elie	92	Vrolik St. Amsterdam	Feb	5	1943	15	Auschwitz
Philips, Grietje Slier-	92	Vrolik St. Amsterdam	Feb	5	1943	50	Auschwitz
Samas, Bram (Abraham)	25	Professor Tulp St. Amsterdam	Feb	12	1943	49	Auschwitz
Samas, Johanna Sophie Salomonson-	25	Professor Tulp St. Amsterdam	Feb	12	1943	55	Auschwitz
Slier, Duifje	291	Vrolik St. Amsterdam	Feb	12	1943	52	Auschwitz
Slier, Betje Benjamins-	291	Vrolik St. Amsterdam	Feb	17	1943	81	Westerbork
Salomonson, Jenny (Jeanie Muriel) Gestetner-	38	Eindenhout St. Haarlem	Mar	6	1943	39	Auschwitz
Salomonson, Martha Sophie	38	Eindenhout St. Haarlem	Mar	6	1943	10	Auschwitz
Salomonson, Philip	38	Eindenhout St. Haarlem	Mar	6	1943	<1	Auschwitz
Salomonson, Rosalie Johanna	42	Honthorst St. Amsterdam	Mar	20	1943	46	Sobibor
Slier, Elisabeth Anna	6	Schelde St. Amsterdam	Apr	9	1943	13	Sobibor
Slier, Philip (Flip)	**128 III**	**Vrolik St. Amsterdam**	**Apr**	**9**	**1943**	**19**	**Sobibor**
Slier, Henri	6	Schelde St. Amsterdam	Apr	9	1943	13	Sobibor
Slier, Joseph	6	Schelde St. Amsterdam	Apr	9	1943	58	Sobibor
Slier, Cato (Catharina) Vleeschhouwer-	6	Schelde St. Amsterdam	Apr	9	1943	45	Sobibor
Slier, David André	44	Uithoorn St. Amsterdam	Apr	30	1943	24	Sobibor
Salomonson, Friedrich	B 132	Hardenberg	May	21	1943	46	Sobibor
Salomonson, Hanni Bertel	B 132	Hardenberg	May	21	1943	11	Sobibor
Salomonson, Lion	B 132	Hardenberg	May	21	1943	12	Sobibor
Salomonson, Esther Philips-	B 132	Hardenberg	May	21	1943	48	Sobibor
de Bruin, Alex Sallie	A 118	Hardenberg	May	28	1943	15	Sobibor
de Bruin, Ru (Rudolf Emanuel)	A 118	Hardenberg	May	28	1943	56	Sobibor
de Bruin, Rosalchen Salomonson-	A 118	Hardenberg	May	28	1943	53	Sobibor
Slier, Leendert (Eliazar)	128 III	Vrolik St. Amsterdam	Jun	4	1943	52	Sobibor
Slier, Seline Salomonson-	128 III	Vrolik St. Amsterdam	Jun	4	1943	53	Sobibor
Slier, Anna Plas-	12	Oude Doelen St. Amsterdam	Jun	4	1943	52	Sobibor
de Bruin, Rosetta	20	Westerhout St. Haarlem	Jul	9	1943	26	Sobibor
Salomonson, Alfred Sallie	38	Eindenhout St. Haarlem	Feb	2	1944	48	The Hague
Samas, Salomo	25	Professor Tulp St. Amsterdam	Feb	29	1944	26	Gräditz
Slier, Philip	44	Uithoorn St. Amsterdam	Feb	2	1945	28	Gross Rosen

If there were no evidence aside from this list, one could infer that the Dutch transports switched from Auschwitz to Sobibor between March 6 and March 20. The actual date of the first transport was March 2. It was inaugurated by the inclusion of Jannetje Philipse-van Buren, age 97 (note 149[F]). And one could infer that the Dutch transports switched back from Sobibor sometime after July 9. The correct date was July 20.

Name	Relationship	Date of birth			Address	Occupation	Date of death		Place of death
Aluin, Henny (Hendrika)	neighbor	Aug	18	1919	171 Derde Oosterp'k St.	Cutter	Sep	24 1943	Auschwitz-
Aluin, Hella (Seliena)	neighbor	Aug	31	1921	171 Derde Oosterp'k St.	Machine stitcher	Aug	27 1943	Auschwitz
Aluin, Stella (Esther)	friend	Jan	10	1924	171 Derde Oosterp'k St.	Artisan	Sep	24 1943	Auschwitz
Amstel, Joop (Samson) van	Molengoot inmate	Jan	8	1922	3 Jodenbree St.	Baker	Jul	2 1943	Sobibor
Amstel, Jacob Leijden van	Molengoot inmate	Jan	5	1898	3 Jodenbree St.	Rag peddler	Jun	4 1943	Sobibor
Beer, Beertje (Vrouwtje) de	Loonstijn's lodger	Jun	12	1875	18 Amsteldijk	Pensioner	Sep	14 1942	Auschwitz
Beets, Walter van	Molengoot inmate?	Jan	3	1922	11 Vrolik St.	Warehouse clerk	Mar	31 1943	Seibersdorf
Beets, Philipp Günter	Molengoot inmate?	Jun	21	1918	11 Vrolik St.	Framemaker	Jun	4 1943	Sobibor
Bienen, Lena (Lea) van	friend	July	20	1924	22 Gaasp St.	Seamstress	Jan	31 1944	Auschwitz
Bleekveld, Barend	neighbor	Dec	30	1903	128 Vrolik St.	Rag peddler	Apr	30 1943	Auschwitz
Bleekveld, Sara Brandon-	wife of Barend	Jun	25	1905	128 Vrolik St.	Housewife	Feb	26 1943	Auschwitz
Blits, David	neighbor	Jun	10	1922	36 Vrolik St.	Diamond worker	Mar	31 1944	East Europe
Blits, Bora (Debora) Prijs-	David Blits' wife	Jan	6	1923	150 Vrolik St.	Saleslady	Oct	31 1943	Sobibor
Blog, Sientje Prijs-	Bora's mother	Jul	8	1902	150 Vrolik St.	Housewife	May	22 1944	Auschwitz
Brave, Abraham der	friend	Nov	29	1921	54 Transvaal St	Bicycle boy	Apr	30 1943	Central Europe
Cohen, Bernard	Molengoot inmate	Feb	13	1923	85 Vijzel St	Office clerk	Aug	31 1944	Auschwitz
Creveld, Sjaak (Isaäc)	friend	Nov	9	1923	9 Alphen aan den Rijn		Mar	31 1944	East Europe
Elzas, Harry (Gerard)	neighbor & friend	Aug	15	1923	148 Vrolik St.	Tailor	Jan	11 1943	Auschwitz
Elzas, Lientje (Vogeltje)	neighbor & friend	Aug	6	1917	148 Vrolik St.	Seamstress	Sep	7 1942	Auschwitz
Elzas, Maurits.	neighbor & friend	Jan	11	1922	148 Vrolik St.	Paper hanger	Aug	14 1942	Auschwitz
Geldere, Eva Nort-van	Arthur's ma-in-law	Sep	10	1897	72 Vrolik Street	Housewife	Oct	12 1942	Auschwitz
va Nort-van	Arthur's ma-in-law	Sep	10	1897	72 Vrolik Street	Housewife	Oct	12 1942	Auschwitz
Groen, Nico	friend				Derde Oosterpk St.	Typographer	arrested in the Hague, ? fate		
Halverstad, Loek (Louis)	friend	Apil	6	1923	7 Smaragd St.	Office clerk	Sep	30 1942	Auschwitz
Halverstad, Klara Pach-	Loek's wife	Jan	28	1924.	7 Smaragd St.	Housewife	Sep	30 1942	Auschwitz
Haringman, Benny (Benjamin)	friend	Sep	12	1922	436 Ceintuurbaan	Apprentice cutter	Sep	30 1942	Auschwitz
Kaas, Jetty (Henrietta)	friend	Sep	1	1923	259 Vrolik St	Seamstress	Sep	30 1942	Auschwitz
Kesnig, Sally (Solomon Saul)	Molengoot inmate	May	20	1906	23 Cilliers St	Rubber processor	Nov	30 1943	Auschwitz
Kleef, Max van	friend	Feb	2	1912	64 Jeker St.	Sales rep	Sep	30 1942	Auschwitz
Kleef, Mietje Haringman-van	Max's mother	Mar	8	1877	64 Jeker St.	Widow	Jan	26 1943	Auschwitz
Klein, Salomon	Molengoot inmate	Nov	13	1923			Jan	25 1943	Auschwitz
Kroonenberg, Reina	friend	Feb	6	1923	46 Miguel St.		Sep	30 1942	Auschwitz
Lampie, Miep	neighbor	Nov	20	1930	62 Vrolik St.	Child	Apr	9 1943	Sobibor
de Lange, Debora	friend	Sep	4	1925	10 Christiaan de Wet St.	Child	Aug	27 1943	Auschwitz
de Lange, Henny (Heintje)	friend	Apr	12	1924	10 Christiaan de Wet St.	Seamstress	Sep	30 1942	Auschwitz
Loonstijn, Mozes	Simon's father	Mar	26	1892	18 Amsteldijk	Guest house keeper	Mar	31 1944	Poland
Loonstijn, Sara Biet-	Simon's mother	Sep	6	1894	18 Amsteldijk	Carer of seniors	Sep	3 1943	Auschwitz
Loonstijn, Simon	Molengoot friend	Aug	9	1922	18 Amsteldijk	Office clerk	Jan	21 1945	Poland
Peekel, Aron	neighbor	Jan	13	1899	128 Vrolik St.	Shopkeeper	Apr	14 1945	Bergen-Belsen
Peekel, Betty	neighbor	Jun	10	1925	128 Vrolik St.		Feb	19 1943	Auschwitz
Presser, Siepora	friend	Jun	7	1924	32 Tugelaweg	Seamstress	Dec	3 1942	Auschwitz
Pimentel, Henriëtte	Suskind colleague	Apr	17	1876	29 Plantaage M'laan	Creche director	Sep	17 1943	Auschwitz
Prijs, Samuel	Bora's brother	Mar	25	1924	150 Vrolik St.	Warehouse clerk	Nov	30 1943	Sobibor
Reis, Ap (Abraham)	Molengoot inmate	Oct	1	1921	97 Tugelaweg	Upholsterer	Feb	26 1944	Auschwitz
Reis, Henny (Henriette)	friend	Apr	8	1920	6 Raamgracht	Saleslady	Sep	30 1942	Auschwitz
Roodveldt, Abraham	Molengoot inmate	Mar	23	1923	303 Vrolik St.	Bicycle assembler	Nov	29 1942	Mauthausen
Scharis, Fanny Colmans-	wife of Jules	Dec	5	1921	90 Vrolik St	Housewife	Oct	8 1942	Auschwitz
Scharis, Jules	Molengoot inmate	Jan	7	1921	92 Vrolik St.				? fate
Schelvis Chelly (Rachel) Borzykowski-	AJC friend	Mar	2	1923	103 Nieuwe Kerk St.	Seamstress	June	4 1943	Sobibor
Schenk, Henk (Hendrik)	friend	Jun	19	1918			Did not survive		
Vogel, Maupie (Michael)	friend	Jul	29	1923	66 Lepel St.	Leather worker	Sep	30 1942	Auschwitz
de Vries, Boetie (Samuel)	Bep's brother	Jun	2	1921	31 Tilanus St.	Typographer	Sep	30 1942	Auschwitz
de Vries, Big Bep (Elisabeth)	AJC friend	Jun	23	1923	80 Vrolik St.	Packer	Sep	30 1942	Auschwitz
de Vries, Jonas	Bep's brother	Nov	6	1919	31 Tilanus St.	Nurse	Feb	28 1944	Warsaw
Waterman, Ap (Abraham)	Molengoot inmate	Jun	7	1916	34 Hofmeyer	Machine cutter	Feb	28 1943	Auschwitz
Waas, Sally (Salomon)	friend	Nov	16	1922	43 Lepel St.	Metal processor	Sep	30 1942	Auschwitz

THE MOLENGOOT MONUMENT

Dick and Salomon Slier at Molengoot dedication

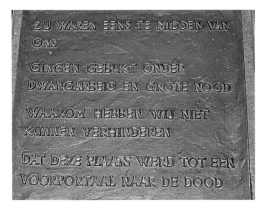

Poem written by Dick Slier

Once they were among us
burdened under forced labor and distress
Why were we not able to prevent
this place become a gateway to their death.

In the first year of the new millennium, about two miles from Hardenberg, a monument was erected at the site of the entrance to Molengoot work camp. It was the brainchild of Dick Slier of Rotterdam (no relation to Flip). He felt an attachment to Hardenberg because the Red Cross had placed him on a farm nearby during the Hunger Winter of 1944. His father's parents, and his father's four brothers and six sisters had been transported to concentration camps in Poland. None of them survived. Because Dick's mother was not Jewish, Dick, his brother Salomon, and his father Jacob survived.

By 2000, Dick had completed two year's work on a book (*Kaddish*) that contains the names of 6,302 Jewish men, women, and children from Rotterdam who did not survive the war. After completing that monument, he turned his attention to the work camps; he established a Molengoot foundation in February 2000, and raised ƒ42,500 for it. The Moor Corporation contributed ƒ20,000 and the government of Hardenberg contributed ƒ20,000. Dick Slier said, "The government was fantastic in the cooperation they gave." The land where the monument now stands belongs to the Bruins family who has granted it on loan for 30 years for a symbolic one euro per year, which they have yet to collect.

The Molengoot monument is a memorial to about 180 men who obeyed their summons to perform what they were told would be "normal work in a normal Dutch labor camp under normal Dutch supervision." The camp was not very comfortable, freedom was restricted, food was inadequate, and the work was hard. The men were often cold and hungry, but there were good days, "We all thoroughly enjoyed the sun and are all red and tanned. I was just called because an ice cream man was at the gate and I ate a delicious ice cream." It was the last place on earth where they could laugh, and keep in touch with their families and friends.

MOLENGOOT INMATES

We hope that eventually there will be a complete list of the Molengoot inmates, but at present we know only the following: of whom the survivors are in bold:

The monument was designed by Kees Huigen, from Den Ham, a village nearby.

Joop van Amstel and his father;
Walter or Philip Günter van Beets;
Bernard Cohen;
I. Cohen (probably Joseph Isidoore);
Matthieu Lopes Cordoza;
Nico Groen;
Walter or Philip Gunter;
(unknown) de Haas;
(unknown) Hart;
Saul Kesnig;
Kiek van Kleef;
Salomon Klein;
Ab van der Linden;
Simon Loonstijn;
Harry Pos?
Abraham Roodveldt;
Jules Scharis;
Flip (Philip) Slier;
Simon van der Sluis;
Gerrit Walvisch;
Abraham (Ap) Waterman;
Ruud (Rudolf) Wolf.

GENOCIDE[A]

It was not the genocide of five to six million Jews that was the catalyst of the UN Genocide Convention;[B] it was Nero feeding Christians to the lions in AD 68, Turkey killing 1,000,000 Armenians in 1915, and Iraq killing 3,000 Christians in 1933.[C] These massacres distressed a young Polish farm boy, Raphael Lemkin, born on June 24, 1901, in eastern Poland, near Bialystok. He became a lawyer, then a public prosecutor. At the League of Nations legal conference in Madrid in 1933, his proposal that attacks on religious, racial, and ethnic groups be made illegal won no support, and the German delegation laughed. When Poland was invaded on September 1, 1939, he fought the Germans, was injured, hid in the forests, and returned to his hometown of Wolkowysk to persuade his family to flee. His father replied: "Jews are used to surviving oppressors." One brother survived but his parents and 47 other family members did not. He fled to Stockholm and from there to the United States, where he taught international law at Duke University and wrote the monumental *Axis Rule in Occupied Europe*.

On August 24, 1941, Churchill described German atrocities in Russia on the BBC: "Since the Mongol invasion of Europe in the 16th century, there has never been methodical, merciless butchery on such a scale, or approaching such a scale . . . We are in the presence of a crime without a name."[D] Lemkin agreed and coined a new name "genocide,"[E] which he proposed should be made illegal. At the Paris Peace conference in 1945, he presented a draft convention on the prevention and punishment of genocide. It was rejected. In Nuremberg in 1946, he tried to persuade the judges to try the Nazis for genocide. He failed, but one of the judges used the word "genocide" in the indictment. In 1946, both at the Peace Conference in Paris and at an international legal conference in Cambridge, England, he failed. However, on December 9, 1948, by unanimous vote, the UN passed the Genocide Convention, the first human rights treaty. Sir Zufrullah Khan, Pakistan's foreign minister, suggested calling it "the Lemkin Convention" in recognition that it was the fruit of Raphael Lemkin's life's work. Lemkin then set out to persuade the signatories to ratify it. He persuaded many, but not the US. In 1959, Raphael Lemkin died in New York. Seven people attended the funeral of the man who laid the foundation for the elimination of genocide, a scourge as disgusting as slavery.

It would take 40 more years and a mighty maverick before the US ratified the treaty. On January 11, 1967, Senator William Proxmire announced that he would give a Senate speech on genocide every single day until the convention was ratified.[A] In 1988, after 3,211 speeches, the US ratified the treaty. It may take another 40 years before the US honors the convention. In 1994 there was Rwanda, and then Bosnia, and then Darfur, where the killing goes on, but we have no Lemkin and no Proxmire.[F] However, in 2001, Radislav Krstic was found guilty of genocide for his role in killing over 7,000 Muslims who were under Dutch UN protection in Srebrenica in 1995. In 2007 several trials were held on the Rwandan genocide. Théonaste Bagosora, the head of the Rwandan army, is awaiting a verdict. If the murderers' accomplices, such as those who blocked the UN from sending troops, should also be brought to justice, would swords be beaten into plowshares, and spears into pruning hooks and would men then not learn war anymore?

Representatives of four states who ratified the Convention on Genocide on October 14, 1948. *Seated left to right:* Dr. John P. Chang of Korea; Dr. Jean Price-Mars of Haiti; Assembly President, Ambassador Nasrollah Entezam of Iran; Ambassador Jean Chauvel of France; and Mr. Ruben Esquivelde la Guardia of Costa Rica. *Standing, left to right*: Dr. Ivan Kerno, Assistant Secretary-General for the Department of Legal Affairs; Mr. Trygve Lie, Secretary-General of the United Nations; Mr. Manuel A. Founier Acuña of Costa Rica; and Dr. Raphael Lemkin, crusader of the Genocide Convention.

Family Tree

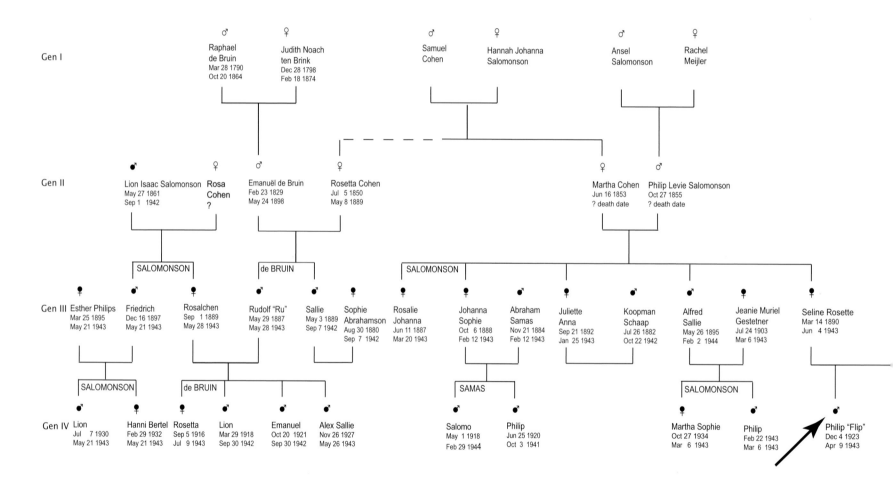

This family tree shows Flip Slier's family in the Netherlands until 1945. It omits Flip's uncle in South Africa and his descendants, as they were not exposed to the German occupation. An aunt who was born and died in 1901, a 14-year-old uncle who died in 1912, and postwar progeny were omitted for the same reason. Male and female symbols, ♀ ♂ are placed above those killed by the Germans; the survivors have clear symbols with the names in blue.

The dates of birth of Flip's family and friends are, like almost all natural events, random; their dates of death however, are non-random. Flip's family tree shows eleven husband and wife pairs in generation III, his parent's generation. Of these eleven, eight died on the same day. The other three pairs died nine, five and three months apart. Because the probability that natural death will occur on any particular day is very small (less than one in 20,000), the probability that a husband and wife will die on the same day is very small indeed. It never happens that eight out of eleven husband and wife pairs in one generation in one family, would die on the same day from any known disease, or from any known natural cause. Those who claim that Jews died of natural causes rather than systematic murder, do not get any help from mathematics.

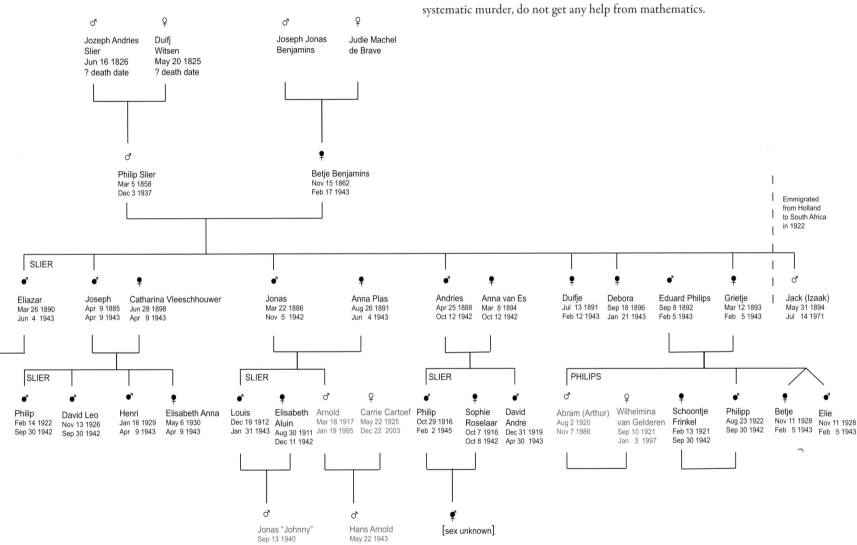

Notes and Sources

Page 11. **A**   Vrolik Street was named for Professor Gerardus Vrolik (1775-1859) and his son, Willem (1801-1863), in gratitude for their donation to the public of a collection of normal and pathological specimens, both human and animal.

11. **B**   Jacob Presser (1988, p.431), *Ashes in the Wind,* quoting A.J. Herzberg.

12. **A**   Death of 22,000 from starvation—that is the number given by the Verzetsmuseum (Resistance Museum), Amsterdam, available at: http://www.scep.nl/verzet/verzetis/153.html. 15,000 is the number given by Walter B. Maass (1970, p.213), *The Netherlands at War: 1940-1945.*

13. **A**   The Reverend Frits Slomp established a national organization that contributed greatly to the survival of many thousands of *onderduikers*. There were probably at least 24,000 Jewish and many more non-Jewish *onderduikers*.

14. **A**   Roth, J. (1933, p.210), *What I Saw: Reports from Berlin 1920-1933.*

14. **B**   William L. Shirer (1984, p.192), *The Nightmare Years, 1930-1940*, noted that Goering appeared to blush when a reporter asked him who started the Reichstag fire.

14. **C**   ibid. (p.245), documents the French response to the violations of the Versailles treaty.

14. **D**   Gestapo is an acronym for *Geheime Staatspolizei,* Secret State Police.

16. **A**   "The atrocities in Poland are unbelievable. They are killing all the young men, driving the old into the fields and sterilising the women. A German Colonel who had been dining with Bob's Swiss friend broke down in the middle of dinner and cried. His nerves had been shattered by what he had seen in Poland." Harold Nicholson (1967, p.62), *The Letters and Diaries of Harold Nicholson, The War Years, 1939-45,* diary entry for March 14, 1940. "Bob" was Robert Boothby, a British member of parliament. Poland lost more people in the war than any other country, more battlefield losses than Britain and America combined, more civilians (17 percent) and more Jews (90 percent).

16. **B**   William L. Shirer (1941, p.245), *Berlin Diary: The Journal of a Foreign Correspondent, 1934-1941.* The German attack on the Netherlands surprised the Dutch but not Shirer, who wrote on November 7, 1939: "Much talk about the Germans pushing through Holland."

17. **A**   Max Nebig was not sent from Buchenwald to Mauthausen with the other 390 men who were seized in the February raid. Alfred Leikam, a German Christian prisoner, working in the camp hospital in Buchenwald, persuaded the hospital to isolate Nebig for tuberculosis, and he "lost" Nebig's prisoner number so that he was able to survive the war hidden in the camp. Alfred Leikam was awarded a Yad Vashem medal. Personal communication, Alice van Keulen-Woudstra to Deborah Slier, October, 2006.

17. **B**   F. J. Goedhart (1941, p.7), "Razzia's op Joden" in *Het Parool*. Despite the Germans executing 13 staff members in February 1943, *Het Parool's* circulation rose to 100,000, more than any of the thousand other underground papers. AJC members distributed it.

18. **A**   Archives available at: http://gemeentearchief.amsterdam.nl/schatkamer/300_schatten/dieren/duiven_als_koeriers/index.nl.html

19. **A**   The *Sicherheitspolizei* was the intelligence department of the SS, the elite Nazi special security force. It began as a subdivision of the SS, which became the controlling police agency in all occupied countries.

22. **A**   Personal communication, Professor Dr. Johannes Houwink ten Cate, October, 2006.

24. **A**   Bob Moore (1997, pp.81-82), *Victims and Survivors: The Nazi Persecution of the Jews in the Netherlands, 1940-1945.*

24. **B**   Maurice Lampe's evidence to Nuremberg Military Tribunal Session 43, January 25, 1946 (Part 5 of 7, p.169), *Crimes against Persons* (Witness examination by M. Dubost). Available at: http://www.nizkor.org/hweb/imt/tgmwc/tgmwc-05/tgmwc-05-43-05.shtml

24. **C**   Available at: http://www.scrapbookpages.com/mauthausen/KZMauthausen/WienerGraben/index.html

24. **D**   Henny E. Dominicus and Alice B. van Keulen-Woudstra (1999), *Mauthausen: een Gedenkboek*; and personal communication, Alice van Keulen-Woudstra; message to Deborah Slier, 2006.

24. **E**   Personal communication, Alice van Keulen-Woudstra to Deborah Slier, November 20, 2006, which explained that the Dutch agents were mostly young boys, students, many of whom had escaped via France and Spain to England where they had been trained to send back messages in Morse code and also to contact the underground. They were betrayed, sent to various camps and eventually killed in Mauthausen. The British government still keeps a part of the archives of this episode closed.

31. **A**   Roel Gritter (1999), "Interview with Egbert de Lange," *De Sallander*, November 10.

Notes and Sources

33. *A*   Before the war the Dutch spelled "Jew" with a capital "J"; it was thus in J.H. van Dale, *Woordenboek der Nederlandse Taal,* (Dictionary of Dutch Language), 1926, pp.312–317, 412–429); in Broers' *Dutch to English Dictionary*, 1940, p.373), in the 1710, and 1926 Dutch Bibles, and in a haphazard selection of prewar books and newspapers. The spelling changed to "jew" around 1941 and that spelling was retained, see the 1970 edition of van Dale, (J.H. van Dale, 1970 pp. 892–895). However, of the Bibles printed in 1946, 1950, 1960, 1961, 1973, 1977, 1978, 1996, and 2004, only one (1973), used the lower case, and then, in part. Professor Dr. G. Kuypers reported in *Trouw* (1997, November 29) that an editor of the newspaper, *De Standaard* had stated that in 1941 the press was ordered to change from upper to lower case "J", "as Jews were not worth a capital 'J'". Kuypers, a non-Jew, questioned why the Dutch commission [1954] in fact legalized a Nazi-spelling of the word "Jew".

35. *A*   Günter Brandorff, personal communication to Deborah Slier, 2004.

35. *B*   Roel Gritter (1998, pp.27-29), *Herinneringen aan Hardenberger joden.*

36. *A*   Selma Leydesdorff (1994), *We Lived With Dignity.* The streets in the Transvaal district of Amsterdam—Tugela, Hofmeyer, Majuba and Christiaan de Wet—are named after Boer heroes and battles in the Boer war.

36. *B*   Jacob Presser (1988, p.296), op. cit. (11B). Presser quoted Dr. A. Lehmann who was quoting a fellow Vught inmate.

37. *A*   The *Digital Monument to the Jewish Community in the Netherlands* (2006) gives names, relatives, occupations, addresses, dates, places of birth and death, photos and biographies on Jews who did not survive. Also used: Yad Vashem. Available at: http://www.yadvashem.org/

38. *A*   Alice van Keulen-Woudstra found the poem which begins and ends: "Een hoge zuil. Kransen met bleek-verdorde bloemen./ Daaronder ligt de heilige soldaat./Mensen die snel in tram of auto naderzoemen,/groeten met onverschillig strak gelaat/en gaan voorbij."

38. *B*   Jacob Presser (1988, p.508), op. cit. (11B).

38. *C*   Vasily Grossman (1985, p.21), *Life and Fate*. His observation was amplified by Labedz (1988, p.240), *Holocaust: Myths & Horrors*: "What is involved in all these 20th century horrors was not only torture, starvation, and violent death upon defenseless people, but also the fact that they were committed not as acts of war, but as civil actions in which the question of personal or individual guilt has not even arisen." Labedz gave three examples of the unconditional extermination of people for no reason except: race (Hitler), political category (Stalin), and literacy (Pol Pot), to whom the wearing of glasses was usually sufficient proof of literacy.

39. *A*   Meyer de Vries, the secretary of the Jewish Council, asked Rabbi Soetendorp to organize the cultural activities in the Work Camps and to tell the people on no account to escape. Soetendorp said: "In those days a boy from Molengoot escaped, and I was ordered to see that the boy would return." [The timing fits with Bernard Cohen's escape.] Soetendorp refused. A heated argument ensued, and de Vries never allowed him into his office again (Knoop, 1983, p.161), *De Joodse Raad*, and David Cohen (1982), *Memoirs prof. Cohen.*

40. *A*   Personal communication, Karel van der Schaaf; message to Deborah Slier, 2006.

41. *A*   See note 37A above.

42. *A*   Waffen SS Captain Josef Mengele was a doctor at Auschwitz from May 1943, until the camp closed in January, 1944. Mengele made selections on new arrivals, and performed many experiments on twins, gypsies and others. The ethics of these experiments matched the science. His Ph.D. from the University of Munich and his M.D. from Frankfurt University were revoked in 1964.

42. *B*   Philip de Vries (1949, pp.254, 263, 324), *Geschiedenis van het verzet der artsen in Nederland.* Of 6,000 practicing Dutch physicians, 4,300 signed the protest against Seyss-Inquart (the Roman Catholics did not sign) and 3,710 wrote Seyss-Inquart a letter of protest. Seyss-Inquart retaliated by putting 400 in prison and fining them each *f*150.-

42. *C*   Jacob Presser (1988, p.470), op. cit. (11B), quoting an unpublished manuscript of Dr. A. Lehmann. Bril did not compete in the 1932 Olympic Games because of anti-Semitism and he boycotted the 1936 Games because Germany was a racist dictatorship. Ireland was the only country to boycott the 1936 Games. In 2008, China, a racist dictatorship, has been awarded the 2008 Olympic Games even while it continues its genocide in Tibet. In the indvidual heptathlon gymnastics competition at the 1908 Games in London, the Netherlands was represented by Jonas Slier, about whom nothing is known except his position in the event—96th out of 97.

44. *A*   Saccharin was discovered by Ira Remsen and Constantine Fahlberg at Johns Hopkins University in 1879. On licking their fingers, they tasted sweetness, traced it to a coal tar derivative, benzoic sulphinide that has no calories but is 300 times sweeter than sucrose. Fahlberg called it "saccharin."

44. *B*   Yad Vashem (2006). Op. cit. (37A).

45. *A*   The first Jew to settle in Hardenberg was Israel Emanuel. He was born in 1710 and died on October 6, 1766. He and his wife, Annigje Rubens, had two surviving children, Jonas Israel, born in 1730, and Emanuel Israel, born about 1739. Jonas took the name Bromet; Emanuel took the name de Bruin. It was from these two people that the Bromets and the de Bruins of Hardenberg were descended. In 1813 there were 16 Jews living in Hardenberg. By 1860 the population had reached 79 and slowly declined thereafter.

46. *A*   Their delightful song can be heard at: http://gemeentearchief.amsterdam.nl/schatkamer/300_schatten/tweede_wereldoorlog/johnny_en_jones/ A one-hour documentary film, *Johnny and Jones,* was released in 2001, directed by Hans Hylkema.

49. *A*   Albert Speer (1970, p.283), *Inside the Third Reich: Memoirs,* added: "The devastation of this series of air raids could be compared only with the effects of a major earthquake. Gauleiter Kaufmann teletyped Hitler repeatedly, begging him to visit the stricken city. When these pleas proved fruitless, he asked Hitler at least to receive a delegation of some of the more heroic rescue crews. But Hitler refused even that."

50. *A*   The statements come from Jan Moor-Jankowski at: http://www.warsawuprising.com/paper/jankowski1.htm. His report is disturbing.

51. *A*   William L. Shirer (1960, p.33), *The Rise and Fall of the Third Reich.*

52. *A*   Jacob Presser (1965, vol. 1, p.194), *Ondergang: De vervolging en verdelging van het Nederlandse Jodendom, 1940-1945.*

59 *A*   Raphael Lemkin (1944, p.601), *Axis Rule in Occupied Europe: Laws of Occupation, Analysis of Government, Proposals for Redress.*

62. *A*   Walter Laqueur (1980, p.96), *Terrible Secret: An Investigation of the Truth About Hitler's "Final Solution,"* and see note 81.

62. *B*   Zygielbojm threw away the dearest thing he owned believing that his suicide would prick the politicians to try to stop the massacres of Jews. Zygielbojm's death "in St Mary's hospital" was promptly and prominently reported by *The Jewish Chronicle*, London (1943, May 14, p.1 and May 21, p.11), which undermined his sacrifice by not reporting the suicide or the suicide note. Whereas *The New York Times* was forthright: "Pole's Suicide Note Pleads for Jews." However, the *Times* delayed three weeks (June 7), and then buried it on page 7.

62. *C*   Richard Rashke (1982, p.128), *Escape from Sobibor,* interviewed Karski, who told him that Jan Ciechanowski, the Polish Ambassador, had been present and protested to Frankfurter, who replied; "I did not say this young man is lying, I said I cannot believe him. There is a difference."

62. *D*   Jan Karski (1944, p.380), *Story of a Secret State.*

62. *E*   The archivists at the World Jewish Congress in Jerusalem, Cincinnati and Washington D.C. have been unable to find the original telegram, which is not mentioned by Aviva Ravel (1980), *Faithful Unto Death: The Story of Arthur Zygielbaum,* nor by Isabelle Tombs' (2000, pp.242-265), *"Moriturivos salutant": Szmul Zygielboim's suicide in May 1943 and the International Socialist Community in London.* However, the telegram is quoted by Samantha Power (2002, p.32), *A Problem From Hell: America and the Age of Genocide,* and by Thomas E. Wood and Stanislaw M. Jankowski (1996), *Karski: How One Man Tried to Stop the Holocaust.* Its text matches a telegram in the British National Archives (FO371/34550, and FO371/31097) and another sent to Churchill in 1942 (Martin Gilbert, 1981, p.108, *Auschwitz and the Allies*).

63. *A*   Marvin Kalb (1996), *The Journalism of The Holocaust,* United States Holocaust Memorial Museum (USHMM). [Accessed 1 May 2005]. Available at: www.ushmm.org/lectures/kalb.html. An extension of Kalb's talk appears in Shapiro (2003, pp.1-13), *Why Didn't the Press Shout? American & International Journalism During the Holocaust.* Both sources cite a Lippmann article in the *New York Herald Tribune,* May 19, 1933, the summary of which is given by Ronald Steel (1980, pp.619, 620), *Walter Lippman and the American Century.* Both Steel (pp.330-373) and David S. Wyman (1984, pp.320, 321, 327), *The Abandonment of the Jews,* elaborate on the common indifference among both Jews and non Jews towards the fate of the Jews. In contrast to the cowardice and indifference of many, Albert Einstein spoke out and petitioned tirelessly on behalf of persecuted Jews. Mandy Katz (2007, p.68), "Was Einstein a Jewish Saint?", *Moment,* April. However, Jews are not alone. Few cared about the fate of the Jews; few cared or care about the fate of the Tibetans, Tutsis, and Timorese. Samantha Power (2001, "Bystanders to Genocide," *Atlantic Monthly,* vol. 288, No. 2). explains why General Romeo Dallaire was abandoned, why the US aggressively blocked UN reinforcements to Rwanda and made the G-word dis appear. Until the genocide convention is implemented, genocide will happen again and again, Terry Allen (2002).

63. *B*   On the 150th anniversary of *The New York Times*, Max Frankel offered an apology: "150th Anniversary: 1851-2001; Turning Away From the Holocaust," *The New York Times,* Nov. 14, p.H10, 2001.

63. *C*   Laurel Leff in "The Holocaust in the New York Times, 1939-1945," *The Harvard International Journal of Press Politics* (2000, pp.52-72), and *Buried by the Times* (2005), gives detailed documentation of the way *The New York Times* distanced itself from Jews by placing articles on inside pages, delaying their appearance, and calling concentration camp victims, Dutch, Poles, Russians, or dentists, but not Jews.

65 *A*   Breitman (1998, p.164) *Official Secrets,* explains how Goebbels responded to the Allied declaration, to the BBC and the leaflets.

65 *B*   Jeffrey Herf (2006, p.265), *The Jewish Enemy,* provides a fascinating insight into Nazi mythology and its propagation.

67. *A*   Saint Nicholas (Santa Claus, *Sinterklaas*) visits Northern Europe with assistant Black Peter for two weeks before December 6 to give presents to

good children and to admonish the bad. St. Nicholas was a very kind Turkish bishop from Myra in the fourth century.

72. **A**   Personal communication, Karel van der Schaaf; message to Deborah Slier, 2006.

75. **A**   This mass shooting, like the one in the photo on p.62, was described by Hermann Graebe, a Rhinelander who had protested against Nazis in 1934 and who protected Jews both during and after the war. Shirer (1960, p.961), op. cit. He was awarded a Yad Vashem medal posthumously.

75. **B**   Walter B. Maass (1970, p.126), op. cit.

75. **C**   Wladyslaw Szpilman (1999, pp.95-6), *The Pianist: The Extraordinary True Story of One Man's Survival in Warsaw, 1939-1945*.

75. **D**   Betty Jean Lifton (1988, pp.339-348), *The King of Children*.

75. **E**   Christopher R. Browning (2004, p.298) quotes Gerlach who quotes Rabbi Tuvia Friedman, *The Origin of the Final Solution: The Evolution of Nazi Jewish Policy, September 1939–March 1942.*

79. **A**   Harm van der Veen (2003), *Westerbork het Verhaal van 1939-1945* is a useful, concise summary of the camp. Philip Mechanicus (1964), *A Year of Fear: A Jewish Prisoner Waits for Auschwitz* is a fascinating objective diary. He describes the OD (p.26); the incremental hardships imposed on the S-prisoners throughout 1943; heads were shaved from August 5 (p.117); they wore indigo and scarlet convict outfits from October (p.181), and from November onwards they were no longer allowed jackets, trousers or overcoats, just the convict overalls and their underwear (p.193). Rood, C. (1949, pp.6-26), *Report* describes how hungry and miserable he was. Jehudith Ilan-Onderwijzer (2003), *Their Image Will Be Forever Before My Eyes,* describes Rosh Hashanah and Chanukah with a little miracle, and Jo Spier (1978) *Dat alles heeft mijn oog gezien: herinneringen aan het concentratiekamp Theresienstadt,* gave affecting fine descriptions and drawings of the people and conditions in prison, Westerbork and Theresienstadt.

79. **B**   In May 1939, 937 German refugees, mostly Jews, left Hamburg for Cuba. The president of Cuba refused to honor the landing certificates of all but 28 passengers. The boat then approached the US, which also refused it entry. It returned to Europe, and in June docked at Antwerp. Belgium, England, France, and the Netherlands admitted the passengers but it is not known how many survived.

81. **A**   Jo Spier (1978) op. cit. (79A).

81. **B**   Philip Mechanicus, September 1943 diary entry (1964, pp. 145, 148, 193, 81). op. cit. (79A). In April 1942, Hosenfeld wrote: "The deeply feared concentration camp . . . [where they] make short work of them by gassing them." Wilm Hosenfeld (2004, p.607, 630, 653), *Ich versuche jeden zu retten: Das Leben eines Deutschen Offiziers in Briefen und Tagebuchern.* The pages quoted are also in Szpilman's *The Pianist* (1999, p.195-201). Jo Spier (1978), op. cit. (79A) described the children arriving at Theresienstadt in 1944, aware that the showers might be sinister, cried "Please don't gas us!". Martin Gilbert (1981, pp.339–341), op. cit. (62E), claimed that the destination of the transports was not known with precision, that the gas chambers of Auschwitz kept their secret until June 1944, and thus the Allies could not bomb them because they were in ignorance. David Wyman (1984, pp.288-307), op. cit. (63A), cites the bombing of Auschwitz factories on August 20, September 13, December 18 and 26, 1944

82. **A**   Walter B. Maass, (1970, pp.123, 124), op. cit. (12A). Maass lived though the war in the Netherlands and has the advantage of personal experience. For example, he described how his wife survived though the kindness of strangers. Bob Moore (1997, p.260), op. cit. (24A) reported 27 years later that: "the majority of Dutch men and women were unlikely to become willingly involved in helping Jews."

86. **A**   Steel (1990), op. cit. (63A); Keegan (1996), "What the Allies Knew," *The New York Times*, 26 Nov.; Walter Laqueur and Richard Breitman (1986), *Breaking the Silence*. The excellent accounts of ignorance and indifference given by Laqueur (1980), *Terrible Secret: An Investigation of the Truth About Hitler's "Final Solution"* and Wyman (1984), op. cit. (63A), ignored the trivializing effect of large numbers. Parkinson observed a committee approve billions for an airport within minutes, whereas a few pennies increase for the morning coffee took an hour's debate. When, as M. Verdoux, Charlie Chaplin was tried for killing thirteen old ladies, he defended himself thus: "One murder makes a villain, millions a hero, numbers sanctify." OJ is shunned; Putin who is responsible for mass murder is invited to Buckingham Palace.

86. **B**   William L. Shirer (1941, p.350), *Berlin Diary: The Journal of a Foreign Correspondent, 1934-1941.*

86. **C**   David Low (1956, p.250), *Low's Autobiography.*

86. **D**   F. H. Hinsley, C. F. G. Ransom, R. C. Knight, E. E. Thomas (1981, pp.669-73), *British Intelligence in the Second World War: Its Influence on Strategy and Operations.*

86. **E**   Victor Klemperer (1999, p.41), *I Will Bear Witness: A Diary of the Nazi Years.*

86. **F**   Szmul Zygielbojm spoke in Yiddish about the fate of the Polish Jews on the World Service of the BBC at 3 p.m. on June 26, 1942, BBC archive (1942). On December 13, 1942, he spoke in English. At times the BBC gave prominence to "Hitler's Pogrom" and at times down-played it, especially on local services. Aviva Ravel (1980), op. cit. (62E), p.167 ff. Isabelle Tombs (2000, pp.242-265), op. cit. (62E).

86. **H**   Hansard (1942), Anthony Eden, December 17, House of Commons, vol. 385, no. 17, 17 Dec. p.2082. The core of Eden's declaration is part of a propaganda leaflet, reproduced on page 63. (Wyman 1984, pp.74,75), op. cit. (63A) showed that the US refused to support the declaration because it was "extremely strong and definite" After weakening the statements about the extermination of Jews, it was approved by 12 governments or governments-in-exile, but not the Vatican, which refused support.

86. **I**   Anthony Eden repeated Lloyd George's remark about the response of Parliament; Jeremy Isaacs (1974), *The World at War*, vol. 5, chap. 3.

86. **J**   Prof. David Cohen's memoirs (1982), op. cit. (39A), in which he wrote: "Not only do I not have any remorse, but also I cannot imagine that I could have acted in a different manner. This would certainly have been the case if I had known what fate was waiting those deported."

86. **K**   Herman Goering (1946). Nuremberg War Crime Trials. Blue Series, vol. 9. Available at;
http://www.yale.edu/lawweb/avalon/imt/proc/033046.htm#Goering

88. **A**   Personal communication, Carry van Lakerfeld; message to Deborah Slier, 2005.

88. **B**   Personal communication (2003) from Flip's cousin, Lionel Slier, who met André van Es in 1955.

90. **A**   Philip Mechanicus (1964, p.23), op. cit. (79C).

90. **B**   Personal communication, Alice van Keulen-Woudstra; message to Deborah Slier, 2006.

95. **A**   Personal communication, Brother Paquette, OCD of the Institute of Carmelite Studies; message to Deborah Slier, 2005.

95. **B**   Jacob Presser (1965, vol. 2, p.261), op. cit. (52A).

95. **C**   Available at: http://www.vatican.va/holy_father/john_paul_ii/homilies/1998/documents/hf_jp-ii_hom_11101998_stein_en.html. "In St. Peter's Square, I am able solemnly to present this eminent daughter of Israel and faithful daughter of the Church as a saint to the whole world."

99. **A**   Tootje Loonstijn-Renger (1998, p.1), *I am Here*.

101. **A**   Elma Verhey wrote (1999) an invaluable introduction to *Tot Ziens in Vrij Mokum; Brieven van Flip Slier uit werkkamp Molengoot (april 1942-oktober 1942)* for which she had done extensive research, and forced attention on the camps. Because the present book is free of the constraints that limited Elma, the family tree now includes an additional 12 de Bruins, 18 Salomonsons and 3 Sliers. And despite being an English translation, these letters more closely resemble the original letters in content, mistakes, corrections, character and layout.

109. **A**   Roel Gritter, (1995, pp.288-290), *Herinneringen aan kamp Molengoot*.

111. **A**   Bert Jan Flim (2005, pp.138, 164), *Saving the Children: History of the Organized Effort to Rescue Jewish Children in the Netherlands, 1942-1945*.

114. **A**   Wladyslaw Szpilman (1999, p.196), op. cit. (75C) and in the complete diary, Wilm Hosenfeld (2004, 626), op. cit. (81A).

114. **B**   Personal communication, Gerrit Renger; message to Deborah Slier, 2007.

115. **A**   Philip Mechanicus (1964, p.155), op. cit. (79C).

115. **B**   Louis de Jong (1969-92, pp.1059-60) vol. V. op. cit. (33A)

119. **A**   Wilhelmina Magdalena van Geldere-Philips, 1995, October 18 interview. Courtesy of Doug Ballman and especially Joanne Rudof, archivist for the Fortunoff Video Archive for Holocaust Testimonies.

121. **A**   Philip Mechanicus (1964, p.23), op. cit. (79C).

121. **B**   Primo Levi (1974) can be seen discussing Auschwitz in Jeremy Isaacs', *The World at War*, op. cit. (86I), vol. 5, chap. 3, "New Arrivals."

124. **A**   The main sources were: William L. Shirer (1988), *The Rise and Fall of the Third Reich*, Vasily Grossman (2006, pp.116-200), *A Writer at War: Vasily Grossman with the Red Army, 1941-1945*, and Alexander Werth (1964, pp.441-563), *Russia at War, 1941-1945*.

124. **B**   ibid., Vasily Grossman (2006, pp.154-156, 159).

124. **C**   Martin Gilbert (1991, p.701), *Churchill: a life*.

124. **D** Winston S. Churchill (1974, p.6427), *Winston S. Churchill: His Complete Speeches 1897-1963*. Robert James, the editor, commented that, "The lack of hesitation with which Churchill allied the British with the Russians marked another major turning point of the war."

126. **A** Winston S. Churchill (1959, pp.509-511), *The Second World War: The Hinge of Fate*.

131. **A** The roommate was Walter or Philip Günter van Beets of 11 Vrolik Street. Their father, Meijer, was dead 4 days later, their mother, Flora, was dead 8 days later. His sisters, Henriette and Margaret, died on the day Auschwitz was liberated and the boys died in June and in March, 1943.

131. **B** Drs. J.M.L. van Bockxmeer (1990, p.115, 178), *The Book of Tears*.

136. **A** Alice van Keulen-Woudstra explained that the authentic Dutch idiom is: "Do not make somebody happy with a dead sparrow."

136. **B** Elma Verhey discovered the Hardenberg police records (1943). Available at: http://www.Hardenbergh.nl/smartsite13467.html

137. **A** Roel Gritter (2005), *Sporen van Joods Verleden* (Tracks of Jewish Past).

137. **B** Wilm Hosenfeld (2004, p.650), op. cit. (81B).

137. **C** Martin Bormann, addressed the Nazi party, adding: "Nazis intend eventually to destroy Christianity." Shirer (1984, p.156).

137. **D** William L. Shirer (1984, pp.154 & 156), op. cit. (14A). Niemöller made his famous apology "First they came for the communists" during a talk he gave in support of Amnesty International, broadcast by the BBC in "Thought for the day" in 1964.

137. **E** Sept 1 1942. Hitler's confidant, Martin Bormann (1946) testified at the Nuremberg Trial of Major War Criminals (vol. VI, p.221), about Hitler's after-dinner conversation on October 2, 1940. It is available at: http://www.nizkor.org/hweb/imt/tgmwc/tgmwc-06/tgmwc-06-55-05.html

137. **F** *The New York Times*, D. T. Brigham (1942, January 3, p.1), "Nazi State Church Plan Proposes To Oust Other Faiths and Ban Bible."

142. **A** Roel Gritter (1995), interview with Ab van der Linden, op. cit. (109A).

142. **B** Jacob Presser (1988, p.412), op. cit.(11B), quoting a baggage handler at Westerbork.

144. **A** Philip Mechanicus (1964 p.95), op. cit.(79C), was quoting a prisoner who had just arrived at Westerbork from Vught in July 1943.

144. **B** Personal communication, Selma Wijnberg-Engel; message to Deborah Slier, Aug. 2006.

144. **C** R.P. Cleveringa (1944), "Zóó is het in Vught," *Het Parool*, 10 Jan, p.5.

144. **D** Philip Mechanicus (1964, p.161), op. cit. (79C).

144. **E** Philips at Eindhoven purposely established a workshop to save Jews at Vught. Personal communication, Jozef Vomberg, 2007.

147. **A** Philip Mechanicus (1964, p.27), op. cit. (79C).

147. **B** Personal communications, Selma Wijnberg-Engel (2006) and Jules Schelvis (2005). Good additional sources are the USHMM recording of Selma on their website, and Jules Schelvis (2003, pp.31-34), *Binnen de poorten*: Ursula Stern's comments were given by Miriam Novitch (1980, p.87), *Sobibor, Martyrdom and Revolt: Documents and Testimonies*. The train went via Bremen, Wittenberg, Berlin, Breslau, and Lublin to Sobibor.

147. **C** Piet Tiggers (1926), *AJC Songs*, Arbeiders Jeugd Centrale, Amsterdam. One of the AJC songs from a booklet of songs. Personal communication (2006) from Joost de Moor of the Stichting Onderzoek AJC to Deborah Slier.

149. **A** Information comes from Laurence Rees (2005), *Auschwitz: A New History*, Debórah Dwork and Robert Jan van Pelt (1996), *Auschwitz 1270 to the Present*, and Primo Levi (2000), *If this is a Man/The Truce*, and *The Drowned and the Saved* (1986).

149. **B** Laurence Rees (2005, p.ix), op. cit. (149A).

149. **C** Irena Strzelecka (1998, p.363), *"Experiments" in Auschwitz 1940-1945*. Primo Levi (1986, p.124), op. cit. (149A), wrote that at a time when the limits of inflicting pain on experimental animals was under review, the limits of inflicting pain in human experiments were ignored by the Germans. For example, they placed people in decompression chambers "to establish at what altitude human blood begins to boil: a datum that can be obtained in any laboratory at minimum expense and without victims." While nothing compares with German medical experiments (except the

Japanese medical experiments), Beecher (1966), *Ethics and Clinical Research,* and Annas, Glanz and Katz (1977), *Informed Consent to Human Experimentation*, discuss experiments on people by American doctors without informed consent. They showed that the rules for informed con sent are much more lax for treatment than for experiment, and the definition of treatment is elastic.

149. **D**   Primo Levi (2000, p.5), op. cit. (149A). When asked why he expressed no hatred of Germans, he responded: "I regard it as bestial, crude . . . Even less do I accept hatred as directed at an ethnic group." If the culprit becomes aware of his crimes and the hateful behavior stops, then Levi would follow the Judeo-Christian precept of forgiving the enemy: "An enemy who sees the error of his ways, ceases to be an enemy" (2000, p. 458).

149. **E**   Wilm Hosenfeld (1999, p.195-6), op. cit. (81A).

149. **F**   Laurence Rees (2005, p.299), op. cit. (149A), who adds "We must judge behavior in the context of the times and judged by the context of the mid-twentieth century sophisticated European culture, Auschwitz and the Nazi's 'Final Solution' represent the lowest act in all history." "Historians generally agree on the uniqueness of the Holocaust." István Deák, (2001, p.81), *The Incomprehensible Holocaust*. But it was not the most efficient, since the Germans had a much lower rate of killing than the Hutus who killed 800,000 Tutsis in 100 days. Perhaps the most unusual feature of the "Final Solution" was that killing was not enough. Primo Levi (1986, p.120), op. cit. (149C), wrote that the reason for deporting 90-year-old women was not just to kill them but to inflict "the greatest physical and moral suffering. The 'enemy' must not only die, he must die in torment." On September 25, 1942, *Het Parool* (No. 43, vol. 7), reported:

> All the crimes we have recorded concerning deportations of our Jewish countrymen pale when compared with the method applied in Amsterdam since the first week in September. Again, Jews are dragged from their homes, but now men and women 60 to 90 years-old are singled out!

149. **G**   Laurence Rees (2005, p.xxi), op. cit. (149A)

149. **H**   Laurence Rees (2005, p.45-46), op. cit. (149A), Rees to a large extent, explains why the SS killed women with children.

150. **A**   Interviewed in 2005-7: Thomas Toivi Blatt, Selma Wijnberg-Engel, Samuel Lerer, Esther Terner-Raab, Jules Schelvis, and Kurt Thomas. Other sources: Thomas Toivi Blatt, *From the Ashes of Sobibor: A Story of Survival* (1999), and *Sobibor: The Forgotten Revolt* (2004); the lecture notes of Chaim and Selma Engel (1988); Ilya Ehrenburg & Vasily Grossman (1993, pp.421-31), *Chernaia kniga* [Black Book]; Esther Terner-Raab (2004), *Tell the World: The Story of the Sobibor Revolt*; Jules Schelvis (1982), op. cit. (147B), and *Vernietigingskamp Sobibor* (1993); Stanislaw Szmajzner (1968), *Inferno Em Sobibor: A Tragédia de um Ado*; Kurt Thomas' manuscript (2006), *My Legacy*; Yitzhak Arad (1987), *Belzec, Sobibor, Treblinka: the Operation Reinhard Death Camps*; Miriam Novitch (1980), op. cit. (147B); Richard Rashke (1982), *Escape from Sobibor*—a reliable report compiled after he interviewed 18 survivors on three continents—and Yuri Suhl (1967), *They Fought Back: The Story of the Jewish Resistance in Nazi Europe*.

Most sources suggest that Flip's transport arrived at Sobibor on Friday, April 9, 1943. Selma Engel wrote in her diary that they arrived at 2 pm on Thursday, April 8. She started her diary on October, 24, 1943 but made this entry in 1944. In 2007, Selma commented: "I think I made a mistake, I am very good at making mistakes." Some sources above claimed that the Dutch often arrived on passenger trains in furs and silk dresses but Mechanicus (1964, p.239), op. cit. (79C), wrote of "the hundred thousand other Jews, most of whom were carried off to Poland in cattle trucks", many who were almost naked and without any baggage, having just the clothes they were wearing, like tramps. Louis de Jong (1978, p.24), *Sobibor*, quoted Jules Schelvis' description of the SS lashing his father-in-law as the doors opened at Sobibor. However, many reports confirm that when some Polish wagon doors were opened, naked, dying, and even decomposed people fell out. Jules arrived at Sobibor on June 4 with Flip's parents, but he did not know them. From this transport, 80 men, including Jules, were selected to work at Dorohucza camp near Lublin, but Jules was in Sobibor long enough to watch his wife, Chelly, go off with the women in the direction of the "showers", talk to some of the Dutch workers who wanted news of their families, and on his way back to the train, to look for the watch that he had suggested that Chelly should hide while they were standing together on the ramp.

150. **B**   SS Sergeant-major Erich Bauer, who had been in charge of the gas chambers, testified at SS Kurt Bolender's trial in 1962. When Treblinka, the sister of Sobibor camp, was liberated, Grossman (2006, p.280 ff.), op. cit. (124A), who was with the Soviet army, interviewed 40 people who had been liberated, from whom he obtained a description that closely resembles Sobibor. He added that "the camp itself covers a very small area, just 80 meters by 600. And if one would have the slightest doubt about the fate of the millions of people who have been brought here, one could have reflected that if these people had not been killed by Germans straight upon arrival, then where would they have lived? These people could have been an entire population of a small country or a small European capital city."

150. **C**   The information came primarily from Selma Engel, Jules Schelvis, Esther Raab and Thomas Blatt (1999, pp.99-102), op. cit. (150A), and also from other sources given in 150A.

150. **D**   Dutch Red Cross pamphlet, SOBIBOR, *Het Nederlandsche Roode Kruis*, Vlamingstraat 2 's-Gravenhage February, (1947, p.8). It uses a capital "J".

150. **E**   Nine women and one man sent cards. One man sent two cards. If he had been offered the opportunity, and had had the strength to hold a pen, that man must surely have been Flip. Ursula Stern was one of the nine women. She collected her card after the war.

150. **F**   Luka's conversation was recorded by Pechersky in 1946, which was translated by Suhl (1967), op. cit. (150A), with Luka's comments on p.23. Pechersky repeated it to Rashke in person in 1981; Rashke (1982, p.185), op.cit. (150A).

150. **G**   ibid. p.123. Psalm 22 is echoed from Golgotha to Sobibor. Here and elsewhere, Tyndale's translation is the first choice.

150. **H**   The letter from Abrao is quoted in Stanislaw Szmajzner (1968, pp.152-154), op. cit. (150A). Abrao bribed Klatt, a Ukrainian guard, to carry the letter to his friend who had come on the same transport. The full letter is given in his book, the few lines here are translated by Vilson Bellim. Szmajzner was born 50 miles from Sobibor. In May 1942, when he was fifteen, he was selected to work as a goldsmith, which he did until the revolt, for which he stole rifles and ammunition. He escaped, fought as a Russian partisan, immigrated to Brazil in 1947, raised cattle, and in 1978, recognized Gustav Wagner on TV news, flew to São Paolo and identified him to the police.

150. **I**   Esther Terner-Raab, personal interview, August 29, 2006 and Esther Terner-Raab (2004, pp210-233), op. cit. (150A).

150. **J**   34,313 people were sent from the Netherlands to Sobibor. On arrival, a few hundred were put back on the train and were transported to work camps around Lublin. Of these, 16 survived. But of the other 34,000, all Sobibor inmates, only three, Selma Wijnberg (Dutch), Ketty (Catharina) Gokkes (Dutch) and Ursula Stern (German) survived the escape. Ursula died in Israel in 1985, aged 57. Ketty died of typhus while fighting with the partisans. Selma is lovely, and is the only Dutch inmate to have survived the war. The number of Sobibor Dutch prisoners who did not survive is not in doubt although, unlike Auschwitz, there is no record of death. All experts agreed that the number of Sobibor Dutch and non-Dutch who died was 250,000 until Peter Witte and Stephen Tyas discovered a Bletchley Park intercept of two January 1943 secret radio messages from Höfle in Lublin to Eichmann and Heim in Berlin (2001, p.468-486), "A New Document on the Deportation and Murder of Jews". Although the radio mesages were cryptic and incomplete, all experts accept this German figure of 101,370 Jews killed at Sobibor in 1942, a killing rate of 16,895 a month. If that rate were continued through 1943, the total number of deaths would have been 253,426. Based on the radio message plus the known transport lists for 1943, Peter Black, senior historian at USHMM, estimates that the total for both years was at least 167,000 and likely to increase, a prediction already proven correct; Jules Schelvis (2007, p.198), *Sobibor*. estimates 170,000.

151. **A**   All the sources (150A) make the same main points, but differ on the details. The direct quotes (line 9) are from Ilya Ehrenburg & Vasily Grossman op. cit. (150A); and (*line 13*) from Selma's diary and Chaim Engel's lecture notes. Although these sources may contain errors, they were honest eye-witness observations. They ring true. Selma's diary is the first Sobibor record known.

151. **B**   When a tall, lean, young Dutchman was not strong enough to split a tree stump, SS Karl Frenzel lashed him on the head. Pechersky put down his axe. Frenzel turned on him:
Frenzel: "Russian soldier, you don't like the way I punish this fool? I give you exactly five minutes to split this stump, or receive 25 lashes."
Pechersky: "I hit the wood as though it was his head."
Frenzel looked at his watch:
Frenzel: "You did it in four and a half minutes."
Frenzel offered Pechersky:a cigarette.
Pechersky: "Thanks, I don't smoke."
In no time everyone knew his name. Many of the sources quoted in note 150A describe this encounter with small variations.

151. **C**   Although Ukraine, as part of the Soviet Union, was fighting against Germany, many guards were Ukrainians with Nazi sympathies. Between 1930 and 1933, Stalin had starved to death between 7 and 11 million of them, and blamed it on the Jews. Grossman (2006), op. cit. (124A).

151. **D**   Sasha was imprisoned for seven years as a traitor, because he had escaped from Sobibor which the Soviets did not believe was possible. They saw his survival as a signal of collaboration. It was Soviet dogma that there had been no war against Jews; that Soviet POWs, not Jews, died at Sobibor.

151 **E**   Misha/Mikhail Lev (1964, pp.78-93), *Almost a Legend*. He expanded this essay into a book, *Kimat a legende* (1973) in Yiddish and recently translated (2006) into English. Alexander Werth (1964, p.989), op. cit. (124A), refers to the profusion of Soviet graffiti in Berlin and gives a few examples but does not quote Rozenfeld's exuberant defiance.

151. **F**   Shaindy Perl (2004), op. cit. (150A), relates Esther's escape and sanctuary, and her testimony at the trial of the SS Bauer.

151. **G**   Kurt Thomas' forthcoming book, is dedicated to Stanislaw and Anna Podsiadly, the kind Polish family who risked their lives to save his.

151. **H**   Karel van der Schaaf remembers Bora Prijs as a naive, combative, resigned person—not the ideal qualities for an escapee.

151. **H**   There is no record or sign of Flip after April 6, 1943, and none of the survivors remember him. However, none of the survivors remember Bora or Samuel Prijs who survived in camp for 7 months.

153. **A**   The map of the camps came from the USHMM (2005). The list of camps came from Presser (1965), op. cit. (52A), NIOD (2006), and the most reliable, Alice van Keulen-Woudstra (2007). Cohen's memoirs (1982), op. cit., describe the events at Ellecom.

most reliable, Alice van Keulen-Woudstra (2007). Cohen's memoirs (1982), op. cit., describe the events at Ellecom.

155. **A**   Laurence Rees (2005, p.263), op. cit. (149A).

157. **A**   Daphne Meijer (2001), *Onbekende Kinderen: De laatste Trein unit Westerbork* [Unknown Children: The Last Train from Westerbork].

157. **B**   Walter B. Maass (1970, chap. 17), op. cit. (12A). When there was no fuel, anything that would burn was pillaged from vacant homes.

157. **C**   The sources of the data for the table below are Raul Hilberg (2003, p.1220), *The Destruction of the European Jews*, and Israel Gutman (1990, p.1799), *Encyclopedia of the Holocaust*, vol. 4. The sources for countries that they did not include, Finland and the Channel Islands (the only part of the UK that Germany occupied during the war), were Hannu Rautkallio (1987), *Finland and the Holocaust,* and Frederick Cohen (2000), *The Jews in the Channel Islands During the German Occupation.* As Gutman provided a minimum and a maximum estimate, an average was calculated. The mean of Gutman's average and Hilberg's estimate was entered into the table. Thus, these data have been compiled in a uniform way that may not increase their reliabilty so much as their comparability. The estimates vary between sources because a Jew is not consistently defined, because foreign Jews are sometimes included in their country of origin, sometimes in their country of residence; because countries are not consistently defined—the borders are not constant; the census was not taken at the same time, and many babies' deaths were not recorded, especially when they were newborn. For example, Sophie Roselaar-Slier was almost nine months pregnant when she arrived at Auschwitz, but there is no record to indicate whether the baby was killed *in* or *ex-utero.* In either case, the child has been included as the fifty-eighth member of Flip's family.

The Dutch Jewish Council and Co-ordination Commission counted 118,295 full Dutch Jews in 1940, and 22,252 foreign Jews. In 1945 they re registered 21,674 survivors, comprising 16,224 *onderduikers*, 4,532 from the concentration camps and 918 at Westerbork. From these Dutch sources, the mortality was 81.7 percent, placing the Netherlands between Lithuania and Poland, number 22 out of 23 countries. The reason that the Netherlands ranks with Poland and Lithuania may be because their chief administrators, Seyss-Inquart and Hans Frank, were civilians, where as all, or almost all, other occupied countries had military governors.

Bulgaria surpassed all other countries. "The church and the professions as well as the general population were all united in the single determi nation to protect Bulgaria's Jewry," Yuri Suhl and Matei Yulzan in Yuri Suhl (1967, p.275), op. cit. (150A). Italy surpassed all other countries in that it was the only country to save the same percentage (80%) of its own and its foreign Jews. The Netherlands was the only country to lose the same percentage (82%) of its own and its foreign Jews.

Country	Prewar Jewish population	Deaths #	Deaths %
Bulgaria	50,000	0	0
Finland	2,000	7	0.4
Denmark	7,800	60	0.8
Italy	44,500	8,340	18.7
France	350,000	76,160	21.8
Germany	566,000	134,000	23.7
Channel Isles	16	4	25.0
Austria	185,000	50,000	27.0
USSR	3,020,000	900,000	29.8
Estonia	4,500	1,375	30.6
Belgium	65,700	26,450	40.3
Hungary	825,000	369,750	44.8
Romania	609,000	274,500	45.1
Luxembourg	3,500	1,725	49.3
Norway	1,700	881	51.8
Czech rump	118,310	78,150	66.1
The Netherlands	140,000	101,000	72.1
Yugoslavia	78,000	59,875	76.8
Latvia	91,500	70,750	77.3
Slovakia	88,950	69,500	78.1
Greece	77,380	61,750	79.8
Lithuania	168,000	135,750	80.8
Poland	3,300,000	2,950,000	89.4

Table showing the fate of Jews during the war in 23 countries.

163. **A**   Samantha Power (2002), *A Problem From Hell: America and the Age of Genocide*, the subtitle of which might well have been: "If a clod be washed away by the sea." Had President Reagan not paid his respects to the 49 SS buried at Bitburg, Proxmire might have had to make 3,000 more speeches.

163. **B** The United Nations General Assembly, 1948, Convention on the Prevention and Punishment of the Crime of Genocide, Resolution 260 A(III)
The General Assembly of the United Nations in its resolution 96 (I) dated 11 December 1946 declared genocide a crime under international law, contrary to the spirit and aims of the United Nations and condemned by the civilized world;
RECOGNIZING that at all periods of history genocide has inflicted great losses on humanity; and
BEING CONVINCED that, in order to liberate mankind from such an odious scourge, international co-operation is required,
HEREBY AGREE AS HEREINAFTER PROVIDED: [Four of the fifteen articles follow:].

Article 1: The Contracting Parties confirm that genocide, whether committed in time of peace or in time of war, is a crime under international law which they undertake to prevent and to punish.

Article 2: In the present Convention, genocide means any of the following acts committed with intent to destroy, in whole or in part, a national, ethnic, racial or religious group, as such:
a. Killing members of the group;
b. Causing serious bodily or mental harm to members of the group;
c. Deliberately inflicting on the group conditions of life calculated to bring about its physical destruction in whole or in part;
d. Imposing measures intended to prevent births within the group;
e. Forcibly transferring children of the group to another group.

Article 3: The following acts shall be punishable:
a. Genocide;
b. Conspiracy to commit genocide;
c. Direct and public incitement to commit genocide;
d. Attempt to commit genocide;
e. Complicity in genocide.

Article 4: Persons committing genocide or any of the other acts enumerated in Article 3 shall be punished, whether they are constitutionally responsible rulers, public officials or private individuals.

Physical Genocide was defined as the outright extermination as well as the imposition of "slow death measures" (i.e., subjection to conditions of life which, owing to lack of proper housing, clothing, food, hygiene, and medical care or excessive work or physical exertion are likely to result in the debilitation and death of individuals; mutilations and biological experiments imposed for other than curative purposes; and deprivation of livelihood by means of looting or confiscation of property).

Biological Genocide was defined as the prevention of births among the target group (i.e., involuntary sterilization or abortion, as well as compulsory segregation of the sexes).

Cultural Genocide was defined as the destruction of the specific characteristics of the group (i.e., forced dispersal of the population; forced transfer of children to another group; suppression of religious practices or the national language; forced exile of writers, artists, religious and political leaders or other individuals representing the culture of the group; destruction of cultural/religious shrines or monuments, or their diversion to alien uses; destruction or dispersion of documents and objects of historical, artistic or religious value, and objects used in religious worship. The USA, Canada and the USSR softened Lemkin's criteria for Cultural Genocide and allowed mass killing of political groups.

163. **C** William Korey (2001), *An Epitaph for Raphael Lemkin.*

163. **D** Winston S. Churchill (1974, p.6474), op. cit.

163 **E** Raphael Lemkin (1944, p.79), op. cit. (59A) wrote: "New conceptions require new terms. By 'genocide' we mean the destruction of a nation or an ethnic group. This new word, coined by the author to denote an old practice in its modern development is made from the Greek word *genos* (race, tribe) and the Latin word *cide* (killing), thus corresponding in its formation to such words as 'tyrannicide,' 'homicide,' 'infanticide,' etc. It is intended rather to signify a coordinated plan of different actions aimed at the destruction of essential foundations of the life of the national groups with the aim of annihilating the groups themselves."

163. **F** One might add, and no Bishop Ambrose of Milan. However, Nicholas D. Kristoff' (2005) "The Secret Genocide Archive," *The New York Times*, and (2006) "Genocide in Slow Motion," *The New York Review of Books*, is a good substitute. Moreover, the entire issue of the *New Republic,* (2006), vol. 234, no. 4,765, was devoted to Darfur. But the world is as unmoved by Darfur as it is by the Chinese genocide in Tibet and Chinese support of genocide in Sudan. Yelena Bonner said of the killing in Chechnya, "if that is not genocide, I do not know what is."

179. **A** Raphael Lemkin (1944, p.478), op. cit. (59A).

Verordnungsblatt
für die
besetzten niederländischen Gebiete
Stück 10

Verordeningenblad
voor het
bezette Nederlandsche gebied
Aflevering 10

Ausgegeben am 25. April 1942   Verschenen 25 April 1942

Article 11

(^{1}) If a person, who according to the provisions of Article 4 of the regulation No. 189/1940 is a jew or is considered a jew, married with a person, who according to said provisions is neither a Jew, nor being considered as a jew, then Article 10 is not applicable in affairs, belonging to:

1) the jewish husband (spouse), for as far as there are children present from the marriage, who, according to the said provisions are not being recognized as jews;

2) the jewish wife (spouse) in the case of childless marriage.

(^{2}) The provisions of the first paragraph under 1, are also applicable if the marriage no longer exists.

(^{3}) The provisions of the first and second paragraph do not apply to marriages that have been entered into after May 9, 1940.

Article 12

Article 10 does not apply with respect to:

1) their own marriage ring and the marriage ring of a deceased partner;

2) silver wrist and pocket watches in personal use;

3) used silver cutlery, meaning that everyone belonging to the family can keep one spoon, desert spoon, knife and fork;

4) dental fillings of precious metal only while in personal use.

Article 13

(^{1}) Objects laid down in Article 10 must also be handed in.

---

§ 11.

(^{1}) Ist eine Person, die nach den Bestimmungen des § 4 der Verordnung Nr. 189/1940 Jude ist oder als Jude gilt, mit einer Person verheiratet, die nach den vorerwähnten Bestimmungen weder Jude ist noch als Jude gilt, so findet § 10 auf solche Sachen keine Anwendung, die gehören

1) dem jüdischen Ehegatten, sofern Abkömmlinge aus der Ehe vorhanden sind, die nach den vorerwähnten Bestimmungen nicht als Juden gelten;

2) der jüdischen Ehefrau bei kinderloser Ehe.

(^{2}) Die Bestimmungen des Absatzes 1, Ziffer 1, gelten auch dann, wenn die Ehe nicht mehr besteht.

(^{3}) Die Bestimmungen der Absätze 1und 2 finden auf Ehen, die nach dem 9. Mai 1940 geschlossen sind, keine Anwendung.

§ 12.

Der § 10 gilt nicht.

1) für die eigenen Trauringe und die eines verstorbenen Ehegatten;

2) für im persönlichen Gebrauch befindliche silberne Armband- und Taschenuhren;

3) für gebrauchtes Tafelsilber mit der Massgabe, dass jeder zum Haushalt des Eigentümers gehörigen Person ein vierteiliges Essbesteck — bestehend aus Messer, Gabel, Löffel und kleinem Löffel — verbleibt;

4) für Zahnersatz aus Edelmetallen, soweit er sich im persönlichen Gebrauch befindet.

§ 13.

(^{1}) Die im § 10 genannten Sachen sind auch dann abzuliefern, wenn daran

---

Artikel 11.

(^{1}) Is een persoon, die volgens de bepalingen van artikel 4 der Verordening No. 189/1940 jood is of als jood wordt aangemerkt, gehuwd met een persoon, die volgens genoemde bepalingen noch jood is, noch als jood wordt aangemerkt, dan is artikel 10 niet van toepassing op zoodanige zaken, welke toebehooren aan:

1) den joodschen echtgenoot, voor zoover er afstammelingen uit het huwelijk aanwezig zijn, die volgens de genoemde bepalingen niet als jood worden aangemerkt;

2) de joodsche echtgenoote in geval van kinderloos huwelijk.

(^{2}) De bepalingen van het eerste lid, onder 1, zijn ook dan van toepassing, indien het huwelijk niet meer bestaat.

(^{3}) De bepalingen van het eerste en tweede lid zijn niet van toepassing op huwelijken, welke na 9 Mei 1940 zijn gesloten.

Artikel 12.

Artikel 10 is niet van toepassing ten aanzien van:

1) eigen trouwringen en die van een overleden echtgenoot;

2) zilveren pols- en zakhorloges in persoonlijk gebruik.

3) gebruikt tafelzilver, met dien verstande, dat elke tot het gezin van den eigenaar behoorende persoon een vierdeelig eetbestek — bestaande uit mes, vork, soeplepel en dessertlepel — behoudt;

4) gebitvullingen uit edele metalen in persoonlijk gebruik.

Artikel 13.

(^{1}) De in artikel 10 genoemde voorwerpen moeten ook dan ingeleverd

295

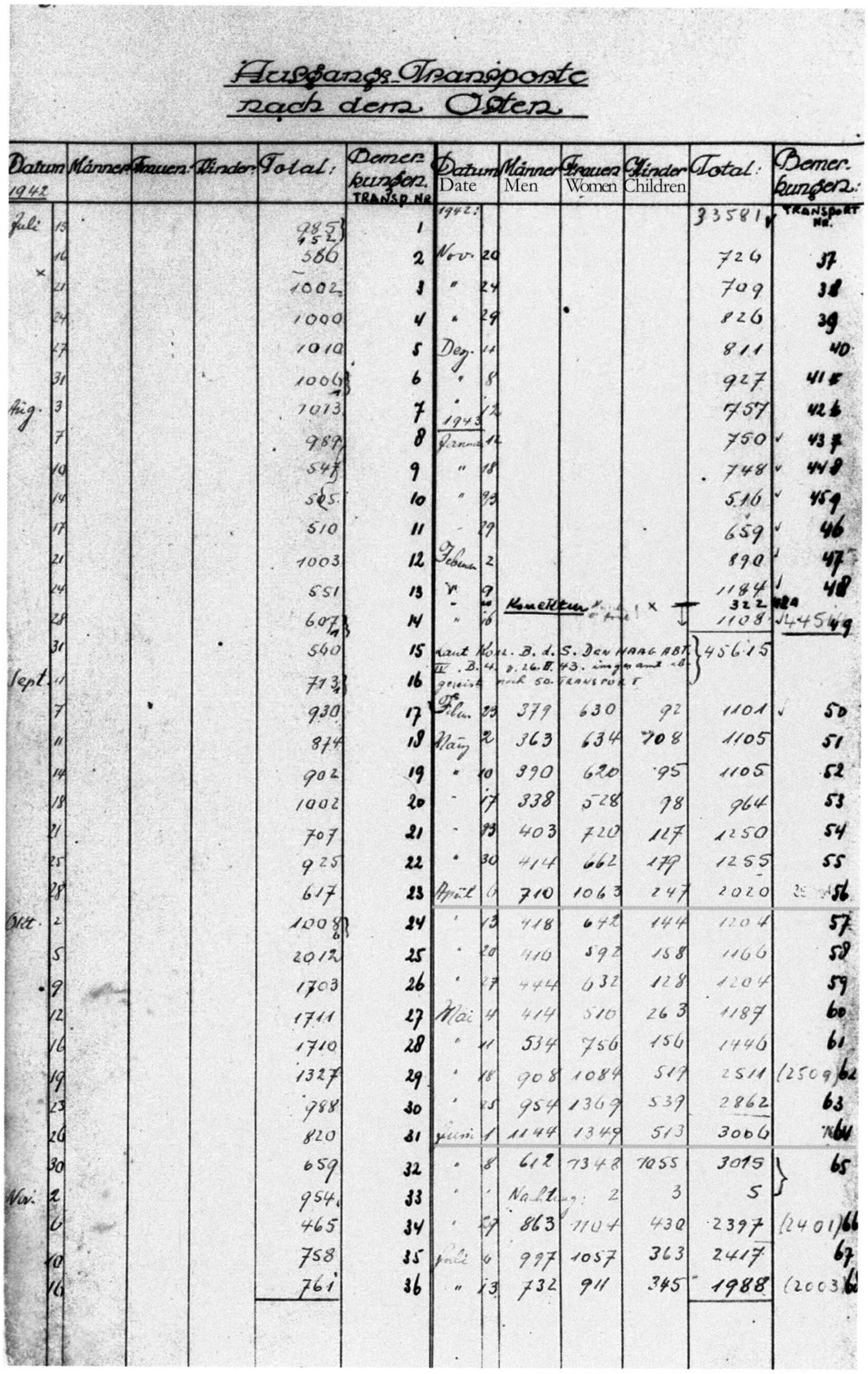

Ausgangs Transporte nach dem Osten

Left section (Transports 1–36):

Datum 1942	Männer	Frauen	Kinder	Total	Transp. Nr
Juli 15				985/452	1
16				586	2
21				1002	3
24				1000	4
27				1010	5
31				1006	6
Aug. 3				1013	7
7				987	8
10				547	9
14				505	10
17				510	11
21				1003	12
24				551	13
28				607	14
31				560	15
Sept. 1				713	16
7				930	17
11				874	18
14				902	19
18				1002	20
21				707	21
25				925	22
28				617	23
Oct. 2				1008	24
5				2012	25
9				1703	26
12				1711	27
16				1710	28
19				1327	29
23				988	30
26				820	31
30				659	32
Nov. 2				954	33
6				465	34
10				758	35
16				761	36

Right section (Transports 37–68):

Datum 1942	Männer / Men	Frauen / Women	Kinder / Children	Total	Transp. Nr
				33581	
Nov. 20				726	37
24				709	38
29				826	39
Dez. 4				811	40
8				927	41
12				757	42
1943 Jan. 11				750	43
18				748	44
23				516	45
29				659	46
Feb. 2				590	47
9				1184	48
16				322 / 1108	49
15				456,5	
Febr. 23	379	630	92	1101	50
März 2	363	634	708	1105	51
10	390	620	95	1105	52
17	338	528	98	964	53
23	403	720	127	1250	54
30	414	662	179	1255	55
April 6	710	1063	247	2020	56
13	418	642	144	1204	57
20	410	592	158	1166	58
27	444	632	128	1204	59
Mai 4	414	510	263	1187	60
11	534	756	156	1446	61
18	908	1084	519	2511 (2509)	62
25	954	1369	539	2862	63
Juni 1	1144	1349	513	3006	64
8	612	1348	1055	3015	65
Nachtrag	2	3		5	
	863	1104	430	2397 (2401)	66
Juli 6	997	1057	363	2417	67
13	732	911	345	1988 (2003)	68

Long term prisoners surreptitiously kept lists of the 104,000 Jews who were transported from Westerbork. This summary list (*left*) of 68 of the transports leaving Westerbork, gives the date, the number of men, women and children and the total on each train. Flip's transport was number 56, his parents were on number 64. Another list was kept of each person leaving Westerbork. One line of this list is given below. Each person is listed alphabetically by surname and first name, giving in addition, the maiden names, dates of birth, home addresses and the dates of departure. Almost everyone on the transport lists was sent to Poland but they also included those who escaped (very few) and those who died. For example, grandma Betje Benjamins-Slier is listed on February 17 when she was taken to be buried in Assen cemetery about five miles away. That was one month after her daughter Debora left on a transport for Auschwitz, two weeks after her daughter Grietje left on a transport for Auschwitz, and one week after her daughter Duifje left on a transport for Auschwitz.

The number transported to Sobibor was 34,313. The survival rate was at most 0.05%. If those who were transferred to other camps on arrival at Sobibor are excluded, then the survival rate was less than 0.009%. At other camps the survival rates were much higher; 1.75% at Auschwitz; 40.5% at Theresienstadt and 58.7% at Bergen-Belsen.

Below: A one line sample of the person by person list of all the people on the transports leaving Westerbork.

| Slier | Philip | 4.12.23 | A-dam | Vrolikstr. 128 | 6. 4.43 |

There were many examples of exemplary behavior, many Good Samaritans and many who hid *onderduikers* and many who accepted household goods, books, and photos for safekeeping. A minority disposed of the goods when they believed the person would not come back or because their family was starving to death. And a small minority, including one or two Jews, betrayed their fellow citizens. One example was reliably reported by someone who knew of a mixed marriage with two children that went sour during the war.

Separating, especially at that time, was difficult and more so if it was a mixed marriage. In 1942, the man was arrested because he was walking outside without wearing his star. He was sent to Amersfoort Camp, but was one of the few who escaped. When he came home, he discovered that his place had been taken by another man and his homecoming was a very unpleasant surprise. But there was a solution, thanks to the war. The wife, together with her new friend, went to the police station and told them about the Jewish escapee at her house. He was fetched from the house at once, taken to Camp Amersfoort, but this time he did not escape; he was transported. He died in his twenties in a concentration camp.

The receipt (*below*) was given to a Dutch subject in 1943 for betraying five Jews for ƒ7,50- each. All five were dead 10 days later. They and several other members of their family members were sent to Sobibor on April 13. The receipt states that: "This amount is paid as an advance from Jewish property." The receipt was acknowledging that the state was to be reimbursed from the sale of Jewish property that the state had acquired by passing a LIRO law (acronym for Lippmann, Rosenthal Bank) that demanded all Jews deposit all that they had in the bank, which then confiscated it. Thus, in effect, the betrayed pay off their betrayers.

Amsterdam on 6 April 1943

The Dutch subject   K------- H-------i--
Room 25_____hands over on___5 April 1943

1 Hartog Waterman	A'dam	24.1.82	Africaner Square 43/5	[age 61]
2. Philip Coster	A'dam	5. 4. 62	Africaner Square 43/5	[age 81]
3. Kaatje Coster-Mok,	Haarlem	26. 9. 68	Africaner Square 54/0	[age 74]
4. Israel Jacobs,	A'dam	23. 5. 73	Majubastraat ΙΙΙΙ	[age 69]
5. Marianne Doof-Pels	A;dam	8. 6. 84	Majubastraat ΙΙ	[age 58]

Amsterdam

For the Central Department for jewish Emigration, Amsterdam, is correctly taken in by;

Wolf SS Stru-
Duty guard

1. For the correctness of the takeover: SS Captain **A. A. Finstom**

2. Administrator

for collecting the payment of 37.50 Guilders, written, thirty seven and ⁵⁰/₁₀₀ Guilders,
Amsterdam   6, April 1943.

Determined by
Police secretary   Found correct
                                    Major illegible (signed)
        The state bank_____on 13 APR 1943
Zahislette-Aussenstelle
        Amsterdam

Acknowledgement of receipt:

Of the cashier's office of the State Bank—branch Amsterdam—I have 37,50 guilders in words thirty seven and ⁵⁰/₁₀₀ Guilders received. This amount is paid as a advancement from Jewish property.

signed

K 372

HET GIROKANTOOR DER GEMEENTE AMSTERDAM

Betr.: V. O. 58/42, betr. de behandeling van joodsche vermogenswaarden.

AMSTERDAM, datum bestelling.

Aan
de Rekeninghouders

Door de firma Lippmann, Rosenthal & Co., Sarphatistraat, Amsterdam is mij medegedeeld, dat volgens een recente beschikking van den Heer Generalkommissar für Finanz und Wirtschaft in verband met de verordening 148/41 en 58/42 van den Heer Rijkscommissaris voor de bezette Nederlandsche gebieden tegoeden van personen, die jood zijn in den zin van art. 4 der verordening 189/40, in alle gevallen, onverschillig of zij meer of minder dan ƒ 250.—bedragen, naar bovengenoemde instelling moeten worden overgebracht.

De rekeningen van de hierbedoelde personen moeten onverwijld worden afgesloten en de saldi bij de firma Lippmann, Rosenthal & Co., Sarphatistraat, Amsterdam ten gunste van deze rekeninghouders worden gestort.

Rekeninghouders welke onder bovenstaande bepalingen vallen worden beleefd verzocht onderstaand formulier in te vullen en aan het Girokantoor in te zenden.

De Directeur van het Gemeente Girokantoor,
M. VAN GIESSEN.

Ondergeteekende.............................
wonende...........................houder van
rekening Letter............, No............, verzoekt op grond van het vorenstaande zijn rekening op te heffen en het saldo over te schrijven op zijn rekening bij de firma Lippmann, Rosenthal & Co., Sarphatistraat, Amsterdam.

AMSTERDAM, ... 1942.
Handteekening,

Aan
het Gemeente Girokantoor
Amsterdam, O.Z. Voorburgwal 274.

Stadsdrukkerij Amsterdam
16622-8-42-51000

I have been informed by the firm Lippmann, Rosenthal, & Co., Sarphati Street, Amsterdam that according to a recent decision of the General Commissioner for finance and business, and in connection with the order 148/41 and 58/42 of the State Commissioner for the occupied Dutch lands, assets of any person who is a jew in the sense of article 4 of the order 189/40, in all cases, regardless of whether they have more or less than ƒ 250.— must be transferred to the above mentioned institution.

The accounts of the identified people must be closed immediately and the money must be delivered to the account holders at the firm of Lippmann, Rosenthal & Co., Sarphati Street, Amsterdam.

Account holders who are in the group to whom the above orders apply are politely requested to fill out the form listed below and send it to the Giro Office.
The Director of the Municipal Giro Office,
M. VAN GIESSEN

The undersigned................................
Address.......................................
......................holder of account
Letter............Number....................req uests that on the basis of what is written above, his account be closed and the balance turned over to his account with Lippmann, Rosenthal & Co., Sarphati Street, Amsterdam

The book of German regulations for the occupation of the Netherlands (page 176), contained some regulations that applied only to Jews. They state that the property of a person who is a Jew, or is considered a Jew, belongs to Germany, with the exception of a watch, a ring, one set of silver cutlery and dental fillings while in personal use; thereby sanctioning the removal of teeth from Jewish dead and anything else from the living.

Another regulation permitted the Germans to sieze anyone's property:

> The property of persons or associations which have furthered activities hostile to the German Reich or Germanism, or of whom it must be assumed that they will further such activities in the future, may be confiscated in whole or in part.[A]

The Germans issued regulations that ensured that it was within the law to arrest Jews, confiscate their homes and possessions, store them in Westerbork, and then transport them to Poland. Mass murder by nation states was never clearly illegal, at least until 1948.

The Dutch spelled "Jew", "Jews", and "Jewish" with an upper case "J" until the German occupation when the lower case became the standard form in newspapers, documents, and dictionaries. Even Flip used the new style. The German regulations on page 176 were printed in German on the left ("Jude" and "jüdischen") and Dutch on the right "jood" and joodschen." Even for the sake of humiliating Jews, the Germans would not forsake their rule that in German, nouns take the upper case and adjectives the lower case. A lower case "J" is the only form seen on all the official Dutch documents of this period, for example on the ID (page 139) or the bank letter (*left*). The note 33A on page 167 amplifies the reasons for supposing that the Germans used orthography as another way to humiliate Jews, albeit a trivial one.

In English the association between anti-Semitism and a lower case "J" was made by T.S. Eliot:

> The rats are underneath the piles
> The jew is underneath the lot.
> *Burbank with a Baedeker:*
> *Bleistein with a cigar*, 1920

> the jew squats on the window sill
> *Gerontion*, 1918

Bibliography

Allen, T. 2002, "The General and the Genocide", *Amnesty International Magazine*, Winter.

Amsterdam City Archives, pigeons 2006, [Accessed 1 June, 2006]. Available at: http://gemeentearchief.amsterdam.nl/schatkamer/300_schatten/

Amsterdam City Archives, Johnny & Jones 2005, [Accessed 10 May, 2005]. Available at: http://gemeentearchief.amsterdam.nl/schatkamer/300_schatten/ /tweede_wereldoorlog/johnny_en_jones/

Annas, G.J. & Glantz, LH, Katz, B. 1977, *Informed Consent to Human Experimentation: The Subject's Dilemma*, Ballinger, Cambridge, Mass.

Arad, Y. 1987, *Belzec, Sobibor, Treblinka: the Operation Reinhard Death Camps*, Indiana University Press, Bloomington and Indianapolis.

Beecher, H.K. 1966, "Ethics and Clinical Research", *The New England Journal of Medicine*, vol. 274, pp.1354–1360.

Blatt, T.T. 1999, *From the Ashes of Sobibor: A Story of Survival*, Northwestern University Press, Evanston.
    2004, *Sobibor The Forgotten Revolt*, Private Printing.

Bockxmeer, Drs. J.M.L. van 1990, *The Book of Tears*, De Ramp bij Hollandia Kattenburg, Amsterdam.

Breitman, R. 1998, *Official Secrets: What the Nazis Planned and What the British and Americans Knew*, Hill & Wang, NY.

Brigham, D.T. 1942, "Nazi State Church Plan Proposes To Oust Other Faiths and Ban Bible," *The New York Times,* 3 Jan. p.1.

Broers, A. 1940, *Engels Woordenboek*, J.B. Wolters Uitgevers-Maatschappij, Groningen.

Browning, C.R. 2004, *The Origins of the Final Solution: The Evolution of Nazi Jewish Policy, September 1939–March 1942,* The University of Nebraska Press, Lincoln.

Churchill, W.S. 1959, *The Second World War: The Hinge of Fate*, Houghton Mifflin Company, Boston.
    1974, *Winston S. Churchill: His Complete Speeches 1897–1963*, ed. Robert Rhodes James, Chelsea House Publishers, New York.

Cleveringa, R.P. 1944, "Zóó is het in Vught," *Het Parool*, 10 Jan, p.5.

Cohen, D. 1982, "Memoires prof. Cohen," trans. J. Vomberg, *Nieuw Israëlitisch Weekblad*, May, p.1–27.

Cohen, F. 2000, *The Jews in the Channel Islands During the German Occupation*, Jersey Heritage Trust and the Wiener Library, 2nd ed., London.

Dale van, J. H. 1926, *Woordenboek der Nederlandse Taal*, vol. J-Keurmede, Ed. A. Beets, Martinus Nijhoff, 's-Gravenhage.
    1970, *Groot woordenboek der Nederlandse taal*, Supplement vol. 1, C. Kruyskamp, Martinus Nijhoff, 's-Gravenhage.

Deák, I. 2001, *Essays on Hitler's Europe,* University of Nebraska Press, Lincoln.

Digital Monument to the Jewish Community in the Netherlands 2006. [Accessed January-December, 2006.] Available at: http://www.joodsmonument.nl/

Dominicus, H.E. & Keulen-Woudstra, A.B. van 1999, *Mauthausen een Gedenkboek*, Stichting Vriendenkring Mauthausen, Amsterdam.

Dwork, D. & Pelt, R.J. van 1996, *Auschwitz 1270 to the Present*, W.W. Norton and Co., New York.

Ehrenburg, I. & Grossman, V. 1993, *Black Book (Chernaia kniga)*, trans. Aleksandr, Yad, Vilnius.

Eliot, T.S. 1952, *Selected Poems*, Penguin books with Faber and Faber, Harmondsworth, Middlesex.

Frank, A. 2003, *The Diary of Anne Frank: The Revised Critical Edition*, eds. D. Barnouw & G. van der Stroom, trans. A.J. Pomerans, B.M. Mooyaart-Doubleday & S. Massotty, Doubleday, New York.

Flim, B.J. 2005, *Saving the Children: History of the Organized Effort to Rescue Jewish Children in the Netherlands 1942–1945*, CLD Press, Bethesda.

Frankel, M. 2001, "1851–2001 A Horror Unexamined; Turning Away From the Holocaust," *The New York Times*, 14 Nov, p.H10.

Gilbert, M. 1981, *Auschwitz and the Allies,* Holt, Rinehart and Winston, New York.
    1991, *Churchill: a life*, Heinemann, London.

Gilbert, M. & Dobroszychi, L. 1995, "The Final Solution," *Oxford Companion to World War II*, eds. I.C.B. Dear & M.R.D. Foot, OUP, NY.

Goedhart, F. J. 1941, "Razzia's op Joden," *Het Parool*, no. 4, 4 March, p.7.

Gritter, R. & Van der Linden, A 1995, "Herinneringen aan kamp Molengoot" *Rondom den Herdenbergh,* vol. 12/3, pp.288–290.
    1998, "Herinneringen aan Hardenberger joden," *Rondom den Herdenbergh*, vol.15, no.3, pp.27–29.
    1999, "Interview with Egbert de Lange," *De* Sallander, 10 Nov.
    2005, "*Sporen van Joods Verleden*" [Tracks of Jewish Past]. Private printing.

Bibliography

Grossman, V. 1985, *Life and Fate*, trans. Robert Chandler, The New York Review of Books, New York.
    2006, *A Writer at War: Vasily Grossman with the Red Army, 1941–1945*, trans. A. Beevor & L. Vinogradova, Pantheon Books, New York.

Gruner, W. 2006, *Jewish Forced Labor under the Nazis: Economic Needs and Racial Aims, 1938-1944*, Cambridge University Press, Cambridge.

Gutman, I. 1990, *Encyclopedia of the Holocaust*, vol.4, Macmillan, New York.

Hansard, 1942, House of Commons, vol. 385, no. 17, 17 December, p.2082.

Hardenberg police records 2006, [Accessed 5 November 2006]. Available at: http://www.Hardenbergh.nl/smartsite13467.html 1943

Herf, J. 2006, *The Jewish Enemy*, Harvard University Press, Cambridge.

Het Parool, 2006, [Accessed 1 June 2006]. Available at: http://www.hetillegaleparool.nl/summary.html and www.hetillegaleparool.nl/archief/1942/420925-7.php

Hilberg, R. 2003, *The Destruction of the European Jews*, Yale University Press, New Haven.

Hinsley, F.H. Ransom, C.F.G. Knight, R.C. & Thomas, E.E. 1981, *British Intelligence in the Second World War: Its Influence on Strategy and Operations*, vol. 2, Cambridge University Press, Cambridge.

Hosenfeld, W. 2004, *Ich versuche jeden zu retten: Das Leben eines Deutschen Offiziers in Briefen and Tagebuchern*, ed. Thomas Vogel, Deutsche Verlags-Anstalt, Munich.

Ilan-Onderwijzer, J. 2003, *Their image will be forever before my eyes*, trans. R. Schloss, Gefen, Lynbrook.

Isaacs, J. 1974, *The World at War*, Thames Television, London.

Jewish Chronicle 1943, 14 May, p.1, London.
    1943, 21 May, p.11, London.

Jong, L. de, 1988, *Het Koninkrijk der Nederlanden in de Tweede Wereldoorlog*, vol. V, Staatsuitgeverij/SDU, The Hague.
    1978, "Sobibor," *Encounter*, London, vol. 52, no 12, December.

Julius, A. 1995, *T.S. Eliot, Anti-Semitism and Literary Form*, Cambridge University Press, Cambridge.

Kahl, J. 1968, *The Misery of Christianity*, Pelican, London.

Kalb, M. 1996, "The Journalism of The Holocaust," *United States Holocaust Memorial Museum*. [Accessed 1 May 2005]. Available at: www.ushmm.org/lectures/kalb.html

Katz, M. 2007, "Was Einstein a Jewish Saint?" *Moment*, Washington, DC. April.

Karski, J. 1944, *Story of a Secret State*, Houghton Mifflin, Boston.

Keegan, J 1996, "What the Allies Knew," *The New York Times*, 26 November.

Klemperer, V. 1999, *I Will Bear Witness: A Diary of the Nazi Years*, trans. by Martin Chalmers, Random House, New York.

Knoop, H. 1983, *De Joodse Raad: Het drama van Abraham Asscher en David Cohen*, Elsevier, Amsterdam.

Korey, W. 2001, *An Epitaph for Raphael Lemkin*, The Jacob Blaustein Institute for the Advancement of Human Rights of the American Jewish Committee, NY.

Kristof, N. D. 2005, "The Secret Genocide Archive," *The New York Times*, 23 February, p.A.19.
    2006, "Genocide in Slow Motion," *The New York Review of Books*, vol. 53, no. 2, 9 February.

Kuypers, G. 1997, "Niet joden, maar Joden," *Trouw*, 29 November.

Labedz, L. 1988, "Holocaust: Myths & Horrors," *Survey*, vol. 30, no. 1/2, London.

Laqueur, W. 1980, *Terrible Secret: An Investigation of the Truth About Hitler's "Final Solution,"* Owl Books, New York.

Laqueur, W. & Breitman, R. 1986, *Breaking the Silence*, Simon & Schuster, New York.

Leff, L. 2000, *The Holocaust in the New York Times, 1939–1945*, The Harvard International Journal of Press Politics, The MIT Press, Cambridge.
    2005, *Buried by the Times: The Holocaust and America's Most Important Newspaper*, Cambridge University Press, New York.

Lemkin, R. 1944, *Axis Rule in Occupied Europe: Laws of Occupation, Analysis of Government, Proposals for Redress*, Carnegie Endowment for International Peace, Division of International Law, Washington D.C.

Bibliography

Lev, M. 1964, "Kimat a legende" [Almost a Legend], *Sovetish heymland*, vol. 1, no. 2, Sovetskii Pisatel, Moscow.

Levi, P. 1986, *The Drowned and the Saved*, trans. Raymond Rosenthal, Summit Books, New York.
    2000, *If this is a Man/The Truce*, trans. Stuart Woolf, The Everyman Library, New York.

Leydesdorff, S. 1994, *We Lived With Dignity: the Jewish proletariat of Amsterdam, 1900–1940*, trans. Frank Heny, Wayne State University Press, Detroit.

Lifton, B.J. 1988, *The King of Children: a biography of Janusz Korczak*, Chatto & Windus, London.

Loonstijn-Renger, T. 1998, *I am Here*, Private printing.

Low, D. 1956, *Low's Autobiography*, Michael Joseph, London.

Maass, W.B. 1970, *The Netherlands at War: 1940–1945,* Abelard-Schuman, London.

Mauthausen, 2006. [Accessed 2 August, 2006]. Available at: http://www.scrapbookpages.com/mauthausen/KZMauthausen/WienerGraben/index.htmldieren/duiven_als_koeriers/index.en.html

Mechanicus, P. 1964, *A Year of Fear: A Jewish Prisoner Waits for Auschwitz,* Hawthorn Books, New York.

Meijer, D. 2001, *Onbekende Kinderen De laatste Trein uit Westerbork,* Mets Schut, Amsterdam.

Hans Moonen, 2006, [Accessed 22 May 2006]. Available at: http://ww2propaganda@home.nl

Moore, B. 1997, *Victims and Survivors: The Nazi Persecution of the Jews in theNetherlands 1940–1945*, Arnold, London.

Nersessian, D. 2005, "Rethinking Cultural Genocide Under International Law," *Human Rights Dialogue,* series 2, no. 12, Spring 2005.

Netherlands 2003, [Accessed 12 December, 2003]. Available at: http://www.edwardvictor.com/Holocaust/Netherlands.htm

New York Times 1943, "Pole's Suicide note pleads for Jews," 4 June, p.7.

Nicholson, H. 1967, *The Letters and Diaries of Harold Nicholson, The War Years, 1939-45*, Atheneum, NewYork.

Novitch, M. 1980, *Sobibor, Martyrdom and Revolt: Documents and Testimonies,* Holocaust Library, New York.

Nuremberg War Crime Trials 1946, *Blue Series*, vol. 9. [Accessed 16 February, 2005]. Available at: http://www.yale.edu/lawweb/avalon/imt/proc/03-30-46.htm
    2006. [Accessed 16 April, 2006]. Available at: http://www.nizkor.org/hweb/imt/tgmwc/tgmwc-06/tgmwc-06-55-05.html

Perl, S. 2004, *Tell the World: The Story of the Sobibor Revolt,* Israel Bookshop, Lakewood, NJ.

Peters, R. 1996, *Historical Atlas of the Holocaust*, MacMillan Reference Books, New York.

Philips, W. M. van Geldere- 1980, Fortunoff Video Archive for Holocaust Testimonies, USC Shoah Foundation, Los Angeles.

Power, S. 2002, *A Problem From Hell: America and the Age of Genocide,* Basic Books, New York.
    2001, Bystanders to Genocide, *Atlantic Monthly*, September. [Accessed January 2005]. Available at: http://www.theatlantic.com/doc/200109/power-genocide

Presser, J. 1965, *Ondergang: De vervolging en verdelging van het Nederlandse Jodendom 1940–1945*, vol. 1, 's-Gravenhage:Staatsuitgeverij.
    1988, *Ashes in the Wind*, trans. Arnold Pomerans, Wayne State University Press, Detroit.

Rashke, R. 1982, *Escape from Sobibor*, University of Illinois Press, Chicago.

Rautkallio, H. 1987, *Finland and the Holocaust: The Rescue of Finland's Jews,* Holocaust Library, New York.

Ravel, A. 1980, *Faithful Unto Death: The Story of Arthur Zygielbaum*, Arthur Zygielbaum Branch Workman's Circle, Montreal.

Rees, L. 2005, *Auschwitz: A New History,* Public Affairs, New York.

Rood, C. 1949, *Report 1942–1945*, NIOD, Amsterdam.
    2002 *Wenn ich es nicht erzählen kann, muss ich weinen*, S Fischer Verlag, Frankfurt.

Roth, J. 1933, *What I Saw: Reports from Berlin 1920–1933*. Trans. Michael Hofmann, Granta Books, London.

Schelvis, J. 1993, *Vernietigingskamp Sobibor*, De Bataafsche Leeuw, Amsterdam.
    2003, *Binnen de poorten: Een verslag van twee jaar Duitse vernietigings- en concentratiekampen,* De Bataafsche Leeuw, Amsterdam.
    2007, *Sobibor: A History of a Nazi Death Camp*, Berg Publishers, Oxford.

Bibliography

Shapiro, M. ed. 2003, *Why Didn't the Press Shout?: American & International Journalism During the Holocaust,* Yeshiva University Press with KTAV Publishing House, New York.

Shirer, W. L. 1941, *Berlin Diary: The Journal of a Foreign Correspondent 1934–1941,* Alfred A. Knopf, New York.
    1960, *The Rise and Fall of the Third Reich*, Secker & Warburg, London.
    1984, *The Nightmare Years 1930–1940,* Little, Brown, Boston.
    1988, *The Rise and Fall of the Third Reich,* Simon & Schuster, New York.

Speer, A. 1970, *Inside the Third Reich: Memoirs,* The Macmillan, New York.

Spier, J.O. 1978, *Dat alles heeft mijn oog gezien: herinneringen aan het concentratiekamp Theresienstadt,* Elsevier, Amsterdam. © Jo Spier estate.

Steel, R. 1980, *Walter Lippman and the American Century,* Little Brown, Boston.

Strzelecka, I. 1998, *"Experiments" in Auschwitz 1940-1945,* Auschwitz State Museum, Auschwitz.

Suhl, Y. 1967, *They Fought Back: The Story of the Jewish Resistance in Nazi Europe,* Crown Publishers, New York.

Szpilman, W. 1999, *The Pianist: The Extraordinary True Story of One Man's Survival in Warsaw, 1939–1945,* Picador, New York.

Szmajzner, S. 1968, *Inferno Em Sobibor: A Tragédia de um Ado,* Edições Bloch, Rio de Janiero.

Tiggers, P. 1926, *AJC Songs,* Arbeiders Jeugd Centrale, Amsterdam.

Tombs, I. 2000, "'Morituri vos salutant': Szmul Zygielboim's suicide in May 1943 and the International Socialist Community in London." *Holocaust and Genocide Studies,* vol.14, no. 2, Fall.

United Nations General Assembly, 1948, Convention on the Prevention and Punishment of the Crime of Genocide, Resolution 260 A (III) Dec. 9. [Accessed 16 February 2005]. Available at: http://www.fordham.edu/halsall/mod/UN-GENO.html

Veen, H. van der 2003, *Westerbork het Verhaal van 1939-1945,* Herrinneringscentrum Kamp Westerbork, Westerbork.

Verhey, E. 1991, *Om het Joodse Kind,* Nijgh & Van Ditmar, Amsterdam.
    1999, *Tot ziens in Mokum. Brieven van Flip Slier uit werkkamp Molengoot (april 1942–oktober 1942),* Minerva, Oudewater, Gieterveen.
    2005, *Kind van de Rekening,* De Bezige Bij, Amsterdam.

Verzetsmuseum Amsterdam 2006, [Accessed 16 June, 2006]. Available at: http://www.scep.nl/verzet/verzetis/153.html

Vries, Ph. de 1949, *MC 1941–1945. geschiedenis van het verzet der artsen in Nederland,* H.D. Tjeenk Willink & Zoon, N.V. Haarlem.

Vries, S. Ph. de 1927, *Joodse Riten en Symbolen* [Jewish Rites and Symbols], Arbeiderspers, Amsterdam.

Werth, A. 1964, *Russia at War, 1941–45,* Barrie and Rockliff, London.

Wessels, B.L. & Bolle, K. W. 2001, *Ben's Story: Holocaust Letters with Selections from the Dutch Underground Press,* Southern Illinois University Press, Carbondale, IL.

Wiesel, E. 2006, *Night,* trans. Marion Wiesel, Hill and Wang, NY.

Witte, P. & Tyas, S. 2001, A New Document on the Deportation and Murder of Jews., *Journal of Holocaust and Genocide Studies,* vol. 15, no. 3, Winter.

Wood, T.E. & Jankowski, S. M. 1996, *Karski: How One Man Tried to Stop the Holocaust,* John Wiley & Son, New York.

Wyman, D.S. 1984, *The Abandonment of the Jews,* Pantheon, New York.

Yad Vashem, 2004, [Accessed 16 February, 2004]. Available at: http://www.yadvashem.org/

Zygielbojm, S. 1942, "Hitler's Pogrom," *BBC World Service,* BBC Archives, London.

We are most grateful for the assistance received from Libraries and Archives:

Amsterdam Municipality Archives, Netherlands
British National Archives, Kew Gardens, London
Dorot Jewish Division, New York Public Library, New York
Dutch Institute for War Documentation, Amsterdam
Hans Moonen Archives, Haelen, NL.
Hardenberg Municipality Archives, Netherlands
Imperial War Museum, London
International Institute of Social History, Amsterdam
Jewish Historical Museum, Amsterdam

National Institute of War Documentation, Amsterdam
RAF Museum, Hendon, England
Senate House Library, London University
Sterling Memorial Library, Yale University
United States Holocaust Memorial Museum, Washington D.C.
Verzetsmuseum, Amsterdam
Vriezenveen Municipality Archives, Netherlands
Weiner Library, London
Yivo, New York

Index

Bold type indicates photos, plain type a text reference; n. indicates the note number on pages 166-173.

Index

Professor David Cohen

Harry Elzas and Flip

Max van Dam, self-portrait

Chaim Engel in 1939 in the
Polish army

Esther Terner-Raab

Karel van der Schaaf and Truus
Tokkie-Sant, October 7, 2007,
in Amsterdamse Bos

Flip hoped (page 90) for an
exemption certificate for his
father like the one above,
which allowed Hendrik Jacob
Visser, born October 27, 1921,
to work as a typographer.

Back left: Bep de Vries; Jetty
Kaas; Henny de Lang;
Front: Henriette Gerritse?; Flip

Index

Karel van der Schaaf (*left*) with granddaughter Sivan in Jerusalem, May 4, 2005

Minke Honij, who hid Arthur Philips

Captain Wilm Hosenfeld

Grietje Slier Philips

In 1949, while in Krautzburg, Samuel Lerer (*above*) seeing SS Bauer walking in the street reported him to a policeman. Bauer was arrested, tried and sentenced to life imprisonment.

Stefka Nowak hid Selma Wijnberg and Chaim Engel.

Philipp Philips

Index

Marion van Binsbergen-Pritchard

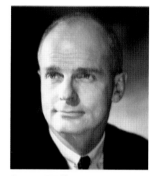

Senator William Proxmire

Wim Prijs

Karel van der Schaaf in 2005, wearing a table napkin to show how the AJC neck-scarf was worn.

Summer 1939, at AJC camp-ground in Vierhouten. *Left to right*: Jetty Kaas; Dick van der Schaaf; Truus Sant; Flip Slier

Jules Schelvis

The Reverend Frits Slomp

Jack (Izaak) Slier in 1922

Index

Lodewijk Ernst Visser, president of the Supreme court

Hendrika Veurink-Jolversma wearing Simon's brooch

Hermina Vrijlink-Broekroelofs

128 Vrolik Street (*right*) in 2006 which used to look like 124 (left).

Credits

PHOTO and DOCUMENT CREDITS

Thanks are due to the following for permission to use the materials as listed.

We have tried to contact all owners of copyright material and apologize if we have missed anybody. If we have inadvertently used copyrighted material without permission, we apologize and hope that the owner will contact us so that we may make amends. We would also have liked to identify the photographers and would be grateful to hear from anyone who has any information. Four photos have been modified; page 45 bottom left, page 147 bottom right, page 191 bottom right, and page 140 bottom left.

Endpaper: © Archives Stichting Onderzoek AJC, Amsterdam, courtesy Joost de Moor. **Frontispiece**: © NIOD (Dutch National Institute of War Documentation). Page **6**: © Choi and Shine. Page **10**: left, © Karel van der Schaaf. Page **14**: top left, Gift of Robert Abels Haskell, Museum of Jewish Heritage-A Living Memorial to the Holocaust, photograph by Jeanette Abels; bottom right, © 1936 David Low; used with permission of Solo Syndication Limited. Page **15**: © Choi and Shine. Page **16**: top and bottom left, © NIOD; bottom right, © National Institute of Social History, Amsterdam. Page **17** and **18**: © NIOD. Page **19**: top right, USHMM (United States Holocaust Memorial Museum), courtesy of U.S. National Archives and Records Administration; bottom, courtesy of Roel Gritter. Page **20**: © Deborah Slier; photo by Jen Foray. Page **22**: Collection of Jewish Historical Museum, Amsterdam. Page **23**: top, Collection of Jewish Historical Museum, Amsterdam; bottom © Family Amsterdam, courtesy of J. de Haas, photographer. Page **24**: courtesy NIOD. Page **25**: left, Collection of Jewish Historical Museum, Amsterdam; top right, © Karel van der Schaaf, middle right, © Truus Tokkie-Sant. Page **27**: top right, © Jane S. Fresco; bottom right, © Tootje Loonstijn-Renger. Page **28**: bottom left, © Karel van der Schaaf. Page **29**: bottom left, © Karel van der Schaaf; bottom right, © Elisabeth Renger; other ration coupons on right, courtesy Karel van der Schaaf. Page **30** and **31**: courtesy of Roel Gritter. Page **32**: top left, © Karel van der Schaaf. Page **32**: bottom left, © Children of Jack Slier. Page **33**: © NIOD. Page **34**: bottom left, © Children of Jack Slier. Page **35**: courtesy Günter Brandorff. Page **36**: © Children of Jack Slier. Page **37**: top right, © Mr. Dijkstra, courtesy of Jo Vomberg; center right, © Karel van der Schaaf. Page **38**: center left, © VARA broadcasting cooperation, courtesy Historical Consultancy 30-45, (www.hab3045.nl), Amsterdam; bottom left, © Marcel van Dam; bottom right, © Karel van der Schaaf. Page **39**: © Children of Jack Slier. Page **40**: center left, © Karel van der Schaaf; bottom left, © Jules Schelvis. Page **42**: left, © Collection of Jewish Historical Museum, Amsterdam; bottom right, © Karel van der Schaaf. Page **43**: bottom left and top right, © Jules and Eddy Philips; bottom right, © Deborah Slier. Page **44**: © NIOD. Page **45**: right, top, © Historical Consultancy 30-45; bottom right, Collection of Jewish Historical Museum, Amsterdam. Page **46**: Collection of Jewish Historical Museum, Amsterdam. Page **47**: bottom left, © Marcel van Dam; top right, © Children of Jack Slier; bottom right, © Hans Heese Cartoef. Page **48**: left top and bottom, © Karel van der Schaaf, right, © Truus Tokkie-Sant. Page **49**: © Imperial War Museum. Page **50**: © Hans Moonen: ww2propaganda@home.nl. Page **51**: courtesy Günter Brandorff. Page **52**: © Children of Jack Slier. Page **53**: left, Collection of Jewish Historical Museum, Amsterdam. Page **54**: top left, © Collection of Jewish Historical Museum, Amsterdam; center © NIOD, photographer Holtzapfel, bottom left, courtesy USHMM; bottom right, © National Foto Archief, Rotterdam. Photographer C. Breyer. Page **55**: bottom left and top right, © NIOD; bottom center, courtesy Gemeente Vriezenveen. Page **56**: left, and bottom right, © NIOD. Page **57**: top right, courtesy of Ross Mellows: ross@spiritburner.com at mellows@freeuk.com>; center right, © Jin Choi; bottom right, © Roel Gritter. Page **58**: top left, © Karel van der Schaaf. Page **59**: top right, © Children of Jack Slier; bottom right, courtesy of Sippy Boersma and Karel van der Schaaf. Page **60**: © Karel van der Schaaf. Page **61**: top right, © Karel van der Schaaf; bottom right, © Children of Jack Slier. Page **62**: top, © USHMM, courtesy of Instytut Pamieci Narodowej; bottom left, © USHMM; bottom right © Jan Karski, courtesy of USHMM. Page **63**: top left and right: British National Archives; bottom, courtesy of Hans Moonen: ww2propaganda@home.nl. Pages **64** and **65**: © NIOD. Page **66**: © Collection of Jewish Historical Museum, Amsterdam. Page **67**: top left, British National Archives; bottom left, © Karel van der Schaaf; right, © Hans Moonen: ww2propaganda@home.nl. Page **68**: © NIOD. Page **70**: © Tootje Loonstijn-Renger. Page **71**: top right, © Karel van der Schaaf; bottom, courtesy Jozef Vomberg. Page **72**: top and bottom, © NIOD. Page **73**: bottom left and center, © Collection of Jewish Historical Museum, Amsterdam; center right, © Edward Victor; bottom right, © NIOD. Page **74**: top © Martin and Riek Veurink-Jolversma; bottom © Karel van der Schaaf. Page **75**: © Ghetto Fighter's House, Israel. Page **76**: top, © Esbit®; bottom, © Historical Consultancy 30-45, Amsterdam. Page **77**: bottom left, USHMM, courtesy of Gedenkstaette Buchenwald; top right, USHMM, courtesy of Trudi Gidan. Page **78**: courtesy USHMM. Page **79**: top and middle, © NIOD; bottom, Westerbork archives. Page **80**: bottom left, courtesy of Jozef Vomberg; bottom right, © NIOD. Page **81**: © NIOD. Page **82**: © Karel van der Schaaf. Page **83**: top right, Collection of Jewish Museum, Amsterdam; bottom, © Karel van der Schaaf. Page **84**: center left, National Institute of Social History, Amsterdam; bottom, © Children of Jack Slier. Page **85**: © Karel van der Schaaf. Page **86**: © 1940 David Low, courtesy of Solo Syndication Limited. Page **87**: top, © Tootje Loonstijn-Renger; bottom, © Karel van der Schaaf. Page **88**: © Children

Credits

of Jack Slier. Page **89**: bottom right, Martin and Riek Veurink-Jolversma; © top right, © Karel van der Schaaf. Page **90**: bottom, © NIOD. Page **91**: © Karel van der Schaaf. Page **92**: Collection of Jewish Historical Museum, Amsterdam. Page **93**: top and bottom, © NIOD. Page **94**: top, © Ian Shine; middle and bottom, © Karel van der Schaaf. Page **95**: © ICS (Institute of Carmelite Studies) Publications, courtesy Brother Bryan Paquette. Page **96** and **97**: © Karel van der Schaaf. Pages **98** and **99**: © Tootje Loonstijn-Renger. Page **100**: top left, © Children of Jack Slier; bottom, © Jules and Joke Philips. Page **101**: courtesy of Roel Gritter. Page **102**: top, © Jewish Historical Museum, Amsterdam; bottom, © Collection NIOD © Family Amsterdam, courtesy J. de Haas, photgrapher. Page **103**: © Jewish Historical Museum, Amsterdam. Page **104**: top and bottom, © Jules and Joke Philips; center, © Children of Jack Slier. Page **105**: top, © Karel van der Schaaf; bottom, © Children of Jack Slier. Page **106**: © NIOD. Page **107**: © Historical Consultancy 30-45, Amsterdam. Page **108**: © Karel van der Schaaf. Page **109**: top, courtesy Günter Brandorff; bottom, © Martin and Riek Veurink-Jolversma. Page **110**: top and center left, © NIOD; bottom left, photo by Lydia Nobelen-Riezouw; © M. van Nobelen; top right, courtesy YIVO. Page **111**: top and center, Collection of Jewish Historical Museum, Amsterdam; bottom left and right, courtesy USHMM, © Hilde Jacobsthal Goldberg; bottom center, © Ian Shine. Page **112**: © NIOD. Page **113**: bottom left, © Karel van der Schaaf; right, © Davitamon. Page **114**: © NIOD. Page **115**: © Jules and Joke Philips. Page **116**: © Children of Jack Slier. Page **117**: top, © Hermina and Jan Vrijlink-Broekroelofs; bottom, © Tootje Loonstijn-Renger. Page **118**: AJC songbook, courtesy Joost de Moor; bottom right © Karel van der Schaaf. Page **119**: bottom left, © Jules and Joke Philips; top right, © Karel van der Schaaf; bottom right, courtesy Gemeente Vriezenveen. Page **120**: top left, © Collection Jewish Historical Museum, Amsterdam; bottom left, © NIOD. Page **121**: top right, © Collection of Jewish Historical Museum, Amsterdam; bottom right, © NIOD. Page **122**: top left, © Collection of Jewish Historical Museum, Amsterdam; bottom left, © NIOD Page **123**: top, © courtesy USHMM; center, Martin and Riek Veurink-Jolversma. Pages **124**: courtesy Hans Moonen: <ww2propaganda@home.nl>. Page **125**: ration coupon, courtesy Karel van der Schaaf; right, © Hermina and Jan Vrijlink-Broekroelofs. Page **126**: courtesy Stapesma Netherlands Collection. Page **127**: top and middle, © Children of Jack Slier; bottom, © Hermina and Jan Vrijlink-Broekroelofs. Page **128**: top, Tootje Loonstijn-Renger; center and bottom, © Karel van der Schaaf. Page **129**: © Hermina and Jan Vrijlink-Broekroelofs. Page **130**: top, © Gemeente Hardenberg; center and bottom, © Gemeente Amsterdam. Page **131**: © Collection of Jewish Historical Museum, Amsterdam. Pages **132** and **133**: © Tootje Loonstijn-Renger. Page **134**: center left, courtesy USHMM; bottom, courtesy J. van der Sleen. Page **135**: © NIOD. Page **136** and **137**: courtesy Günter Brandorff. Page **138**: top and bottom left, © Tootje Loonstijn-Renger; bottom right, Hermina and Jan Vrijlink-Broekroelofs. Page **139**: center and bottom right, © Jozef Vomberg. Page **140**: top © Karel van der Schaaf; center, center © Gemeentearchief Amsterdam, courtesy of Historical Consultancy 30-45; bottom left, © Ian Shine; bottom right, © Karel van der Schaaf. Page **141**: © NIOD. Page **142**: © J. Presser, used with permission of Wayne State University Press, Detroit, **143**: top, © Westerbork archives; bottom, courtesy Günter Brandorff. Page **144** and **145**: © NIOD. Page **146**: footnote, © Westerbork archives; top, © Children of Jack Slier; center, © Daughters of Philip Mechanicus. Page **147**: top and center right, © Selma Wijnberg-Engel; center left, AJC songbook, courtesy Joost de Moor; center, and bottom right, © Jules Schelvis. Pages **148** and **149**: © NIOD. Page **151**: center, © Selma Wijnberg-Engel. Page **152**: © USHMM. (The USHMM map has been modified). Page **153**: © NIOD. Page **154**: © Hermina and Jan Vrijlink-Broekroelofs. Page **155**: © Tootje Loonstijn-Renger. Page **156**: top left, top right, and bottom right, © Tootje Loonstijn-Renger; bottom left, © Karel van der Schaaf. Page **157**: top, © NIOD; center, courtesy J. van der Sleen; bottom, © Karel van der Schaaf. Page **158**: top left and right, and bottom right, © Children of Jack Slier; bottom left, © Hans Hesse Cartoef. Page **162**: top, © Dick Slier; center and bottom, © Ian Shine. Page **163**: © United Nations archive. Pages **176**: top left © NIOD; others, courtesy Hans Moonen: ww2propaganda@home.nl. **177**:© NIOD. Page **178**: © NIOD. Page **179**: Collection of Jewish Historical Museum, Amsterdam. Page **184**: from top to bottom, © Jules and Joke Philips; © Karel van der Schaaf; © Ian Shine; Collection of Jewish Historical Museum, Amsterdam. Page **185**: top to bottom: © NIOD; © Karel van der Schaaf; © Collection of Jewish Historical Museum; © Selma Wijnberg-Engel. Page **186**: top to bottom, © Esther Terner-Raab; © Karel van der Schaaf; © Edward Victor: "edwardvictor.com", ©Karel van der Schaaf. Page **187**: top, © Karel van der Schaaf; center, ©Jules and Joke Philips; bottom, © family of Captain Wilm Hosenfeld. Page **188**: top to bottom: © Children of Jack Slier; © Samuel Lerer; © Selma Wijnberg-Engel; © Children of Jack Slier. Page **189**: top to bottom: © Marion van Binsbergen-Pritchard; courtesy U.S. Senate Historical Office; © Karel van der Schaaf; © Ian Shine. Page **190**: top to bottom: © Truus Tokkie-Sant; © Ian Shine; © Hermina and Jan Vrijlink-Broekroelofs; © Children of Jack Slier. Page **191**: top to bottom: collection of Jewish Historical Museum, Amsterdam; © Hendrika Veurink-Jolversma; © Ian Shine; © Ian Shine. Page **194**: © Alice van Keulen-Woudstra.

PHILIP SLIER

Detail from the AJC monument shown on the front endpaper.